Jazz

James Lincoln Collier

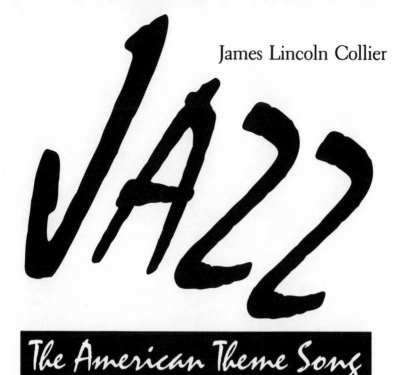

JAZZ

The American Theme Song

New York   Oxford
Oxford University Press
1993

Oxford University Press

Oxford New York Toronto
Delhi Bombay Calcutta Madras Karachi
Kuala Lumpur Singapore Hong Kong Tokyo
Nairobi Dar es Salaam Cape Town
Melbourne Auckland Madrid

and associated companies in
Berlin Ibadan

Copyright © 1993 by James Lincoln Collier

Published by Oxford University Press, Inc.
200 Madison Avenue, New York, New York 10016

Library of Congress Cataloging-in-Publication Data
Collier, James Lincoln, 1928–
Jazz : the American theme song / James Lincoln Collier.
p. cm.   Includes bibliographical references and index.
ISBN 0–19–507943–4
1. Jazz—History and criticism.
2. Music and society.
I. Title. ML3508.C62 1993
781.65—dc20 92–43644

1 2 3 4 5 6 7 8 9

Printed in the United States of America
on acid-free paper

For Barbara and John

Preface

Most of my writing about jazz has been historical and bio-graphical; and while I find this sort of work absorbing, it is limiting, in the sense that a lot of interesting material that turns up in the course of researching a Louis Armstrong or the development of a certain style of playing is not really germane to the subject and has to be discarded—or rather, put aside for the moment. This, I think, is likely to be the case for re-searchers in any field: there is always the hope that somehow, this or that little *gatherum* of information will someday find a home.

The present book is such a home for material about jazz I have been mulling for a good many years. It is not simply a grab bag of previously published work, but has been researched and written expressly for this book. My aim has been to exam-ine jazz from a variety of positions, in hopes of more fully illuminating a subject I consider a fascinating mirror of America. This book, then, is as much about America as it is about jazz.

Needless to say, it could not have been written without help. I am grateful to Dan Morgenstern and the staff of the Institute of Jazz Studies at Rutgers, Bruce Boyd Raeburn and his staff at the Hogan Jazz Archive, and the staff of the music library at Lincoln Center, for considerable aid. The manuscript was read in full by John L. Fell, who provided much useful comment, and also ferreted out a number of musical examples that were critical to the examination of jazz rhythm.

Gerald Early, Krin Gabbard, Curt Jerde, and Bruce Boyd Raeburn also read portions of the manuscript, and offered criticisms and suggestions that helped give the book its final shape. Additionally, I would like to thank a number of people with whom I have held conversations on many of the subjects herein, among them Christopher Collier, Geoffrey L. Collier, H. Wiley Hitchcock, William H. Kenney III, Gene Lees, James T. Maher, Lewis Porter, Grover Sales, and Christopher Waterman.

I owe a substantial debt to the musicians I have worked with and talked with over many years. They have been the real source for my knowledge of jazz.

Finally, as ever, I must thank my editor, Sheldon Meyer, and his exemplary staff for sympathetic guidance.

Contents

Jazz

1

The

Inevitability

of Jazz

in America

Jazz happened in America, and it could have happened only there. There existed there a unique set of conditions—social, economic, intellectual—that allowed it to take root and grow. Jazz was not an accident. It appeared when it did because of what had gone before, and it spread through the culture with amazing speed because the American people were prepared for it—in fact, were actively searching for it, or something like it. As a consequence, we cannot really understand it in the abstract, isolated from the world around it. Jazz is part of the social history of the United States, and must be seen in that context. What, then, were the social conditions that made jazz possible, indeed, almost inevitable?

To begin with, there is the fact that the United States housed a black subculture, constituting at that time about ten percent of the American people, which had proven extremely difficult to assimilate into the mainstream. These people had developed for their own use a musical system that had proven attractive to white Americans, and had been adapted for them by both blacks and whites in the form of the plantation songs of the minstrel shows, the spirituals made popular by the Fisk Jubilee Singers and similar groups, and ragtime, which by 1900 was widely popular in America.

This black music in its various forms was particularly abundant in the unique city of New Orleans, which had long seen pleasure-seeking as a legitimate concern of life, unlike much of the North, still dominated by residual Calvinism through much of the nineteenth century and even beyond.[1] Music and dance were a regular part of the social life of New Orleans; and because whites and blacks there lived in closer physical contact than they did in many other places, they were thoroughly aware of each other's music. I have written at length elsewhere about what made New Orleans the breeding ground for jazz.[2] Suffice it to say here that the people of New Orleans of both races were, by 1900, hearing a great deal of ragtime, both in its popularized version and the rhythmically denser black version, and they were prepared for the next development, which proved to be jazz. This new "hot" music became widely popular in the city. Somewhat later, the *New Orleans Times-Picayune* editorialized against jazz, comparing it to "the dime novel or the grease-dripping doughnut."[3] This attack provoked a flurry of letters from local jazz lovers, presumably middle-class white readers of the newspaper, one of whom wrote, "It is typical American music . . . filled with the spirit and bustle of American life."[4]

But New Orleans was *sui generis,* a city unlike any other in the United States—a Caribbean city more akin in many respects to Port au Prince and Kingston than to Boston and Philadelphia. Jazz might well have remained a local phenomenon, a New Orleans specialty like jambalaya and the Creole patois, had it not been for currents moving through the United States at almost precisely the moment that jazz came into being.[5]

Essentially, in the years around 1900, there appeared in America a dramatic shift in attitude, followed a decade or so later by an equally dramatic shift in behavior, which continues to have consequences for us today. This was the arrival of what is now called "modernism." The genesis of this new Zeitgeist was complex. But to simplify, perhaps too much, it begins with the fact that through much of the nineteenth century, the United States—and indeed other parts of the Western world—was dominated by a way of thinking and doing called Victorianism. This attitude was based on the notions of responsibility and self-control.[6] Its watchwords were "order" and "decency." Proper Victorians drank little or no alcohol, at least attempted to confine sex to the marriage bed, disapproved of any but the most decorous sort of dancing, frowned on swearing, nudity, and even prize-fighting and uncleanliness. Women ruled in the home but not outside of it, and children were raised to be proper Victorians themselves.

All of this makes Victorianism sound appalling—indeed psychotic—but there was another side to the story, for these people worked very hard at doing right by family, friends, community, and country. Honor, truth-telling, respect for the rights of others, were insisted upon.

But by the end of the century, a lot of young people, especially, had lost sight of the useful aspects of Victorianism; all they saw was its heavy hand barring from life anything that was unfettered and joyous. By itself, a simple reaction to Victorianism might not have shattered the old attitude. But in the years from about 1880 to 1920, the United States underwent a change even more dramatic—and to some people simply devastating—than the shift in spirit that followed in its train. This was the movement from the old rural, agrarian system, built around independent farm families, villages, and small towns, to the big-city industrial economy, which has been the way of the Western world in the twentieth century. "Industrialism," to employ the generally accepted term, was driven by several intermeshed forces. One of these was an explosion of technology, which produced oil, gas, and the internal combustion engine; the telegraph, wireless, the telephone, and eventually radio; new ways of mass producing steel and other metals; techniques for high-rise building; and, in time, the trolley car, the automobile, the airplane.[7]

A second force impinging on the America of the time was the massive influx of immigrants, beginning in the 1840s with a flood of Germans and Irish, and continuing through the latter decades of the nineteenth century and into the twentieth, with the inpouring of so-called "new" immigrants from south and east Europe, along with substantial numbers from China and elsewhere in the Far East.[8] The immigrants were by no means all of a piece, and they brought with them a congeries of attitudes, religions, and lifestyles. But the bulk of them had come from impoverished peasant cultures, and they tended to have a *carpe diem* attitude that urged them to seize what pleasure they could in the brief hours away from the sweatshops, mines, and factories where most of them got their livings. God-fearing they may have been, and hard-working they certainly were, but when it came to drink, dancing, and sex, they were resolutely anti-Victorian.

At the same time, for a variety of economic and social reasons, the old family farm economy was falling apart. Native-born sons and daughters of families who had been farmers for generations flooded into the burgeoning new cities, where they found work in the factories inspired by the new technologies. The cities grew at an alarming speed, racing outwards across forests and farms at a pace that was almost visible. Chicago, which in 1850 had been described by one visitor as "unfinished, ragged and uncouth," with streets so muddy in wet weather that rough plank bridges had to be put up so people could cross them, was by 1890 a vast, flourishing industrial city.[9] By 1920, the old rural structure was diminished, and the city was dominant.[10]

Precisely how the mere fact of city dwelling would change human attitudes is not easy to get at. Nonetheless, it is obvious that people living in anonymity, where the neighbors across the hall are strangers, are freer to do what they want to do than they are in a village or small town where everybody knows them, and where Aunt Meddling, Doctor Straitlace, and Preacher Godfearing are liable to be lurking just around the next corner. People in cities could come home drunk with somebody else's spouse at three in the morning because nobody around them cared. Thus, the city itself encouraged an anti-Victorianism in the youths from the farms that reinforced that of the immigrants.

Yet one more factor that would have immense effects on the century aborning was feminism.[11] The Victorian Age had its woman's movement, but it was focussed mainly on social reform: closing the saloons, reforming prostitutes, cleaning up the political system. The new feminism of the twentieth century had as its primary goal the liberating of women. The Victorian shackles must be cast off, so that women could be free to drink, smoke, dress comfortably, and sleep with people of either sex without benefit of marriage. Feminism, too, was anti-Victorian in its thrust.

Again, for reasons that are difficult to tease out of the social fabric, an anti-Victorian system of thought was growing in philosophy, psychology, painting, literature, and music. In philosophy, it was the notion of William James, John Dewey, and others that the free flow of emotion was a desired objective of human life. In psychology, it was the idea of Sigmund Freud, John B. Watson, and others that "repressing" the emotions was not a good idea. (This of course is a gross over-simplification; but that is how many lay people interpreted the new psychology.[12]) In painting it was the approach of the so-called Ashcan School, which, in the words of one of them, was to "stop studying water pitchers and bananas and paint every day life": the idea was to be spontaneous, to "work at great speed."[13] In literature it was the new realism of Theodore Dreiser, Stephan Crane, and others, who took for their subject matter the underclass, and brought sex and drunkenness into their novels.[14]

All of this intellectual ferment was tending in the same direction, and by 1910–1915, it had given rise to a new attitude toward life among artists, intellectuals, and the bohemians rolling into Greenwich Village and similar places. This attitude said that people ought to be free to express themselves as they liked; be themselves; live fully and for the moment; be spontaneous; and above all enjoy themselves.[15]

It would take ten years for this attitude to spread through the general populace; but already the new spirit was pushing itself through the surface of the society: in the years around 1912, feminism was breaking into the open, Margaret Sanger was publishing her first articles on female sexuality; the famous left-wing publication *The Masses* was founded; the new psychology was proclaimed; the magazine *Poetry*, the standard-bearer for the new literature, was founded; the Armory Show that introduced Americans to modern art was mounted.

It was all of a piece: the new thought, the new art, the attitude of the immigrants, the lifestyle encouraged by the industrial city, were pushing Americans in the same direction—toward lives that—so they hoped in any case—would be free, expressive, spontaneous. There was, many young people thought, to be a new world.

It should not therefore surprise us to learn that the word "jazz" first found its way into print in 1913.[16] The music,

obviously, fit exactly into this new spirit of a new age. It was—
at least supposedly—spontaneous, improvised on the moment.
It was certainly "expressive," however we define that term, and
by virtue of both its spontaneity and its expressiveness, it was
almost by definition free, apparently unrestricted by the standard rules and regulations of musical theory.

Thus, jazz appealed to those partaking of the new modern
spirit, *simply for what it was seen to be*, regardless of musical
considerations. This phenomenon has been noted in art by
Robert L. Herbert, who has pointed out that the rather sketchy
early Impressionist paintings that Monet and Renoir made
together at Grenouillère in 1869 were not seen as significant
until well into the twentieth century, which "so prized spontaneity and daring, that we have elevated the Grenouillère compositions to a high place in modern art."[17]

The point is that a particular style or form in art gains adher-
ents not simply from purely aesthetic considerations, but also
from how well it appears to agree with fashionable social,
philosophic, or even political considerations, as the uproar
over "political correctness" in literature makes clear. Jazz benefitted substantially from the new free spirit of the modern age.

That same spirit helped give rise to an institution that was
not only important to jazz, but has had an overwhelming effect
on American society. As pleasure-seeking became increasingly
acceptable, entrepreneurs jumped in to exploit it. Very rapidly, from about 1880, there came into being the huge entertainment industry that so dominates American life today.[18] It
is difficult for us to realize, given the extent to which we are
enmeshed in show business, that professional entertainment
has been, for most of human history, a rare thing. As long as
people were living in peasant villages, small towns, and isolated farms, there was really no easy way to make professional
entertainment profitable on a large scale, simply because it was
hard to gather audiences regularly in sufficient numbers to

make a show or a concert pay. Touring shows might struggle across the countryside from time to time, putting on performances of one kind or another in barns and village halls, but these did not come to most places often. Only in the cities was it possible to collect enough people to establish theaters and concert halls, and until the rise of the industrial city after the middle of the nineteenth century, only a small minority of human beings—less than ten percent in most places—lived in cities. For the vast majority of humans of an earlier time, entertainment was homemade—a sing around the pump organ, a dance to Uncle Fred's fiddle, a card game, a foot race, a hayride, a story told before the tavern fire.

But with the growth of the city, mass entertainment was possible. One of the earliest building blocks leading directly to the enormous entertainment industry of today was the institution of the concert saloon. It was derived from the European *cafés-concerts*, to employ the French term, which were an important feature of major cities in the second half of the nineteenth century. [19] These European *cafés-concerts* were often open-air. They presented entertainment, frequently a female vocalist, and served drinks to customers who sat at long tables or wandered about looking for friends. Many of them provided space for dancing as well, and it is important to note that they were attended by all classes of people, from the wealthy, through the middle class and working people, down to the pimps and prostitutes at the bottom of the society. These *cafés-concerts* were seen as characteristic of the modern city aborning, the prototype of which was Paris, and they were painted again and again by the Impressionists, who were beginning to make their mark in France in the 1870s and 1880s.

The idea of providing entertainment in drinking places was brought to the United States by the immigrants, and flourished here as the concert saloon, or concert garden. According to Kathy Peiss, in her study of working women's amusements: "In the 1850s some saloon owners converted their back rooms and cellars into small concert halls and hired specialty acts to amuse their patrons and encourage drinking. By the 1860s over two hundred concert-saloons had spread along Broadway [in New York], the Bowery, and the waterfronts, catering to a heterogeneous male clientele of laborers, soldiers, sailors and 'slumming' society gentlemen. The conventions of polite society were put aside in these male sanctuaries, where crude jokes, bawdy comedy sketches, and scantily clad singers entertained the drinkers."[20]

Very quickly it occurred to entrepreneurs to dress up this entertainment a little and present it in theaters. Thus was vaudeville, or variety, created.[21] It was still fairly rough saloon entertainment, however. Then, in 1881, a showman named Tony Pastor, aware of an untapped audience of the middle class, especially middle-class women, introduced "clean" vaudeville, and within a decade vaudeville had become a rage, the primary entertainment medium of the big cities.

Riding on the back of variety was a new music industry built around the large sales of sheet music of "hit" songs meant to sell fast and have short lives. By the early nineteen-hundreds the phonograph was well developed, and was being bought by increasing numbers of the middle class, and then, as prices went down, the working class. At the same time there appeared another product of the technological boom of the time, the motion picture. It grew at exponential speed, and by 1920 was on the way to killing its parent, variety. And in the 1920s there appeared yet another technical miracle, radio, which rapidly became a major presence in the society.[22]

Taken together, variety, the movies, radio, and the phonograph record made up a huge system of professional entertainment, which increasingly engaged Americans' minds and their leisure time.

The role of the immigrants in the development of modern

show business was substantial.[23] They provided the first audience for the movies. They brought in the concert saloon, which vaudeville developed out of. They were major consumers of popular music, and when the phonograph became cheap enough, major buyers of phonograph records.

But beyond this, the immigrants, and to a lesser extent blacks, discovered in the new show business an industry they were acceptable in. The established industries, like steel and banking, were not eager to bring immigrants, and especially blacks, into the executive offices. But show business, during the years in which the immigrants poured in, was still being invented, and it was open to new people. Indeed, the middle and upper classes looked upon show business with considerable disdain; their offspring did not aspire to be movie producers or music publishers. There was an entrepreneurial gap, and the immigrants rushed in to fill it. Among other things, there were ways to get into the business with small amounts of capital: it has been estimated that a storefront movie theater—the so-called nickelodeon—could be opened with six hundred dollars.[24] Both as entrepreneurs and as performers, the immigrants and some blacks became a major—perhaps the major—element in the new entertainment industry. Just look at the names: Irving Berlin, Samuel Goldwyn, George Gershwin, George M. Cohan, Jerome Kern, Jesse Lasky—the list could go on and on.

It is obvious, as we shall see in more detail later, that jazz could not have spread, or perhaps even come into being, had it not been for the emergence of this new show business machine. Critical to the music's development were the record industry, the popular music business of Tin Pan Alley, radio, the concert saloons, and, to a lesser extent, variety and the movies.

A second institution that was to have an important effect on jazz was the semi-formal vice district.[25] One of the great facts of the Victorian era was the ubiquity of venereal disease. It was hard to cure and could lead to sterility, blindness, insanity, and death. Rarely mentioned in polite circles, it was everywhere a silent specter.

During the Civil War, Union army officials, faced with a considerable number of troops *hors de combat* because of venereal diseases, decided that a system of "regulated" prostitution might help control infection. Prostitutes were to be regularly inspected; if they were disease-free, they would be certified to ply their trade; if not, they were to be banned until cured.

This idea seemed a good one to a lot of people, and in 1870, the city of St. Louis instituted its own plan of regulated vice. Reformers objected: the answer to venereal disease was abstention: men would simply have to learn to control themselves. The St. Louis law was repealed.

It did not matter, however. Whatever the reformers wanted, the laws were inforced by city officials and the police, and in many cities around the nation, those in power believed that regulating vice was a good idea. For one thing, it confined the evil to specific areas, usually the poorer ones, and kept it out of neighborhoods where it would be visible to the middle class and, not incidentally, would not lower property values. For another, the officially illegal but tolerated vice district offered prodigious opportunities for graft. Through the latter decades of the nineteenth century, the institution of the vice district swept across the nation. Big cities like New York and Chicago had two or three such districts; every middle-sized city had at least one; and there were others in small cities, towns, and even villages. The best-remembered today are New Orleans' Storyville and San Francisco's Barbary Coast, but at the time there were many others as famous, among them New York's Tenderloin and Chicago's Levee.

The vice districts were centered around the brothels, which ranged from fifty-cent houses where working men enjoyed a woman (the majority were in fact teenagers) for five minutes or so—to the grand parlor houses where prices were five dollars and up and bogus champagne was sold for twenty-five dollars a bottle. But the brothels were only part of it, for they were surrounded by adjunctive institutions, including saloons, drug parlors, gambling houses, and perhaps a theater and dance halls.

The vice districts attracted a clientele that ranged through the social system from the very bottom to the very top. Parties of wealthy gentlemen often concluded a well-lubricated evening with a visit to a fancy fifty-dollar whorehouse, like the famous Everleigh Club in Chicago. Only doors away, drunken sailors on a spree were having a five-minute fling for fifty cents, or even less: there are reports of Storyville prostitutes selling themselves to newsboys for a nickel.

While differing social classes as a rule segregated themselves according to the price of the brothels they frequented, they all met under the same roof in saloons and dance halls.[26] This is worth a moment's comment. As I have said, the European *café-concerts* the American vice district saloons and dance halls were based on, catered to wealthy boulevardiers, the new middle class of clerks, and ordinary working people. It appears that this mixing of classes was some of the appeal of these places. Upper-class males in particular were predatory, looking for mistresses among the entertainers or the working-class women who served as waitresses and barmaids. For the middle class there was a certain titillation at mingling with working people, whom they ordinarily kept at a distance. And many of the working class-women who came to drink and dance at the *café-concerts* hoped to make contact with a wealthy man who had money to spend on them.

Something of these same attitudes obtained in the American vice districts. For the middle classes especially, there was the sense of dipping into a different world, where different rules applied. Here was the open display of sexuality; a lot of drinking, gambling, erotic, indeed pornographic, display; and even drugs. It was all in marked contrast to the decorous ways of the middle-class homes they came from, and there was an excitement to it that went beyond the mere availability of sex and drink.

One important feature of most of the vice districts, which would play a considerable role in the development of jazz, was the "black and tan"—a saloon or cabaret ostensibly intended for a black clientele, but actually designed to draw a substantial white patronage, the idea being that whites as a rule had a lot more money to spend than blacks did.[27] The black and tans featured black entertainment, and usually had black waiters and bartenders. Some of them were owned by blacks, like Barron Wilkins' famous Exclusive Club in Harlem; others, like the Sunset Cafe in Chicago, where Armstrong played for a period, were run by whites.

The institution of the black and tan was a manifestation of the interest white Americans have taken in the black subculture. As far back as the eighteenth century, slaveholders went out to the cabins to watch the blacks dance and make music, and even at times to join in. Whites routinely visited black brothels, and even in the Northern cities, blacks and white laborers, like sailors and casual workers, might frequent the same saloons. These low dives were sometimes visited by wealthy slummers; Charles Dickens gives a report of a visit to a black and tan in New York during his American tour of 1842.[28] This interest in black culture was responsible for making minstrelsy a major component of nineteeth-century entertainment, and produced the boom in black entertainment of the 1920s that helped make jazz popular, as we shall see in more detail later.[29]

The black and tans were commonplace in the vice districts and in ordinary black enclaves. Among the best known were

Purcell's in the Barbary Coast;[30] the aforementioned Barron's, where what became the Duke Ellington Orchestra made its New York debut;[31] the Nest, also in Harlem, where many important jazz musicians played; and the Sunset, Plantation, and another Nest in Chicago, where Oliver, Armstrong, Noone, Hines, and others played. In fact, the honky-tonks of the Liberty–Perdido Street area in New Orleans, where jazz at least in part was developed, were effectively black and tans, for they attracted many whites. The New Orleans bass player Pops Foster said, "Most saloons had two sides, one for whites and one for colored. The colored had so much fun on their side dancing, singing, and guitar playing, that you couldn't get in for the whites. It was the same way at Lincoln Park for the colored; you couldn't tell who it was for, there were so many whites there."[32]

The tradition of the black and tan was carried on for decades. As late as 1926, *Variety* reported that at Small's, "To see the 'high hats' [whites] mingle with the native steppers [blacks] is nothing unusual."[33] The San Francisco musician Charles Turner said that in the 1920s, "We played many places where the whites mingled with the colored."[34] Earl Hines, speaking of the Grand Terrace in Chicago, where he was a fixture during much of the 1930s, said, "The audiences were mixed. Segregation never crossed anyone's mind."[35]

Paralleling the black and the tan was the institution of the "midnight ramble"; that is, a special performance for whites of a show in a black theater or club. These midnight rambles were given after the regular performance for blacks, with prices usually raised. A good many midnight rambles were put on at Lincoln Gardens, so that white musicians could hear the King Oliver band, with Armstrong, after their own jobs were over;[36] and Doc Cheatham reported that the Bijou Theater, where he played when he was young, routinely put on midnight rambles for whites.[37]

The attraction of these midnight rambles was to a considerable extent an eroticism that was not usually present in mainstream vaudeville. Some blacks objected to the midnight rambles. In 1925, *The Southwestern Christian Advocate* ran comments by a Reverend L. H. King, who I presume to have been black, which said in part, "One degrading phase of this same practice is the popular midnight show staged by Negro theatricals for whites in the large towns and cities of the South. These are riotous exhibitions of vulgarity and obscenity too shocking to decent sensibilities to be described. . . . It is destructive of racial self respect . . . for the Negroes . . ." to engage in these "lewd" and "smutty" productions. And the black actor Clarence Muse concurred, saying, "It may be the demand of our public that the stage produce obscene productions, but I do not believe it for we are at heart a clean people."[38] But the midnight ramble continued to be practiced, especially in the South, for some time.

White interest in black entertainment was not evinced only in black and tans and midnight rambles. White bohemians and intellectuals at times attended black performances by themselves or in small parties. Carl Van Vechten, who had grown up among blacks and was interested in black culture, used to take parties of his friends to black theaters to hear Bessie Smith and other blues singers;[39] John Hammond, even as an adolescent, frequently visited the Harlem theaters and clubs on his own.[40] Not all black and tans were situated in vice districts, but most of the big-city vice districts contained at least one black and tan; they were a standard feature.

The popularity of the black and tans among whites was at least in part a consequence of yet one more aspect of the new spirit of the age: primitivism. This was the idea, widely held not merely by intellectuals and artists, but by many in the general populace, that primitive people, who had not been repressed by the rules of civilization, were better able to express their feelings spontaneously than were the civilized. Blacks, according to many whites, were essentially primitives.[41] Once again, jazz benefitted. It was widely agreed that the music had come out of the black subculture. Gilbert Seldes, who popularized the term "the lively arts," wrote in 1924 that jazz came from "genuine folk music of the Negro slave";[42] in 1925 Virgil Thomson said flatly that "Africa has made profound alterations in our European inheritance";[43] Olin Downes, in his oft-quoted review of the Paul Whiteman Aeolian Hall concert, said that jazz had "Negro" origins.[44]

The point to be made about this was that, to many people, especially those breathing in the new spirit of the age, the idea that jazz was, or at least appeared to be, black music was an attraction. This was hardly true of everybody. Probably the majority of white Americans saw blacks as inferior, and the fact that they had invented jazz militated against it in many minds.

But a substantial number of people believed that the black roots of jazz were what gave it value. An advertisement in *Billboard* in 1917 for Clarence M. Jones' "The Dirty Dozen" said that the piece had "caused a sensation in the 'Black Belt,'" suggesting that its very blackness was a virtue.[45] (This number was outright boogie-woogie—there was something of a vogue for boogie at the time.)

Similarly, the black element in the vice districts was an attraction for many whites, and through the early days of jazz's development, it was almost taken for granted that you would find it in the black and tans. Right through the 1920s the black and tans continued to flourish, dying out only when black entertainers and black-derived entertainment had moved so completely into the mainstream that the black and tans had nothing to offer that could not be found elsewhere.

The vice districts also were becoming obsolete as jazz came to its first maturity. Under attack from the reformers from the beginning, by the years after 1900, one after another, they were closed down. The last one to go was Storyville, which was shut by order of the Navy Department during World War I. But they lingered on clandestinely into the 1920s, and died finally with the demise of Victorianism, when people were freer to drink, dance, and enjoy sex out of wedlock, making the vice district unnecessary.

But while it lasted, the big-city vice district played an important role in the making of jazz. It has been argued that, contrary to legend, jazz did not originate in Storyville, the New Orleans vice district, and that few of the major pioneers of the music ever played there.[46] And that does, in fact, seem to be the case: not much jazz was played in the famous vice district.

But it must be borne in mind that there were two Storyvilles: the one of song and legend for whites, and a shabbier, uncelebrated one for blacks in the above-mentioned Liberty–Perdido Street area. This quarter was awash with honky-tonks, where there was drinking and gambling, and where prostitutes danced the slow drag to attract customers.[47] These places featured small, usually very rough, two-to-four-piece bands, which played a lot of blues mixed with a limited repertory of the simpler popular tunes of the time. Louis Armstrong apprenticed in these honky-tonks, and it is clear that jazz was in part shaped in these haunts of prostitution.

And when it began to spead out, it flowed naturally into the Northern vice districts. The music did not go into them only; jazz was being played on the vaudeville circuits, and in dance halls and ordinary cabarets as well. But after, say, 1915, there was always jazz in the dives and saloons of the vice districts, and this is where, in the main, Americans outside of New Orleans were hearing it. In most places where jazz was played in the early days, sex was not far from people's minds. Sid LeProtti, a black band leader working the Barbary Coast at the time, speaks of getting requests for the slow drag from the prostitutes who frequented the clubs he played in.[48]

The movement of jazz out of New Orleans, beginning in 1908 or 1909, was fostered by an astonishing boom in social dancing, which was underway by 1907. Americans had, of course, danced before, but their dances had been relatively decorous, as befitted the Victorian morality. In many places they were still dancing the reels and set dances we now call "square" dances, in which body contact was limited. The dances of the boom were different, done by couples in a more or less close embrace, who whirled around the floor according to the dictates of their feelings. One observer said, "Couples stand very close together, the girl with her hands around the man's neck, the man with both his arms around the girl or on her hips; their cheeks are pressed close together, their bodies touch each other."[49] This was a description of a working-class dance; but even among the middle classes these dances more than hinted at sexuality. Here, exactly, was the spontaneity and expressiveness of spirit the new age was calling for. Irene Castle, of the celebrated Castle dance team, wrote, "By the fall of 1913 America had gone absolutely dance-mad. The whole nation seemed to be divided into two equal forces, those who were for it, and those who were against it."[50]

Many of the new dances had animal names: the Buzzard Lope, the Turkey Trot, the Grizzly Bear, and of course the Fox Trot, and they have been termed collectively "the trots." At first they were danced to ragtime, then at the peak of its popularity. These dances seemed to call for dotted rhythms, and it has been pointed out by Edward A. Berlin, in his study of ragtime, that beginning in about 1911 there was a rapid shift in published rags to dotted rhythms.[51] Jazz, however, was essentially *about* dotted rhythms, and it was seized on by dancers everywhere as soon as they came upon it. It had a lilt that went beyond ragtime, and very quickly it took over. In 1913 *Variety* like the Cotton Club, where Duke Ellington developed his music and became celebrated; the Club Alabam, which provided the first home for the Fletcher Henderson Orchestra; Reisenweber's, where the Original Dixieland Jazz Band introduced jazz to mainstream America; the colleges where Beiderbecke, Oliver, and other groups got much of their employment in the early 1920s.

We have to understand, then, that while a substantial proportion of the American middle class did not like jazz—was indeed threatened by it—probably the majority at least tolerated it, and a large minority were excited by it. Conversely, a great many religious blacks, and religious working people in general, were as hostile to the music as was the middle-class opposition. Jazz was astonishingly democratic: both its friends and its foes came from the whole spectrum of the American class system. William Howland Kenney III, in a recent study of Chicago jazz, has pointed out that the Lawrence Duhé band, with King Oliver, played at the Chicago White Sox home games in about 1920;[55] interest in baseball cut across all classes.

It was, really, all of a piece: the dance craze, Tin Pan Alley, the rise of the new show business, feminism, coming along together in a boiling mass, fired by the new spirit of modernism that informed everything. It is impossible to see jazz outside of this elaborate context, because it quite literally could not have existed without it. True, jazz could probably have gone on as a specialized folk music in a hidden subculture of New Orleans; but it certainly could not have become what it did without the new dances, the feminism that allowed women to do them, the proliferating entertainment industry that gave it a format in which to be exposed, the technology that produced not only the phonograph, but the big city in which the new show business was possible. It could have happened only in America, and only when it did.

2

The Rise of

Individualism

and the

Jazz Solo

In the minds of most people, at the heart of jazz is the improvised solo. Critical attention is almost invariably devoted to the analysis of solos by the great jazz musicians. Discussions of ensemble work are rare indeed in jazz literature, and I am at a loss to think of even one short critical essay on the work of some unsung master of ensemble playing—Hymie Schertzer's brilliant lead alto in the Goodman saxophone section, Georg Brunis' carefully constructed ensemble trombone with various Eddie Condon groups. It is always the soloist who is written about, always the solo that is analyzed; and if an ensemble is talked about at all, it is from the point of view of the arranger, the individual creator, rather than the group.

So much is the improvised solo seen as the essence of the music that listeners feel cheated when they discover that a solo is not the sudden outpouring of an open heart but has been memorized and repeated night after night, or even written out and played from sheet music. Most jazz fans do not feel a solo with the same force if they believe it is not spontaneous, even though the music itself would be no different. Clearly, the circumstances surrounding the music have much to do with how we perceive it; for the jazz fan, it must be seen as spontaneous—"improvised."

To an extent, of course, all music is improvised, in that the nuances of dynamics, shifts of timbre, shadings of pitch and vibrato, so important in giving life to a musical line, can be notated only roughly and depend on the inspiration of the moment. But it is difficult to think of any music that is improvised to the extent that jazz usually is. In much modern jazz, soloists are free to produce any sound their instrument is capable of making, in any order they wish. Even in music that is built on a preset harmonic pattern—the chord changes—there remains a great deal of liberty to play at some distance from the harmonic structure. For example, Lester Young, who tended to play what are ostensibly very basic harmonies, emphasizing tonics and fifths, used a great many lowered thirds, ninths, elevenths, and substitutions of the augmented dominant for the dominant seventh, according to Lewis Porter, in his thorough analysis of Young's work.[1] Indeed, it goes farther than that. According to his brother Lee, he would say, "Don't call the chords to me. Just play the chords and I'll play. . . . He would say it confines you too much if you know it's a D♭7, you know, you start thinking of the only notes that will go in that chord, and he would say that's not what he would hear."[2] The implication is that Young was working from a harmonic system he had internalized, which was different in some respects from standard harmony. And I think that something like this is the case with many jazz improvisers.

As this all suggests, in an improvised jazz solo, *any* note is permissible at *any* given point, provided that there is sufficient reference to the chord changes so that the listener can grasp the basic harmonic shape of the piece. And this degree of freedom is allowed even when six, seven, or eight musicians are all playing at once, although it is customary for some of them, especially the rhythm players, to conform fairly closely to the chords.

Jazz, then, is a highly improvised music dominated by solos. Given this, it is an astonishing paradox of the music that when it first became known to the American public, it was not essentially improvised, nor did it contain very many solos. It was instead an ensemble music tied to the limited forms of ragtime and the marches much of ragtime was built on. Ensemble lines were in the main worked out in advance, and played more or less the same, night after night, although the musicians were allowed to "embellish" the music here and there as it suited them.[3] The idea, as Chink Martin (Martin Abraham) said, was to play together. Each instrument had a role to play, and nobody was to be a star.[4]

Virtually without exception, from 1917, when the first jazz records were recorded, until 1923, there was no significant amount of soloing on any jazz record; and this was as true of the Northern bands trying to catch hold of the new music, like the Earl Fuller Jazz Band, as it was of the New Orleans pioneers. In fact, of several hundred jazz and pseudo-jazz recordings made before mid-1923, there was only one single significant jazz solo, Oliver's three plunger-mute choruses on "Dippermouth Blues." And that solo was not improvised, but was played the same night after night, not only by Oliver, but by others who copied it.

We should not be surprised by any of this. For one thing, the Victorian nineteenth century was the great age of the massive ensemble. It saw the swelling of the symphony orchestra into a huge instrument, which might be combined, as in the work of Berlioz and Liszt, with massive choruses to provide even larger "instruments." In popular music, it was the time of the large marching band. John Philip Sousa's famous bands had nearly fifty pieces, and grew to seventy over his career.[5] The nineteenth century did have its solo music; for example, operatic arias, or solos performed by Sousa's virtuoso brass players like Arthur Pryor and Herbert L. Clarke, who stepped forward from time to time to perform florid concert pieces designed to display their brilliant techniques. Nonetheless, the solo was the spice in the stew; the meat and potatoes was the ensemble; the larger, the better.

The early jazz bands owed a great deal to the marching band—they were in a sense, marching bands in miniature—and were thus part of the ensemble style of the day. But there was also the black element; and crucial to the black tradition was the idea of *community*. To simplify considerably, one of the functions of West African tribal music was to affirm the solidarity of the group.[6] It was not there just to offer pleasure, or to supply a beat for dancing, or to provide religious uplift; it was also supposed to create a sense of the group bond. The music was not received passively, as in a concert hall. The tribe's people danced, sang, clapped, or simply moved their bodies to it; they were as much a part of the performance as the musicians. John Miller Chernoff, who has studied African drumming intensively, says, "In African music, it is the listener or dancer who has to supply the beat; the listener must be actively engaged in making sense of the music."[7]

This sense that music was a communal effort continued to be part of the black tradition in America well into the present century, and is probably still true today. Blacks did not sit quietly in a circle around a singer or small band, listening. Music instead was participatory, as in the ring shout of the black church, the dances that went on in Congo Square until well into the second half of the nineteenth century, in the work song, in the custom of the "second line" in the New Orleans funeral parade, where the band was accompanied on all sides by dancers.[8] In black music, essentially, there was no audience; everybody had a part in the performance.

Participatory music of this kind cannot be largely improvised. It must conform to known patterns and practices. In the work song, for example, the song leader—who was often exempted from work—had a certain freedom to vary his line, but the workers who constituted the ensemble had to sing more-or-less-preset melodies in their responses.[9] The same was true of the church ring shouts, where the music was well-known spirituals, with standard words and melodies.

There was always some room for variation, as there was in West African tribal music. Members of the congregation or labor gang could sing a parallel line, usually an octave or a fifth away from the main melody; they could sing occasional notes at some distance from the melody; and they could add melisma in the spirit of the moment if they wished. Sometimes an inspired member of the congregation might venture a new lyric, which, if it were successful, might become a regular part of the piece. But these were only variations; in general, the music hewed to preset melodies and lyrics.[10]

The pioneering jazz musicians drew on both the tradition of the participatory music and the European preference for the ensemble. This was best exemplified in the parade bands often hired, or sponsored by, the fraternal organizations that were characteristic of black society in New Orleans. These groups, which might consist of ten to twenty pieces, mostly brass, clarinets, and drums, played a rough ensemble music in which small instrumental groups—cornets, E♭ horns, trombones, and so forth—played arranged contrapuntal parts.[11] Whether the three or four instruments in a given section were harmonized is not certain; I am inclined to believe that in the rougher of these bands, each section played in unison simply because it would have required a good deal of training, which many of them did not have, for them all to work out three-part harmonies for even the simpler tunes they featured, like "Listen to the Mocking Bird" or "Home, Sweet Home."

This idea is supported by the fact that there is no tradition of harmony in the European sense in either West African tribal music or the black American folk music derived from it. Given that, what happened next in the development of jazz should come as no surprise. Precisely how the dixieland jazz band evolved out of the parade bands we are not sure. It is probable that the evolution came naturally, when ensembles had to be cut down to suit a small dance hall, a party in somebody's front yard, or the dimensions of a wagon carrying a band around for advertising purposes.

In creating the dixieland jazz band, they simply shifted to a reduced version of the contrapuntal interchange of sections they used in the marching groups, except that now each "section" consisted of a single instrument. (Although not always: a photograph of the early Buddy Bolden band shows two clarinetists, and of course King Oliver brought in Armstrong as a second cornetist in the famous Creole Jazz Band.[12]) In the earliest stages a violin was usually added to double the lead, in part because a violin was traditional for dance music, and in part because violinists could usually read music and were thus able to easily pick up the new tunes a dance orchestra had to have in its repertory. As a rule, in the earliest of these bands, guitar and string bass substituted for the drums and tubas that provided the ground beat in the marching band, but there might also be a drum or even a piano.[13]

These early jazz bands thus grew out of a tradition that was resolutely ensemble, and not essentially improvisatory. The musicians could "embellish," as the term was; but as in the marching band, they were expected to play a more or less preset line; for it was the byplay between the instruments that gave the music its interest, leaving aside the rhythmic element.

This was the music that swept America after the enormous success of the Original Dixieland Jazz Band in 1917. There were virtually no solos. Everything was built around swift, instrumental byplays: one- and two-measure breaks smacking suddenly out of nowhere, sometimes several by various instruments successively; trombone smears dashed into the gaps; shrill clarinet plunging from high above into the instrumental turmoil. And all, of course, set to the infectious new hot rhythm that made people leap to the dance floor.

The recording of these groups was somewhat haphazard at first: the only New Orleans groups to be extensively recorded in the early days were the Original Dixieland Jazz Band and the Louisiana Five, whose members, however, were not all New Orleanians. Nor were any of these groups black. But when the black New Orleanians began to record, first the Kid Ory band in 1921, and then the Oliver band in 1923, the music was little changed. The black bands may have been rhythmically a little looser, but the difference was not large. The Kid Ory band, at one point the most celebrated hot band in New Orleans, recorded only two sides in Los Angeles. The music is a little hotter than that of the Original Dixieland Jazz Band, but otherwise much the same, and worked out in advance. Ory's clarinetist, Dink Johnson, appears to be somewhat freer than the others to vary his line, sometimes playing different phrases over repeated portions of the piece. He is not, however, improvising novel melodies, but reshuffling a small stock of standard figures, which he alters as necessary to fit the passing harmonies. Even a fairly well-trained ear would be hard pressed to find much difference between his method and that of Larry Shields, the Original Dixieland Jazz Band's clarinetist.

The next year saw the extensive recording of the King Oliver Creole Jazz Band, with Louis Armstrong on second cornet. These are generally considered the first important set of jazz records made, and we can therefore assume that they were definitive. Once again there is very little soloing, many arranged breaks, and ensemble parts played much the same from chorus to chorus. Because of the way records were made in this early day, there are few second masters available for comparison. We have two takes of "Mabel's Dream" and "Southern Stomps," however, and two versions of "Riverside Blues" and "Dippermouth Blues." A comparison of these various cuts makes it clear that ensembles are played much the same each time.

More significantly, so are the solos. Oliver's famous "Dippermouth Blues" solo was a carefully worked-out set piece designed to showcase his plunger work, and was played the same both times in the series. Armstrong's solos on the two cuts of "Riverside Blues" are straightforward renderings of a simple melody, played virtually identically in both cases. Again, on "Chimes Blues," Armstrong has a solo made up of two choruses of the blues. Once again it is straightforward playing of a simple melody, both choruses almost identical, down to a rhythmic hitch in the middle.

Only Armstrong's solo on "Froggie Moore" can be even loosely described as improvised. To begin with, it is not a "solo" in the way the word is used today, for the trombone and clarinet continue to accompany Armstrong in a manner that at times slides into ordinary ensemble playing. In the early New Orleans days, especially during a parade, the musicians were expected to work more or less steadily for two or three or more hours: it was, after all, an ensemble music requiring all parts to be present. Few players, however, could keep going without respite, and this was especially true of the brass players, many of whom were badly trained and were using too much pressure on the lips for support of high notes. It was the custom, therefore, for one of the other musicians to come forward for a period in a song so that those who had been carrying the burden could "take down," as the expression was.[14] What we appear to have in "Froggie Moore" is precisely this, rather than a true solo, with Armstrong coming forward while Oliver takes down. Oliver was beginning to have trouble with his embouchure, which would dog him for the rest of his career; there is some suspicion that he brought Armstrong north from New Orleans specifically to cover for him.[15] "Froggie Moore" was the eighth record cut at this particular session, and it had been immediately preceded by Oliver's specialty, "Dippermouth Blues." The band had made at least two takes of some numbers, including "Dippermouth Blues," and three of some others (none, regrettably, preserved). Oliver had been playing lead almost constantly throughout, and he had every reason to take down and let Armstrong come forward. But Armstrong used the opportunity to substantially embellish the melody and the effect is more of a solo than a cornet lead. Nonetheless, it is not a purely improvised line in the modern sense, but is built to the general shape of the tune—more than a simple embellishment, but nonetheless confined by the tune.

Johnny Dodds' treatment of his clarinet solo on "Dippermouth Blues," which also became a set piece, is instructive. According to Dan Havens, who has studied these recordings, "Dodds takes his first chorus, repeating what he had played on the Gennett in April, and then on the second chorus repeats the first. This suggests that, in his view, the first chorus was the better invention; at any rate, it has in two short months become crystallized as part of the tune and the arrangement."[16] This, really, is how it worked: players would from time to time try something new in the heat of the action—one of those embellishments—and if it worked, they would leave it in and go on to perfect it.

But the solos on these Oliver records are few, probably not constituting more than ten percent of the band's entire recorded output. The same is true of the other early recordings by the New Orleans players. The consistency is remarkable: this was an ensemble music, on the whole not improvised but played from preset, rehearsed arrangements.

It has been suggested by some writers that on location in cabarets and dance halls these bands opened up the music to allow more soloing.[17] There is no good evidence for it. Tom Thibeau, a pianist who heard the Oliver band at Lincoln Gardens, has said that it sounded much the same live as on records.[18] Marshall Stearns, who heard the Original Dixieland Jazz Band at Reisenweber's, said the same.[19] And why, when a band was having success with one manner of playing in the clubs, would it change to a different style when it recorded?

This ensemble style was what young musicians all over the United States were trying to grasp. It was what was imitated by the established bandleaders, like the white Earl Fuller and the black Wilbur Sweatman, who leapt to get in on the fad. It was also what young musicians, many of them teenagers, set about learning. Jimmy McPartland, cornetist with a group of Chicago teenagers known today as the Austin High Gang, had heard the Original Dixieland Jazz Band records and the Oliver group at Lincoln Gardens, but the main influence was the New Orleans Rhythm Kings, a group of whites, mostly from New Orleans, who were working around Chicago in the early 1920s. McPartland said: "What we used to do was put the record on—one of the Rhythm Kings', naturally—play a few bars, and then all get our notes. We'd have to tune our instruments up to the record machine, to the pitch, and go ahead with a few notes. Then stop! A few more bars of the record, each guy would pick out his notes and boom! we would go on and play it. Two bars, or four bars, or eight—we would get in on each phrase and then play it."[20] It is clear from this that these youngsters were not simply learning to play jazz solos, but were "catching" the parts of an instrumental ensemble.

This was distinctly not what young jazz apprentices would be doing a few years later. They would still be working from the records, but if they were copying anything, it would be classic solos—Oliver's "Dippermouth" chorus, Noone's "I Know that You Know," Armstrong's "West End Blues." But they were really more likely just to jam with the records, as young jazz apprentices have done ever since, learning how to improvise.

The goal of the earlier players, however, was different. They wanted to learn how to play the dixieland ensemble of the New Orleans bands they were hearing; and when they began to record, this is what they played. The earliest recordings of the Original Memphis Five, with Miff Mole and Phil Napoleon, made in 1922; the first records of the Wolverines with Beiderbecke, from 1924; were primarily devoted to the dixieland ensemble, with occasional brief solos added for the sake of variety.

That the improvised solo was not considered to be the main point of jazz is also made clear by the development of the large dance orchestra playing what was thought at the time to be an arranged version of jazz. The concept was first worked out in San Francisco, probably by 1915, by Ferde Grofé, and developed by the band leader Art Hickman in conjunction with Grofé and later, Paul Whiteman, who also had Grofé as his primary arranger.[21] This new kind of dance music, which Whiteman, who had a keen eye for publicity, called "symphonic jazz," was built mainly around the arranged passages or the dixieland ensemble. The improvised solo had little part in the music of the larger dance band at the beginning. Solos, where they existed, were straightforward expositions of the melody, although, as ever, the soloist was free to embellish the line here and there if he wished. For example, on Paul Whiteman's "Way Down Yonder in New Orleans," recorded in 1923, trumpeter Henry Busse plays what is supposed to be a jazz solo. The first note is a rasp, and is followed by a few accent shifts in the first two or three measures, but otherwise it is straight melody, lightly inflected with a feeling of swing. In a few years no soloist in what was thought to be a jazz performance would consider presenting an unimprovised solo of this kind; but in 1923 the idea of the improvised jazz solo was still aborning.

How then, and why, did jazz become the soloist's music it has been since, let us say, 1927? It has usually been said—by me, among others—that Louis Armstrong was responsible for making jazz a soloist's music, and I think, as I shall attempt to show, that this is at least partly true.[22] But I believe that the initial impetus came from another man. That is Sidney Bechet, who began as a clarinetist but who made his largest mark playing the soprano saxophone.

Bechet was a New Orleanian Creole, who had imbibed the music firsthand.[23] Something of a prodigy, and mainly self-taught, he is reliably reported to have been playing in amateur contests at ten, gigging around the city by the time he was fourteen, and playing with top New Orleans jazzmen by the time he was sixteen. Danny Barker, a New Orleans guitarist who was born in 1909, said, "When I was a child [Bechet] was already a legend in New Orleans." And he added, "Nobody at that time was spoken of with the same level of sensation as Sidney Bechet," referring to the years just before 1920.[24]

Bechet left home early to travel. He eventually landed in Chicago as part of the general movement of New Orleans jazz musicians to that city in the 1915 to 1920 period. He instantly made his mark: as early as 1916 the *Chicago Defender*, a nationally circulated black newspaper, reported that Bechet was "screamin' 'em every night with his sensational playing."[25] In 1919 he was heard by both Will Marion Cook and James Reese Europe, important black musicians who were putting together musical groups—not jazz bands—to tour England and the Continent. Cook and Europe were both well-schooled musicians—Cook was a composer, arranger, and violinist of symphonic quality—and both of them offered Bechet jobs, even though he could not read music and would have to appear as a soloist. It is significant that neither of them signed any of the other black jazz musicians around Chicago at the moment, although by this time many of the best of the New Orleanians were there.

Bechet eventually went with the Cook group. He was heard in London by Ernest Ansermet, an important European conductor of the time, who termed Bechet "an extraordinary clarinet virtuoso" and an "artist of genius."[26] Ansermet had little experience of jazz, and could not judge how Bechet stacked up against others in the genre, but he knew what a clarinet virtuoso was.

Bechet's European sojourn ended when he got into a scrape with the law in London, and by 1922 he was back in New York. He was immediately hired by Ford Dabney, one of the best-known society bandleaders in New York, and shortly thereafter was booked into a Broadway show as a featured soloist. Duke Ellington heard him when the show reached Washington, D.C., where Ellington was still an apprentice musician. Ellington was stunned by the experience. He later said:

> Bechet. The greatest of all originators, Bechet, symbol of jazz.
> . . . He had a wonderful clarinet tone—all wood, a sound you
> don't hear anymore. The New Orleans guys absorbed something
> down there along with the Albert system. I consider Bechet the
> foundation. His things were all soul, all from the inside. It was
> very, very difficult to find anyone who could really keep up with
> him. He'd get something organized in his mind while someone
> else was playing and then he'd play one or two choruses—or
> more—that would be just too much.[27]

Ellington, over a long lifetime in music, worked with some of the greatest jazz musicians who have ever lived; in a fair amount of study of Ellington, I have not come across praise of any other musician from him as strong as this. That he would still feel that way toward the end of his life, when Bechet was dead, and the memory of listening to him live was forty years old, is striking.

It is clear from all of this testimony that Sidney Bechet was, in this early day, having a substantial impact on jazz musicians. With people diverse as Danny Barker, Will Marion Cook, Ernest Ansermet, and Duke Ellington singling him out for this kind of praise, it is obvious that he was somebody special. There is no record of any other musician of that time being so admired. There were others, like Oliver, who were looked to as examples; but Bechet stood above them all.

Sidney Bechet was by temperament a maverick, a very independent man who did not take orders easily, and spent most of the first part of his life wandering from place to place, from one musical situation to the next. Inclined to be intractable, and given to turning up for engagements in his own good time, he worked best under his own leadership. He was, in sum, ill suited for playing a cooperative role in a dixieland ensemble. It was always necessary for his voice to be out front. In essence, no matter what the circumstances, he always played solo. Trumpet players who worked with him regularly understood this and tailored their playing to his demands, as can be heard on the series of records he made for Victor in the 1930s with Tommy Ladnier and Sidney DeParis, both of whom knew how to stay out of his way. Louis Armstrong, to the contrary, although by nature somewhat shy in his personal dealings, tried never to let anyone dominate him on stage. The few efforts that were made to bring the two New Orleans giants together left bad blood between them. [28]

Bechet did not record until 1923, presumably because of his peripatetic habits. His first recordings were "Kansas City Man Blues" and "Wild Cat Blues," under the leadership of Clarence Williams, whom he continued to record for into 1925, mainly as either the Red Onion Jazz Babies or the Clarence Williams Blue Five. These records show a fully matured jazz soloist—smoking hot, fervent, and in total command of his instrument, mainly the soprano saxophone here. There is no question in my mind that at this moment Sidney Bechet was the finest jazz player alive. Even Louis Armstrong, who appeared with Bechet on some of the Williams' sides, was overmatched. Furthermore, Armstrong was still developing; Bechet had found his métier. And in these records we can see why Bechet was held in such high regard by everybody who heard him: he was simply better than everybody else.

This is a judgment that is somewhat difficult to make. The records we have from before 1924 are very patchy, and probably not truly representative. Only the Oliver band, the Louisiana Five, and the group of mainly Northern whites best known as the Original Memphis Five, had done enough recording to leave us a fair idea of how they played. Yet we do have enough to suggest that when Bechet began recording with Williams in 1923, the jazz solo was still in its infancy. Armstrong cut his "Froggie Moore" solo that year, and by 1924, with the Fletcher Henderson orchestra, he was developing rapidly as the master soloist he would become. In some instances he was still using paraphrase as method, as for example on "How Come You Do Me Like You Do," but in others, as on "Go 'Long Mule," he was making new melodies. In New York, Miff Mole was showing promise of the virtuoso soloist he would become later in the decade, as in his solos on "Hot Lips" and "Sister Kate," with the Cotton Pickers in 1922; by late 1923, trumpeter Bill Moore and reed player Bobby Davis were improvising fairly well, and Adrian Rollini was becoming a fine soloist, as in The Varsity Eight "Mean Blues."

But Mole, Armstrong, and others were still searching. Bechet had already found the way, and apparently had done so some time before, if the opinions of Ansermet, Cook, and others are to be believed.

It should be pointed out that Bechet was not riding on pure

inspiration of the moment. Following New Orleans practice, he frequently worked out figures in advance that were suitable to this or that passage of a tune. According to Bob Wilber, who not only studied with Bechet, but actually lived with him for a period, "Generally speaking, although Sidney improvised freely when playing the blues, he would nevertheless follow the theme and variation form and make a definite development from chorus to chorus."[29] That is to say, he was not merely embellishing a preset line, but creating fresh melodies; however many of the elements in a solo were planned, and used again and again.

It would not be safe to say that Sidney Bechet invented the concept of improvising from the chord changes. Many of the ragtime pianists, for example, knew a good deal of music theory, and would certainly have understood the principles involved. Edward A. Berlin even suggests that a lot of the ragtimers improvised, although it is not clear whether they were improvising in the jazz sense, or simply interpolating set variations of one kind or another on certain strains.[30]

Nor can we say with certainty even that Bechet was the first jazz soloist. The bands in the New Orleans honky-tonks often consisted of a wind instrument backed by one or two rhythm players—Armstrong apprenticed with such a group—and in these bands the wind player was perforce a soloist. But, on the strength of the recordings we have, and what was being said about him, we can say that he was the first truly accomplished jazz soloist. It is very significant that the much-admired King Oliver, in the course of cutting some forty sides with the Creole Jazz Band, chose to feature himself only once. He obviously saw himself primarily as the lead cornetist in the dixieland ensemble, not as a soloist. But Sidney Bechet was, from the beginning, a soloist.

Why, then, did he not have more impact; why is he not today recognized as the first true jazz soloist? The answer is quite simple: from 1919 to 1922, when jazz was washing out of the vice districts and honky-tonks into the mainstream, and drawing to it thousands of aspiring musicians looking for models to emulate, Bechet was in Europe. Interest in jazz there at the time was virtually nonexistent. Although the word had some currency in Europe by 1922, there is no record of anybody who knew what it really was.[31] The 1919 English tour of the Original Dixieland Jazz Band was a failure.[32] Bechet did attract a little attention in England and France, but it was as a novelty, and he left no circle of adulators. The Bechet boom in Europe would begin only after World War II.

Had Bechet been in the United States in those years he would almost certainly have been playing in major locations and probably making records. If so, he would have become the central figure in jazz, the position Louis Armstrong would hold by the end of the 1920s. He had a second chance to make a real mark when he was in New York from 1922 to 1925. In particular, Ellington brought him into his band, and would have showcased him on his radio broadcasts, which would soon make Ellington one of the heroes of the new music. But Bechet chafed under even the loose discipline of the Ellington group, and left. Through these years he wandered, making only a few sides, at the moment when jazz records were beginning to flood onto the market. Then he was gone to Europe again, and by the time he returned, Armstrong, Beiderbecke, and others had caught up, and Sidney Bechet was nearly forgotten. During the 1930s, when Armstrong, Ellington, Goodman, Red Allen, and others were recording incessantly and playing top locations, Bechet was at times hard-pressed to make a living in music.[33]

Nonetheless, despite everything, I am convinced that during his sporadic Chicago and New York stays, Bechet had a great influence in jazz. According to Chilton, Barney Bigard, Harry Carney, and Lionel Hampton all said that they had listened hard to the Clarence Williams sides, especially those first two cuts, "Wild Cat Blues" and "Kansas City Man Blues."[34] It is also true that Johnny Hodges, Ellington's premier saxophonist, directly emulated Bechet, whom he worked with at times before joining Ellington.[35] And these musicians in turn influenced a great many others who came after. Bechet's influence was therefore indirect, generalized. Chilton says, "In many distant parts young musicians listened to Bechet's playing on the recording and gained the conception of jazz improvising from it."[36]

This was not true of everybody: Bix Beiderbecke arrived at a method of improvising that was independent of the Bechet influence, and created a school of followers who were playing in a more dispassionate, reflective style. But it was Bechet's approach—fiery, driving, fluid, exciting—that became what the jazz solo was supposed to be all about.

Yet Bechet by himself could not have changed jazz from being an ensemble music to a soloist's art. Bechet may have had an effect on musicians and close fans of the music, but his records were hardly best-sellers in the way the Original Dixieland Jazz Band or the Original Memphis Five records were. What happened, I think, was that by the middle of the decade the new spirit of modernism, with its crying-up of freedom, emotionalism, and expressiveness, had escaped bohemian and artistic circles and was rushing into the mainstream. The call was no longer for community, but for individualism, for self-expression. The shift was certainly apparent everywhere in art.[37] For example, the old Victorian novel was about social systems, if it was about anything. Dickens, Tolstoy, Balzac, and Thackery, were creating large circuses that showed the relationships between people through the whole range of the social structure, and focussed on basic institutions like marriage, the law, religion, and industry. The new novel of Hemingway, Fitzgerald, and Joyce centered on the fate of an individual, frequently a suffering hero like Stephan Daedalus or Jake Barnes. Society was no longer seen as the structure within which the individual worked out his fate, but as the enemy.

Similarly, the new dances of Loie Fuller, Ruth St. Denis, and Isadora Duncan were not the ensembles of classical ballet, but solos. The new music of Stravinsky, Ravel, and Debussy was not built on the tight, highly formal structures of the classical period, but was looser, associative rather than carefully woven, more fluid and purely "expressive." In the Victorian Age, Thoreau's *Walden, or Life in the Woods*, the quintessential call for individualism, sold about two thousand copies in its first edition and was out of print within four years;[38] in the twentieth century it became a central work, required reading for anybody with intellectual pretensions.

As I have pointed out, the way music is perceived affects how we feel it. The idea of the jazz soloist throwing off music from a full heart exactly suited the new mood. It was the individual, not the community, that counted. Jazz people were quite explicit about this. Jimmy McPartland, one of the members of the Austin High Gang who leapt into jazz early, said, "One thing we talked about a lot was the freedom of jazz. People used to ask Bix to play a chorus just as he had recorded it. He couldn't do it. 'It's impossible,' he told me once. 'I don't feel the same way twice. That's one of the things I like about jazz, kid. I don't know what's going to happen next. Do you?'"[39]

Another member of the group, Bud Freeman, summed up a great deal of the new way of thinking when he reflected years later on the experience of hearing Oliver at Lincoln Gardens:

> I was not only hearing a new form of music, but was experiencing a whole new way of life. Here were these beautiful people, not allowed any of the privileges of the white man, and yet they

seemed to be so much freer in spirit and so much more relaxed than the white man. I think I was impressed with the black man's way of life at an early age because he seemed so much wiser than the white man. . . . Certainly there can be no doubt that guilt and ego have done more to destroy man than anything else. In the many years I've been associated with the black man I've found that he takes each day as it comes and doesn't worry about tomorrow.[40]

It is all here: the call for freedom of the spirit, the virtues of primitivism, belief in living spontaneously. Jazz, and by implication all of art, was to arise from the individual expression of feeling. Indeed, Ornette Coleman has said flatly that in jazz "the essential quality is the right to be an individual"—in essence, to do what you want to do.[41]

Today this seems obvious. And yet, it is an idea that, before the arrival of the new spirit of modernism, would have puzzled a great many earlier artists. As we shall see in more detail later, as a general rule in Western art, the point has not been to express an individual psyche, but to perform certain functions in relationship to an audience. The great painting of the Renaissance was meant to inspire viewers with awe, pity, terror, love, and most especially, religious feelings of one kind or another. Similarly, prior to the late nineteenth century, the composers whose names still ring with greatness worked by a whole array of formulas, rules, and systems to create unified wholes. Bach, says Donald Jay Grout, "regarded himself as a conscientious craftsman doing a job to the best of his ability for the satisfaction of his superiors, for the pleasure and edification of his fellow men, and to the glory of God."[42] The idea that his music ought to be an expression of his individual soul would have sounded exceedingly strange to Bach.

Nor was it any different in literature. The great dramatists, from Shakespeare and the Elizabethans through the Victorian novelists, worked from well understood, if never really codified, ideas about how the dramatic form worked. Stories were built around conflict growing out of the nature of the people who figured in the work. Incidents built to climaxes, and the whole boiled to an end meant to leave the audience at once shaken and satisfied. What mattered was not the individuality of the artist, but the effect the work had on the audience.

The idea of art as the expression of an individual psyche is the product of the Romantic movement, about which I will have more to say later, and by the time of the Impressionist painters it was widely accepted. Renoir, according to Robert L. Herbert, hated the "finish" of the Salon art he and his confrères were struggling against, "because it was the product of mindless labor, rather than the spontaneous product of instinct. In this Renoir continued the view held by so many artists and writers of the romantic era, that instinctual freedom is the source of creativity. . . . Spontaneity, freedom, and nature became the watchwords of the avant-garde. . . ."[43] And this spontaneity expressed itself in a certain roughness and irregularity, that lack of "finish" that Renoir sought.

By the time that jazz was spreading across America, this view of the artist was thoroughly accepted. One of the great appeals of jazz for intellectuals in the first instance was its very roughness and crudity, which were seen as outcomes of the spontaneous way it was supposed to be made. This was understood: the members of the Original Dixieland Jazz Band went to great pains to conceal the fact that their trombonist, "Daddy" Edwards, could read music, for fear that audiences would suspect there was something calculated about the music.[44] Even today there are musicians who refuse to learn to read, study theory, rehearse, or even practice, for fear that a conscious knowledge of what they are doing will inhibit spontaneity and the free flow of feeling.

But although dixieland jazz certainly appeared to be spontaneous, it was not individual, but communal. It was that byplay between the instruments that mattered. A soloist, however, fit precisely the image of the romantic, even tortured, hero who so appealed to the twentieth century. It is startling how frequently jazz writers today speak of an improvising soloist's "risk taking" or "accepting challenges," as if he were climbing a mountain in a blizzard. We have wanted to see our jazz soloists as Hemingway heroes, and we have waved as banners alcoholism and drug addiction as proof that they were tormented geniuses—as if the suffering itself certified their genius.

But suffering or not, in the middle years of the 1920s, the soloist emerged from the dixieland ensemble. The shift can be seen quite clearly in Armstrong's seminal Hot Five series, which ran from late 1925 to the end of 1928.[45] By 1925, Armstrong had spent a year as jazz specialist with the Fletcher Henderson Orchestra, and had recorded a number of solos that had excited musicians. The point of the new Hot Five series was to show off Armstrong's improvising power, and he would therefore play solos. Nonetheless, the early Hot Five recordings are firmly in the dixieland style: the important members of the group, especially trombonist Kid Ory and clarinetist Johnny Dodds, were New Orleanians, and the ensemble predominated. Very quickly, however, the record producers, responding to what they took to be the public's wish, pushed Armstrong forward. By the end of the series, the New Orleanians had been replaced by ordinary musicians who could provide backing (in many cases written out) to showcase Armstrong.

My reference to these records should not blind us to the fact that they were, as far as the working jazz musician was concerned, adjunctive: the real business was done in the dance hall, theaters, and cabarets. To study jazz solely through records, as has so often been done, badly distorts its history, as William Howland Kenney has pointed out.[46] Kenney insists that the jazz solo was developed in considerable measure in cabarets and elsewhere, by Armstrong and others, as "acts" intended to display virtuosity as much as anything else.[47]

But it was not just Armstrong. By 1926, a whole troupe of orchestras featuring a lot of soloing were coming forward: Fletcher Henderson, Jean Goldkette, Duke Ellington, Ben Pollack; and they were followed by McKinney's Cotton Pickers, Casa Loma, Bennie Moten, and more. In 1927, even Paul Whiteman saw what was happening, and he reached out for the best white soloists he could find, among them Beiderbecke, Jimmy Dorsey, and Frank Trumbauer.

It cannot be only coincidence that jazz changed swiftly from an ensemble to a solo art in precisely those years of the mid-1920s when the new spirit of the new age was catching hold of the young American generation, which would be the primary audience for jazz at the time. Given the cry for individualism, there was no way that the dixieland ensemble could stand up against the romantic hero, trumpet pointed to the sky, flinging his feelings into the midnight air. And when Louis Armstrong began cutting the solo masterpieces of the 1927–1928 period, the New Orleans ensemble was dead.

Beiderbecke's remark, quoted by Jimmy McPartland above, is instructive: "That's one of the things I like about jazz, kid. I don't know what's going to happen next." It was not something that men such as King Oliver, Jelly Roll Morton, or others trained in the ensemble style would have said: they knew what was going to happen next because they had planned it. That was the New Orleans idea, the conception on which jazz was founded. Bob Wilber said of Bechet, "Like Jelly Roll Morton, he wanted discipline in his music, and never went for complete freedom of expression without regard to how each part fitted in with the others."[48]

But by 1925, not knowing what was going to happen next had a great appeal for young Americans escaping from the well-ordered life of the Victorians. And the jazz solo seemed the embodiment of that idea.

3

Going

It

Alone

"That was what we believed, in the Austin High Gang in Chicago: play the way you feel, yourself."[1] So said Jimmy McPartland, talking about the days of his apprenticeship in Chicago in the early 1920s. It is a statement hardly anybody connected with jazz would begin to question. It has had such uncritical acceptance that, as far as I have been able to discover, nobody has ever stopped to ask what it means.

It is, however, an interesting question to examine. Why is it better for a musician to play what he feels, rather than something he has previously worked out? And what sort of feeling is it, exactly, that a musician is supposed to play from?

Before we can answer this question, we must see what it is that the jazz musician actually does when he is improvising.[2] The process is not nearly so mysterious as it may sometimes seem to ordinary listeners. It depends on the fact that human beings have the ability to "hear" sounds in their heads in the same way that most of us are able to visualize in our minds scenes from the past or scenes that are set for us in books. Whether everybody has this capacity to hear music in their heads to the same degree has not been, to my knowledge, tested, but I assume that it is true of most people.

It is certainly true of jazz musicians, for it is essential to good improvisation. The jazz musician has taught himself, or gained through simple experience, the ability to play on his chosen instrument more or less anything he hears, and this is true whether the sound is actual or only exists in his head. (It may be that cognitively these are similar processes.) This is not nearly so difficult to do as it sounds; like the ability to sight-read quickly, it can be acquired through training over time. It is probable that some people are more naturally gifted this way than others, just as some people have better hand-eye coordination, or greater dexterity with tools. Jazz musicians do not have to be able to identify a chord upon hearing it; but they must be able to hear chord *relationships:* that is to say, given a starting point, usually the tonic, they can tell by the sound what the chords are as they come along, without really having to think about it very much. Once again, musicians' ears vary: some musicians are able to "spell out" a whole chord on the staff, with its inversions, doublings, omissions, and the like, a talent that is mainly acquired by arrangers and composers who constantly work in these terms. The ordinary improvisers do not need to be so highly trained, especially those who are working with a single melodic line; but in general, the more a musician can hear, the better.

It should be understood that the musician is not so much hearing the individual notes in a chord, although the well-schooled musician can do that, too, with a little concentration. He is instead getting an "impression," taking in the unified sound of the chord, in the same way that most people can recognize a familiar voice without breaking it down into its components. Actually, the cognitive process at work in hearing the chord changes is probably exceedingly complex, for there are several aspects to the cluster of notes termed a "chord" that the musician must recognize: the tonic, the mode (whether it is major or minor), and various extensions of the basic triad like sevenths, minor ninths, and others. The question for the cognitive psychologist is whether the musician has one mental apparatus for hearing tonics, another for discriminating between major and minor modes, a third for judging what sort of seventh is being played, and so forth; or learns separately each of the (roughly) dozen chord types that most jazz improvising is based on. Intuitively, I suspect that it is the latter; for example, major and minor seventh chords vary quantitatively only by one half step in four notes, and yet they are heard as qualitatively quite different.

However he does it, the jazz musician at work is embedded in a world of sound that is saying things to him. He is like a naturalist who is able to instantly decipher the sounds coming to him from the woods, fields, and ponds surrounding him. And it is the musician's job to provide an additional voice that makes sense in terms of what is happening around him. This is true whether he is the soloist of the moment, an accompanist, or a member of the rhythm section. Even a drummer, who is supposed to set time independently of anyone else (although, as we shall see in another chapter, this is probably not wholly the case), must be responsive to the whirl of sound he is working in. Not all musicians listen carefully: some soloists as well as accompanying players plow ahead on their own course in disregard of their musical surroundings. When Louis Armstrong was playing second cornet with the Oliver Creole Jazz Band, he very carefully tailored his line to Oliver's lead: but later, when he was fronting bands of inexperienced and usually inadequately rehearsed musicians in the early 1930s, he was almost forced to ignore his accompaniment, say damn the torpedoes, and full speed ahead.[3] But in general, one of the worst accusations that can be flung at a musician by other musicians is that "he doesn't listen." The unwillingness to take into account what everybody else is doing is taken as arrogance, a mark of disrespect for one's fellow players, and is seen as damaging the music.

And this, finally, is where the ability of the musician to hear notes in his head comes in. The jazz musician is not simply spilling unconsidered notes from an open psyche; instead, he hears in his head the notes he is going to play before he plays them. There are two reasons for doing so. To begin with, it is usually necessary, especially for players of wind instruments, to hear the note fractionally beforehand in order to hit it clearly. Why this should be true, nobody seems to know, but it is generally taken for granted by teachers of wind instruments. It is akin, in a way, to the idea of hand-eye coordination. As baseball players understand, the better you are able to see the ball, the more likely you are to hit it. A great hitter like Ted Williams is said to have been able to see the stitches on the ball as it raced toward him. There is, similarly, something in the process of hearing the note in advance that prepares the muscles of the mouth, face, fingers, or feet to instantly take on the right configuration.

But more important, the jazz musician must hear what he is about to play so as to give him an opportunity to judge its aesthetic merits. Now, we must be cautious about this. Given the speed at which everything is happening, there is not much time for a lot of conscious thought. Indeed, perhaps most of the time the improviser does not have time to do anything more than simply play the idea that he has come up with. A lot depends on how far ahead the player is able to think. It has been said that Charlie Parker was able to think so far ahead that he could change the music several times in his head before he came to it. The story may be apocryphal, but the idea behind it is correct: the improviser who has something to say is not just carving out patterns he knows will fit the tune; instead, musical phrases arise into his consciousness, which he can then accept, reject, or modify. It is a process very similar to writing. The writer does not simply bang on the keys, but shapes and re-shapes phrases and whole sentences that come into his head through association with what has gone before.

It is worth saying a little more about this. It is often said that people cannot think without language; that they need words in order to think, and that the limits of the language available to them shape what they are able to think about.

But, as should be apparent, musicians can think entirely in musical terms, without recourse to words. They hear patterns in sounds, and can concoct related patterns without thinking in words at all.

The process of improvising has some very interesting analogies to sports. Both the improvising jazz musician and the athlete must train intensely to build up sets of conditioned reflexes that enable them to respond without thinking to events that are unfolding around them in fractions of seconds. A quarterback usually has no more than three or four seconds to check his receivers, decide which one to throw to, if any, and get the ball off; a batter has about a second, or less, to decide what to do about an oncoming baseball. Similarly, the jazz musician must frequently deal with chord changes coming along as fast as one a second. Like the athlete, he must deal with them *now*. There is no tomorrow, no rehearsing.

That, of course, is true of any musician, whether he is reading an orchestral score, playing a piano concerto got by memory, or improvising. But unlike the symphonic violinist, the improviser must also create. And paradoxically, in this sense the jazz musician resembles the athlete more than he does the symphonic violinist. The athlete, too, must often "create" in response to the immediate circumstances he is in, because the circumstances are never quite the same.

But that jazz musician has an added burden: he must invent on the spur of the moment, yet he must also invent something that is of aesthetic worth—a "thing of beauty," as the term used to be. It is as if the shortstop were told not only to race into the hole, snatch the ball out of the air, pivot, and throw accurately to first base, but that he must do it so that the movements of his body, the flight of the ball, and other elements in the picture are as beautifully patterned as a ballet. Some athletes, lacking special physical skills, manage to get by on bull strength or sheer doggedness; as long as they get the job done, it does not really matter how they look. But jazz musicians cannot get by on bull strength, although some try; they need the imagination that provides gracious lines and the aesthetic sensibility to reject one idea in favor of another.

Critical to the process is that mental apparatus called the imagination, which produces the musical ideas the whole thing depends upon. Where do these ideas come from? How are they coaxed forth? All artists of course have their own ways of working, although they do not always understand their own methods very well. Painters and writers have an advantage, in that they have a real world to play off of. Monet found in his haystacks and water lilies a world of possibilities, and the human figure has been a major subject dating back at least to the Willendorf Venus of prehistoric times. Writers often begin with an incident from real life—sometimes grand ones, like the French Revolution and Napoleonic wars, which formed the basis of A *Tale of Two Cities* and *War and Peace*, sometimes something as trivial as a line of conversation at a dinner party.

The musician does not have a real world to work from in the same sense, but he does have a universe of sound that is thoroughly alive and meaningful to him. His head is stuffed with a congeries of motifs, instrumental sounds, tiny figures, large structures, scales, chords, modes, and the rest of it. Like the writer and painter, he works through association: one fragment draws forth another, or perhaps several other orbiting ideas, which in turn draw forth others. By sorting through these ideas, the musician hopes to find things that form novel relationships—this piece will relate to that one by means of elements in each that have hitherto seemed unimportant. Music, as has been said often enough, is the most abstract of the arts; it is not about ways of seeing the world, or the sudden recognition of something familiar in different clothing, but about relationships.

By way of example, consider Louis Armstrong's famous "Muggles" solo, cut in 1928. In measure ten, he plays two quarter notes followed by a rip up an octave; in bar twelve he plays the same idea backwards, so that the rip comes out upside down and in a different place in the measure. One figure was obviously drawn from the other, and the associative process of itself gave rise to the relationship.

Or consider another of Armstrong's great solos, the mute chorus that comes after the guitar on "Mahogany Hall Stomp," a solo Armstrong would continue to play on the tune, with variations, for many years. It is built around variations on a brief figure that features a sudden accent jumping out of a quieter cluster. It is my sense that Armstrong did not bring the solo into the studio the first time he cut it but developed it on the spot, for the central idea is not clearly defined from the beginning, but is only prefigured.

Similarly, it is very easy to hear the relationship of ideas in Bix Beiderbecke's classic "Singing the Blues," especially in the opening bars; in Parker's "Ko-ko," in which a figure across the first three bars is followed by a contrasting one that fills out the first eight measures, and in turn is followed by a three-measure figure reflecting the opening one; in Lester Young's

"Cherokee" with Basie, in which a variation on the opening figure appears twice in the remainder of the solo.

This ability to come up with related musical ideas is one of the characteristics of the great soloist. But the process I have been describing, in which one idea draws forth related ones in an endless stream, is, as any experienced jazz player knows, the ideal. The reality is often—indeed usually—different. Few jazz musicians can count on having a steady flow of interesting ideas. In fact, it is probable that only the geniuses of the music—the Armstrongs, Parkers, Ellingtons, and a few others—were able to come up with as many as one or two novel ideas each night.

The result is that jazz musicians depend on various systems to get them through the night. In the early days of the music, a great many of the players knew little formal music theory; some, in fact, could not even name the notes they were playing, much less the chords; they knew only that a given combination of keys or valves would produce certain melodic fragments.

Today, however, professional jazz musicians have studied their instruments formally, can read well, and have a good grasp of music theory. Thus, when inspiration flags or the ear fails, they can fall back on their knowledge of chords, scales, modes, and the like for notes to play. As a rule they will have got by memory the chord changes of the tunes they play often, and they can usually quickly recall in a first go-around tunes they had once known but had forgotten. They also know that most of the standard tunes they are likely to be confronted with are built around combinations of chords that come up again and again. Faced with, to choose an obvious example, the chord sequence $G^7/C^7/F^7/$, the improviser can be fairly certain that a $B\flat$ is coming next, although of course an imaginative songwriter will sometimes surprise him. The trained professional knows what notes are in a G-minor ninth, for example, and furthermore has probably practiced playing this chord again and again. He also knows one or more admissible substitutions for it. He hardly has to think to find acceptable notes to play, even though the resulting melodic fragment may not by itself be particularly interesting.

For another, there are certain basic phrases that are suggested by the technical aspects of the instrument itself. For example, certain figures can be played on brass instruments by the embouchure alone, without any movement of the valves or slide. Brass players inevitably tend to fall back on these when at a loss for something better. Saxophones overblow an octave, clarinets overblow a twelfth. As a consequence, octave leaps come easier to saxophonists, who use them a lot, than to clarinetists, who do not. Similarly, some kinds of melodic figures are "pianistic," arising from natural movements of the fingers, and inevitably pianists fall back on them when at a loss for something to play.

Again, jazz musicians develop, over the course of time, stock figures that fit well against specific chord changes at given tempos, and they constantly sort and resort this material. It is probable that more than half of the material in any jazz solo consists of variations on stock ideas the player has used before, frequently many times. This is not quite the same thing as developing a set solo to be played more or less the same each night, as in the case of Oliver's "Dippermouth Blues," because the material is constantly being reshuffled. But there is an inevitable tendency for ideas that have been used in a given place before to come to mind each time the passage is played, and the improviser may have to consciously fight the tendency to repeat himself. In total, improvising jazz musicians develop a sizeable grab bag of melodic fragments to draw upon in the heat of playing.

But beyond these, there are strategies they use to suggest things to play. One common system is parallelism, a very basic concept, which has a long history in Western music. There are several different kinds of parallels that can be employed. One of the most common is imitation—the repetition of a brief figure several times successively higher or lower, a device worked to death by the dixieland clarinetists like Dodds, Shields, and Ropollo, and by the Baroque composers as well. Or, to provide additional interest, the figure can be repeated both higher and lower: Lester Young does this in the last eight bars of his classic 1936 recording of "Lady Be Good."

A second sort of parallel commonly used by jazz musicians is the repetition of a rhythmic figure in different harmonic guises, a device that is basic to popular songwriting.

Another way of providing structure to an improvised jazz chorus is in the use of contrast—a patch of quick notes followed by a group of longer ones, high phrases set against low ones, loud against soft, or some combination of several of these, such as long, high, loud notes followed by a patch of busy little figures in the low register, as for example in the celebrated last chorus of Armstrong's "West End Blues," which begins with a high note stretched over almost four bars, and is then broken off with a rapid falling figure repeated several times. Armstrong, in fact, was the master of this sort of contrast. In "Go 'Long Mule," one of the first records he made with Fletcher Henderson in 1924, he builds his solo around contrasts of three emphatic quarter notes followed by patches of dotted eights and sixteenths; and his heart-wrenching solo on the mawkish "Sweethearts on Parade" is made up of quiet, sweetish passages alternating with rapid, tense, double-time ones.

Another way of producing material and giving a solo some kind of continuity, if not an actual shape, is to repeat at appropriate intervals a phrase or a variation on a phrase. This sometimes happens serendipitously when a player from time to time returns to the written melody of the tune he is working from. In

Ellington's small-band recording of a version of "The Farmer in the Dell," called "Swinging in the Dell," (1938) the soloists from time to time drop in fragments from the well-known nursery rhyme. But some players have made a more conscious practice of scattering a brief figure through a solo. Sonny Rollins is particularly noted for this practice, as for example in "The Blue Room," from 1966–1967, in which he uses quarter-note triplets on one tone, often the tonic, a number of times in his solo.

It is interesting that these practices have not been exploited by soloists more than they have. Only parallelism has been widely used, and even that device is almost entirely absent from the work of some major soloists, such as Armstrong and Parker, because, I suspect, these giants of the music felt at some level that it was too easy and glib a way to form a solo; which, in the hands of many players, it is. Why jazz musicians have not chosen to use, let us say, contrast, in their work more frequently is hard to understand. There is nothing terribly complex about following a busy passage with a spare one, a dynamic one by a static one. Contrast of these kinds have been routine in classical music for centuries, and, as the journey-man composer quickly discovers, they can make otherwise undistinguished musical material more interesting. Jazz musicians are constantly dealing with undistinguished melodic material, and one might think that they would find contrast, and the other devices I have briefly discussed, very useful.

But they have had substantially less recourse to these schemes than they could have, and I suspect it has something to do with the fear that too much conscious control will inhibit the free expression of feeling they are supposed to be exhibiting. The idea that you should not talk about the creative process or even think about it too much appears to have been endemic to jazz for a long time. I have read scores of oral histories of jazz players, and probably hundreds of interviews with them, and it is difficult to think of more than a tiny handful of musicians who have had anything to say about how they approach the problem of improvising. Probably the best-known analyses of the art of jazz playing by a well-known musician are the various comments on music by Jelly Roll Morton in the Library of Congress interviews by Alan Lomax, and these, if gathered together, would not amount to more than a few pages of typescript. Jazz musicians can talk endlessly about technical matters like chord substitutions and clarinet facings; but ask one how he achieves this or that effect, or what sort of thing he thinks about when he is improvising, and you are certain to get an evasive answer. Duke Ellington was interviewed thousands of times in the course of his long career, and while I have hardly read all of this material, much of which appeared in local newspapers across the United States, I have read a good deal of it, and I have come across virtually no discussion of his composing methods, except for impressionistic statements about beginning with a picture or an image of a flame at night, or a distant line of hills. Similarly, I once had the chance to play for Dizzy Gillespie one of his pre-bop records, in which he twice played emphatic major thirds over a minor chord. He was clearly trying something out, and I suspected it might have been an early experiment with the dissonant devices that went into the making of bop. His reply, simply, was, "It was a mistake, man." Needless to say, a musician of Gillespie's skill does not make this sort of mistake.

Why are jazz musicians so loath to discuss the essentials of their own creative processes? In part it is out of fear of appearing to boast; they are wary of the constant use of the pronoun "I" that any such discussion necessitates. But I think the basic reason for this unwillingness to be too explicit about what they are doing is that they are afraid analysis will kill the spirit of the music. Jazz is supposed to be spontaneous, supposed to be a product of the feeling of the moment: if you deliberately set out to impose some sort of scheme on the music, will that not interfere with the direct expression of feeling?

Yet withal I think jazz musicians are making a mistake by avoiding too much conscious analysis of the improvising process. Artists in other fields take it for granted that thinking about their métier is not merely helpful, but essential. The Greeks, in classical antiquity, devised all kinds of rules about proportion in architecture and sculpture, and unities of time and place in drama; and they built the basis for Western music on mathematical lines. The painters of the Renaissance studied anatomy in detail and devised rules of proportion that are taught in art schools today. Bach and his contemporaries worked out the idea of the tempered scale, which allowed a composer to wander freely through the full range of keys, and set up formal rules for writing fugues. The Impressionist painters attempted to apply the science of chromatics to their work, and Arnold Schoenberg created a whole system of composition on an intellectual base. Monet did not get from the rather sunny disposition of Grenouillière to the depth of the last water lilies, or Dickens from "Pickwick Papers" to "Bleak House," without deep thought. I do not mean by this critical analysis—the sort of thing critics and art historians do. Artists and critics do not think about a piece of work in the same way. The artist has his own reasons for putting things in and leaving things out, which have more to do with questions of internal design than philosophy or social commentary. As an artist matures—perhaps it would be safer to say *if* an artist matures— he becomes more and more interested in the nature of the work itself. That is to say, *how* a thing is said, rather than *what* is said, comes to preoccupy him, to the point where the method itself often becomes the subject of the work of art.

It is true, of course, that the composer or painter has time to reflect, to make changes, or even to scrap a work that does not seem to be succeeding, which the improvising jazz musician does not. Still, there is nothing to prevent a jazz musician from reflecting in tranquillity upon what exactly he does, or might do, when he is improvising. The fear of analysis, I think, has prevented jazz from enriching itself in a way it might have done. I think the music has gone as far as it can go on sheer intuition, an idea borne out by the fact that young musicians today are looking back over their shoulders to find models for their work. I suspect that when a new commanding figure comes along to reshape the music, it will not be yet another intuitive player like Parker, but somebody who has studied music carefully in order to see how it works, and has thought deeply about his own art.

Even so, there are limits to what intellectual rigor can do for jazz. Critical to the music is the way that it is inflected. The amount and kind of vibrato, the sharpness of attack, alternations of staccato and legato; the rise and fall of dynamic weight, the patterns of accents, the dips and bends of pitch, timbral shadings, the placement of note and accent against the ground beat—these give the melody line the variety and life that are essential to jazz feeling. These inflections are often minute, lasting for tiny fractions of a second, and involving shadings of one kind or another that are measurable only with the finest of instruments. Given their extreme subtlety, it is not likely that an improvising jazz musician can apply them consciously. They have to "happen," which means that the musician must count on his unconscious to supply them for him.

Consider Charlie Parker's first solo on "She Rote," from 1951, with Miles Davis on trumpet. There are in this solo none of the melodic devices I have been discussing—no parallel figures, no deliberate contrasts, no variations on a repeated idea, as in Armstrong's "Mahogany Hall Stomp." It is all one long, sweeping statement, which depends for its effectiveness on a swift, endless variety of melodic fragments, alternations of legato and staccato, and a full spectrum of dynamic shading.

To be sure, there is a certain amount of contrast from one passage to the next, simply because an improviser of Parker's immense fecundity is bound to vary his line from moment to moment, so that here are showers of quick, sharply snapped off notes, there, slurred passages. But there are none of the deliberately conceived contrasts that Armstrong worked out in "Sweethearts on Parade." It is a race, a charge, all unreflected forward motion. Or, to choose another metaphor, it has the effect of speech—not the formal exposition of a lecturer offering a line of consecutive thought spiced with planned effect, but the spontaneous talk of somebody in a bar arguing a point, describing an event of consequence to him.

Indeed, the inflections in solos of this sort are not just spontaneous, but to an extent accidental. Like many, if not most, wind players, Parker allows the natural dynamics of his instrument to emerge, with the line becoming louder as it rises, softer as it falls. Similarly, fast passages tend to blur towards a continuous rise and fall of pitch, while longer notes in slower areas are more emphatically stated, simply because it is easier to articulate clearly at slower speeds. Once again, especially with wind players, there is a natural tendency, in playing strings of eighth notes, to accent the first of each pair at the expense of the second. These subtle inflections, whether accidental or added without much conscious thought, are essential to jazz. Most solos, when written out, are less coherent than they sound when heard. That is to say, the soloist's melodic line, stripped of inflection, very frequently does not say much to us. There are exceptions, of course: Armstrong's "West End Blues," Beiderbecke's "Singing the Blues," and Parker's "Just Friends" are coherent melodic constructions.

But the great bulk of jazz solos, like the aforementioned "She Rote," are dependent on more than their melodies for their effects. Evidence for this lies in the attempts by one instrumentalist to reproduce somebody else's famous solo:

Cootie Williams' version of "West End Blues," Rex Stewart's "Singing the Blues," the Supersax-arranged version of Parker's "Ko-ko." These effects are often interesting and get a certain life from the reflection they form of the original solo. But in no case has it ever been widely believed that the recreations are the equal of the original. And this is because the recreation of the melody alone will not do it; the subtle inflections in the original must be there, too.

Herein lies one reason why it is so difficult to play jazz very well. Because these subtleties are not really under conscious control, because they have to "happen," the player is at the mercy of his own unconscious. If his unconscious will not help him, there is little he can do about it.

It is therefore not surprising that jazz musicians, like athletes, are always concerned about the psychological state they carry to the bandstand. I doubt that very many of them have ever thought this through, exactly, in line with their general distaste for analysis. Nonetheless, they are quite aware that they have had days when they couldn't "get loose," when their minds were clogged, their fingers stiff. But like the athlete, good day or bad, jazz musicians must perform, and they reach for expedients to get them going. Some of them perform little rituals before going on the stand. Some eat, or do not eat, before playing; or drink a carefully programmed amount they have found—or believe they have found—will loosen them up without inhibiting muscle control.

The problem is to relax enough to let the ideas flow freely and the fingers to fly without thought, while at the same time not becoming too unconcerned or offhand. Too much tension will interfere with the smooth flow of physical response of muscles and nerves, which at moments may shift several times a second. Just as the tense shortstop becomes stone-fingered and drops the ball, so the tense improviser becomes stiff-muscled, fluffs, misfingers.

Yet the jazz musician cannot play well if he is completely relaxed, as if lying half-somnolent in a Jacuzzi. He must be highly concentrated, alert to the whirling world of sound he is working within. He is not, as the romantics sometimes believed, merely a conduit through which his "genius"—that is to say, his attendant spirit—passes the poem or melody. The artist *works* at what he is doing; trying effects, making conscious choices; and so does the improvising jazz musician.

Once again, the analogy to the athlete is useful. There has recently come into sports the concept of "zoning" or "getting into the zone." This means achieving such a high level of concentration that anything but the immediate aspects of the game are barred from consciousness. A baseball pitcher who gets into the zone becomes unaware of the crowd, of the players behind him, of the weather, of the time of day. His conscious world consists of the baseball, the batter, home plate, the catcher. It has been said that when a pitcher gets into the zone he is almost impossible to beat.

In my own experience, something similar happens to a writer when he is at his best. This is especially true in writing fiction, where there is no need to refer to anything but the writer's inner world. A writer who is utterly immersed in the world of his characters, so that it is alive to him, more real than the world of his daily life, is able to convey it with understanding and rich and subtle detail, because he is actively experiencing it.

It is admittedly not easy for most people to achieve this highly concentrated condition. It requires the loss of self-consciousness, and this is something most people resist: we fear giving up the continuous monitoring of ourselves—where we are, what we are doing and feeling, who and what is around us—because to do so puts us at risk of stepping off the edge, or missing the creak in the snow that signals the approach of wolves. The fear is irrational, of course, as much fear is: the writer hunched over his keyboard in his attic study is not likely to encounter wolves—real ones, anyway. Nonetheless, self-consciousness undoubtedly has a real protective advantage, and we inevitably fear the loss of it.

But for the improvising jazz musician the abandonment of self-consciousness has great value, for it allows him to focus himself entirely on the music, barring from consciousness the audience, unpaid bills, his dislike of the club owner, the clatter of knives and forks. This is why jazz musicians so often close their eyes when they are playing.

It is particularly hard for the jazz musician to achieve this high state of concentration—to get into the zone—for there are likely to be extraneous conditions that keep intruding—a sticky valve, a bad piano key, a too-aggressive drummer, a rhythm section that keeps speeding up, a clarinetist who persists in going sharp in the upper register. These often-small things can be more troubling than a noisy or inattentive audience, for they are part of the world of sound the musician is supposed to be concentrating on. As I have said, Armstrong claimed to be able to ignore the poor accompaniments he so frequently worked with, but most musicians find musical problems distracting. And distractions keep them from being attentive to the subtleties of playing that are critical to jazz.

It is these subtleties, more than melodic shape, that provide the individuality that allows us, in the case of the great players at least, to say instantly whom we are hearing. This individuality, this ability to identify players, is essential to the jazz experience. Once I was in a café in Venice, only vaguely aware of the music coming out of the speakers on the wall, when I was suddenly stopped dead in my conversation by a single note, which I recognized instantly as coming from Louis Armstrong. Out of context as this note was, I could not mistake it. This was not due to any special sensitivity on my part; any fan of Armstrong's would have known it was he.

The great players are almost always instantly recognizable. We know immediately that we are hearing Parker, Young, Armstrong, Davis, Coltrane. And it is very much to the point that we have more difficulty identifying the lesser players. We are usually sure it is Young. We are not always so sure that it is Wardell Gray, Paul Quinichette, or any of the many others of the Young school.

I do not really know why this should be so, but I suspect that it has to do with the fact that the greatest jazz musicians produce music that is, not surprisingly, intensely personal. It is not constructed simply according to rules of harmony and rhythmic conventions, although of course these will apply; nor is it manufactured solely to suit the wishes of an audience, although many fine jazz musicians take audiences into account. Rather, it is put together to please the artist himself. The best jazz musicians like to listen to themselves play. They enjoy the sound they are producing, the melodic figures they have constructed, the inflections they have added to the line. Ellington said again and again that he kept his orchestra together, when it was costing him hundreds of thousands of dollars a year to do so, so that he could immediately hear the music he had written. Armstrong, in talking about shutting out of his mind the inferior bands he often played with, made it clear that he could do this because he was listening to his own horn.

These great jazz musicians, then, are for the most part playing something that they want to hear, and they are playing it the *way* they play it precisely because that is *what* they want to hear. Their music, then, is a direct reflection of their own musical preferences. It tells us what they like.

Lesser players—at least so I believe—are more likely to work from rules and conventions than to listen to the dictates of their own minds, in good measure, probably, because their own minds are not throwing up to them a lot of musical ideas with the clarity good soloing calls for. Instead they work from a sense that this or that musical phrase is appropriate to the context of the moment. It is not their own hearts that are telling them what to play, but notions taken in from outside.

We must not exaggerate this. I think that even fairly inept amateur players from time to time play something that they like to hear. But it is a sign of greatness to do it consistently.

None of this implies that what they want to hear is always fresh invention. As we have seen, the earlier players especially liked to develop set pieces that suited them. But once put together, it was what they wanted to hear.

And now, finally, we can see what it really means to "play what you feel." It is not a question of making some sort of statement about the travails of life, about racism, about the joys of communal effort, or troubles at home. It means simply that the musician plays what he *feels* like hearing.

Yes, musicians have been quoted as saying that they are trying to "tell a story" in their playing, or express some sort of mood. Duke Ellington was given to explaining that his compositions were inspired by something visual—the sight of flames at night, a particular woman, or whatever.

But all of this has to be taken with a grain of salt: it is the sort of thing jazz musicians tell unsuspecting interviewers when they are faced with questions they cannot answer, like, "Where do you get your ideas from?" or "What inspired you to write thus and such?"

As a general rule jazz musicians have no idea why they choose to play this or that, except that this is what they want to hear at the moment. The truth is that jazz musicians rarely play what they "feel" in the sense of expressing a mood or making a statement. The musician who walks into a job after a fight with a spouse, a bad review, or a hangover, is not trying to express what he feels. Instead he is hoping that the music will cheer him up, help him forget his troubles. A melancholy jazz musician does not want to play the blues, but a nice easy swinger that will lift his spirit.

And this brings us to yet one more aspect of jazz playing: it is taken for granted by almost everybody connected to jazz that one goal of the process is to make the musicians feel good. It is all part and parcel of playing the thing you want to hear. Indeed, it goes further than this, for a great many musicians, and fans as well, believe that the music is best when it makes the musicians happiest. If it feels good, it must be good.

Now that, I submit, is a fairly curious idea in art. Few novelists or poets are on record as saying that their work was best when they thrilled to the process of composition. Indeed, few have ever said that the process of writing was in the least enjoyable. Similarly, it is taken for granted by composers that composition is hard work, and involves a lot of tedious labor. The same is true of painting, and certainly ballet is usually physically very demanding. In sum, few artists of any kind have ever insisted that creating was a pleasure, and the more they enjoyed it, the better the work was.

But jazz musicians believe that playing music ought to feel good; this is, in fact, why most of them bother with jazz at all, and this inevitably leads them at times to confuse how they are feeling with what sort of music they are making.

In fact, I have never seen any evidence that the music is best when it is most enjoyable to the players—or rather, to put it more concretely, that audiences like the music most when the musicians are having fun. My own guess, based on common experience, is that the two conditions are unrelated. Sometimes, I am sure, when a musician is pleased with how things are going, the audience is, too. But it seems to me equally true that the music may come out better when the musicians are working hard, a little nervous, keyed up, and concentrating, than when they are relaxed and enjoying it.

Yet it is difficult to entirely dismiss the idea that a jazz improviser is likely to feel better when he is playing well than otherwise, for he is likely to play well when he has a flow of ideas, when he is hearing in his head a lot of things he wants to play. Thus, he can really never be wrong when he judges the music by how he feels; for in the end, he is the audience.

4

Hot

Rhythm

It has always been understood that the central characteristics of jazz, the *sine qua non* that distinguishes it from all other known kinds of music, is the rhythmic quality generally called "swing." Jazz can be played in all sorts of harmonic systems—the standard European diatonic scheme, modes of various kinds, the pentatonic blues scale with its microtonal blue notes. It can be played on virtually any combination of instruments you want to name, employing the available range of instrumental timbres, including a number that were developed specifically for jazz music; and it can be played in almost any kind of metric system the musicians can master. But if it doesn't swing, it isn't jazz.

This being the case, it is startling to realize that rhythm is the least studied, and inevitably, the least un derstood aspect of jazz. Whole books are written about jazz without the subject of rhythm being mentioned except in the most impressionistic way, usually in terms of this or that player's "sense of swing," or some similar phrase. Dozens of carefully crafted musicological analyses of the melodic and harmonic tendencies of the work of famous improvisers have been produced in which the master's approach to rhythm will be passed over in a page or two, if that.

Musicians and critics justify their inattention to rhythm by saying that it is beyond analysis. Where chords and melody are based on discrete and usually readily identifiable pitches that can be fitted into standard harmonic schemes, rhythmic differences from note to note are too small to be measured, but can only be felt in the aggregate as either swinging or not swinging. This belief—indeed, article of faith—was succinctly expressed in the story, perhaps apocryphal, that Fats Waller, when asked what swing was, replied, "If you gotta ask, you'll never know."

The idea that in jazz, harmony can be analyzed, but rhythm cannot, is open to a good deal of question. For one thing, analyses by mechanical means of sung or played melody dating back to at least the 1920s show beyond a doubt that, especially in solo performance, musicians have an extremely flexible approach to pitch. [1] This is as true of operatic divas as of jazz trumpet players. Musicians slur from pitch to pitch, indeed, through long strings of pitches. They approach pitches from above and below, sometimes from as much as an octave below. They allow pitches to rise and fall. Plotted on a graph or a computer screen, a melody line will not appear as a series of steps of varying heights up and down, but as a fairly continuous, waving line.

As a consequence, the analysis made of a mezzo's vocal line, or a jazz trombonist's improvised melody, is really an abstraction—a scheme drawn from the Western notational system that reduces the melodic line to a rough approximation of what is actually being sung or played. Thus, melody and harmony are not really any more susceptible to accurate analysis by the ordinary tools of musicology than is rhythm.

But both rhythm and melody are aspects of a physical artifact, music. If we are today capable of measuring the infinitely small frequencies of light, surely we ought to be able to measure the much larger units of time that distinguish melodies that swing from those that do not.

Interestingly enough, the best efforts to analyze jazz rhythms were the very first ones. It was recognized right from the time jazz became widely known to Americans that there was something special about its rhythms that distinguished it from even its close relative, ragtime. As early as 1917, a Columbia University English professor named William Morrison Patterson produced an analysis of jazz rhythm that was not surpassed for decades. Patterson had recently published his dissertation on the rhythms of prose, and it was natural for him to turn his attention to jazz.[2] After "months of laboratory experiments in drum-beating and syncopation," he concluded:

> Jazz is based upon the savage musician's wonderful gift for progressive retardation and acceleration guided by his sense of "swing." He finds syncopation easy and pleasant. He plays to an inner series of time—joyfully elastic because not necessarily grouped in successions of twos and threes. The highly gifted jazz artist can get away with five beats where there were but two before. Of course besides the thirty-seconds scored for tympani in some of the modern Russian music, this doesn't seem so intricate, but just try to beat in between the beats on your kettledrum and make rhythm and you will think better of it. . . . With these elastic unitary pulses any haphazard series by means of syncopation can be readily, because instinctively, coordinated. The result is that a rhythmic tune compounded of time and stress and pitch relations is created, the chief characteristic of which is likely to be a complicated syncopation. An arabesque of accentual differences, group-forming in their nature, is superimposed upon the fundamental time divisions.[3]

This was an astonishing piece of work. Patterson was the first, as far as I am aware, to use the term "swing" in its modern sense, and he did so years before it had any currency in the jazz world. And it would be at least fifty years before anyone devised a more accurate description of jazz rhythms: "an arabesque of accentual differences . . . superimposed upon the fundamental time divisions."

Patterson was not alone in attempting to analyze jazz rhythm. It was clear to many people that jazz produced a particular feeling in the blood and the bones, and the great puzzle was to find out how the effect was created. What, exactly, was going on? Another contemporary writer, Walter J. Kingsley, also from Columbia, was reported to be "scientifically investigating the variations in all forms of rhythm." Kingsley concluded that "jazz experts put in anywhere from five to ten extra beats between the notes of a composition."[4] This observation is not as keen as Patterson's, but it is clear that Kingsley was onto something.

This idea that jazz rhythms were created by putting in "extra beats" was believed by other critics of the day. Virgil Thomson expressed more or less the same idea when he said (as quoted by Aaron Copland), "Jazz is a certain way of sounding two rhythms at once . . . a counterpoint of regular against irregular beats," with an emphasis on second and fourth beats.[5]

A more common idea, however, was that the peculiar rhythmic feel to jazz was created by "anticipation." Don Knowlton, writing in *Harper's* in 1926, defined anticipation as "a sort of hurrying of the melody."[6] Thomson said that to jazz up a piece was to "start [a note] a little ahead of the beat."[7] And Winthrop Sargeant, in his 1938 book, wrote, "Anticipations of long notes by small fractions of their values (in performance sometimes the fractions turn out to be nearly infinitesimal) are quite common."[8]

Finally, there developed a third view, expressed in 1939 by

Wilder Hobson in his book *American Jazz Music*, that "the rhythms developed around the beat" or were "variously suspended around the beat,"[9] and this last opinion, that an important element in swing is the placing of melody notes away from the beat in some fashion, to create tension between the ground beat and the improvised line, is most widely accepted today.

Then, in 1949, the ethnomusicologist Richard Alan Waterman, who was also a jazz bass player, produced what was one of the first scholarly papers on jazz, in which he posited the existence of a "metronome sense."[10] Waterman, after considerable study of African tribal music, hypothesized that the tribespeople, both musicians and fellow tribesmen, possessed an ability which allowed them to abstract from a complex set of polyrhythms a basic beat to which everything related. "The assumption by an African musician that his audience is supplying these fundamental beats permits him to elaborate his rhythms with these as a base. . . ."[11]And Waterman went on to say that jazz musicians also depend upon developing the same sort of metronome sense to allow them to keep track of the ground beat while playing away from it. Although, as far as I know, this hypothesis has never been tested in the laboratory, it is widely accepted.

All of this, however, was speculative. Writers were working from their ears alone; and while a sensitive analyst with a good deal of training can frequently judge where a note falls in relationship to the beat, it is doubtful that anyone can do this consistently enough to be able to characterize the rhythmic principle employed by a given musician, or group of musicians in a particular school. The problems are daunting. Many, if not most, tones in jazz do not begin and end with the abruptness of a note played by an electronic instrument. Wind players in particular often articulate notes in such a way that they swell into existence, and may become audible to different auditors at different times. Most tones in jazz of any duration are likely to be inflected partway along by the addition of vibrato, accent, pitch sag, and the like, which can create a secondary pulse. And how do we deal with long, continuous lines of melody, as in the singing of Billie Holiday, which are difficult to break down into discrete tones?

Indeed, jazz musicians themselves are frequently at a loss to explain what is happening rhythmically when they are playing. Again and again they will refer to playing "on top of the beat," "behind the beat," "pushing the beat"; but in the same breath they will insist that they are keeping accurate time. Marian McPartland once wrote: "We'd often discuss playing 'on the beat,' 'behind the beat,' 'laying back,' 'on top,' etc. Joe [Morello, her drummer] would say, 'That's all bullshit. There's only one way—either you're playing on the beat, or you're not. Laying back means you're dragging. On top means you're rushing.'"[12]

Given the problems, it is easy to sympathize with critics who simply shrug off as beyond solution questions of rhythm. It will therefore surprise many readers to learn that there has been in existence for some time a technology for analyzing jazz rhythms in far subtler ways than it is possible to do with the ear alone.[13] The technology is employed regularly by experimental psychologists in their studies of what they call "time," and of other areas, like speech perception and motor control. Moreover, people interested in electronic music have used the technology for their own experiments with rhythm, as, indeed, have occasional hobbyists.

But the experimental psychologists have brought the study of time to a particularly sophisticated level, using computers that not only measure very fine pieces of time, but allow complex mathematical manipulation of the results. The psychologists are primarily interested (to simplify a good deal) in discovering how the brain processes time, which has no readily measurable physical dimensions—that is, it cannot be seen, touched, heard, or smelled. How is it that we can tell, even roughly, when a second, a minute, an hour has elapsed?

These studies of time have a fairly long history: the noted Carl Seashore published his classic *Psychology of Music* in 1938, and he had been working intensively in the field for at least a decade by that time.[14] Until very recently these studies have been almost entirely concerned with classical—or at least "non-jazz"—music. What is curious about this is that neither jazz musicologists nor experimental psychologists are aware of how much they have to learn from each other. Musicologists— and especially jazz critics—have for decades been writing about matters like "a natural sense of rhythm," playing "on top of the beat" or "behind the beat," and much more, totally unaware that there are relatively simple ways of studying many of these problems in the psychology laboratory. On the other side, few psychologists have understood what a rich field for investigation jazz rhythms can be: jazz musicians know, if only intuitively, a great deal about how time is measured, because they routinely deal with units of time as small as a tenth or even a twentieth of a second.

One of the few full-dress studies of jazz rhythm is a doctoral dissertation by musicologist Richard F. Rose.[15] Rose analyzed the length and placement of beats, and other phenomena, in three recorded jazz performances, using advanced technology. His results are too technical to be discussed in detail here, but they suggest that jazz musicians do not strive for an even flow of beats, but vary significantly, if subtly, the length and place-ment of what appear to be even notes. Among other things, he calls into question the widely accepted idea that jazz musicians tend to subdivide a beat by a two-to-one "triplet" ratio. He also found a strong tendency for his subjects to make second and fourth beats slightly longer than first and third.

A second interesting study is one by psychologist Mark C. Ellis, published in 1991.[16] Students of jazz have long been aware that putative "eighth" notes played in jazz are in fact unevenly weighted. Almost invariably, the first of each pair that make up a beat is longer and more heavily accented than the second.

Ellis brought three professional jazz musicians into the laboratory, and using available technology, he studied the way they divided the beat. Although, as we would expect, each player had his own way of dividing the beat, the differences were "with an average grand ratio of 1.701 to 1," which is consistent with the Rose results.

The work of these and other investigators is a good indication of what can be done in the laboratory to help us understand the phenomenon of swing. The weakness of the Rose and Ellis papers is the small size of their samples. In an independent study, psychologist Geoffrey L. Collier ran a lengthy series of tests—several thousand trials—on both jazz and classical musicians, as well as many musically untrained ones. Collier's results indicated that people, at least those in his sample, routinely divided beats by a ratio of about 1.8 to 1, and this was true when they had no interest in jazz at all. Therefore, it appears likely that the tendency to subdivide the beat in this fashion has little or nothing to do with swing in particular, and might be related to the brain processes that generate time.

Conveniently enough, Geoff Collier is my son, and we have combined forces to examine in more detail what actually goes on rhythmically in jazz performance. At this stage in our investigations we are not prepared to offer much beyond some working hypotheses, but it is already clear that a lot of what is commonly believed on the subject will not hold up to rigorous examination.

By way of background, we can begin with the fact that ordinary humans are able to tap out beats with surprising accuracy. In fact, there is evidence that people can measure time at least as accurately as, and trained musicians sometimes more accurately than, they can judge dimension in other modalities, like size or weight.

What is most interesting about this is that if you set a subject to tapping a key attached to a computer capable of making very fine time discriminations, the distance from one tap to the next can, and usually will, vary noticeably, and this is true even of jazz drummers who would prefer to think that they keep near-perfect time. Yet surprisingly, over a sequence of, say, twenty beats, the errors may—and to some extent usually do—even out. That is to say, the twentieth beat will come out closer to where it mathematically ought to, than might be expected from the beat-to-beat variations.

This immediately suggests that the subject is not being guided by the line of taps he has laid down behind him, but by a very accurate internal timer, which the actual taps only approximate. The existence of some sort of internal timer is now widely accepted by psychologists working in this area, although there is disagreement about the details of how it works, which tends to support Waterman's idea of the metronome sense. And it has been shown that the deviations from beat to beat that subjects invariably manifest are due in part to "mechanical error." That is to say, there is a certain slackness in the neural and muscular machinery that prevents the hand or foot from responding with machinelike precision to the directions of the internal timer. The timer itself, psychologists believe, is highly accurate.

Jazz musicians, then, come equipped with mental devices that allow them to maintain a steady beat over a fairly long time. Studies by Geoff Collier[17] and others have shown that this ability can be enhanced by training; that is, the well-schooled jazz drummer will usually be able to keep far better time than the novice.

In order to examine this phenomenon further, it makes sense to look at the larger parameters first, especially tempo.

The "beat," after all, is the spine on which everything else hangs, and it must therefore be of critical importance. Experience tells us that jazz musicians usually have very definite ideas about tempos for specific tunes in specific circumstances. Given this, at the outset we suspected that we would find musicians preferred certain tempos to other ones. But experience also indicates that very slow and very fast tempos are more rarely used, and it occurred to us that, alternatively, we might find tempos arrayed along a "bell" or "normal" curve, with the largest number of them coming in the midranges, and growing less frequent at the extremes.

In order to test these hypotheses, we timed a hundred recorded jazz performances carefully selected to represent a balance of styles and historical periods. Such a sampling can only be approximate, as younger players may work in older styles, and older players continue to play in outdated styles. The sampling was based on long study of jazz history, however, and was presumed to be as representative as any other sample would be.

To our surprise, when plotted, the tempos of these one hundred performances were normally distributed over a wide range. As we had expected, extremely fast and slow tempos were rare. For this sample, at least, the number of tempos used tapered off rapidly below MM 80 (MM stands for "metronome marking," or beats per minute), and a similar tapering off above MM 275. Within these limits, though, tempos were normally distributed. There was a slight clustering in the MM 160 to MM 210 range, but it was not statistically significant. All of this suggests that the usual range for jazz tempos is from as low as MM 80, a slow ballad tempo, to MM 275, which will tax any but the best jazz musicians. Surprisingly, we found some of the oldest groups using very fast tempos: a Beiderbecke group at MM 253, two Jelly Roll Morton performances in the same range, and startlingly, a 1917 Original Dixieland Jazz Band recording at MM 252.

It is hard to know how to interpret these findings, but it is our guess that in each case of tempo selection so many factors come into play, like the health of the musician setting the tempo, the need to find a tempo different from a previous one, compromises among the musicians, and in the case of the older seventy-eight records, time limits, that inevitably it all evened out. But this is of course speculative.

Yet despite this tendency for tempo preferences to follow the "normal" or "bell" curve, for a number of technical reasons, Geoff Collier has concluded that there is a gap from MM 160 to MM 190. That is to say, while musicians did at times choose tempos in this range, they did not do so as frequently as the mathematical analysis predicted they would. And the piano soloists we timed avoided this gap almost entirely. We believe that there is a clear tendency for jazz musicians to think in broad ranges of "fast" and "slow" tempos—they like to feel that they're either playing "up-tempo," or "down," and that what they think of as "medium" tempo is below this divide: the area in the gap appears ambiguous to musicians, neither really "fast" nor "slow."

Our study of tempos chosen by jazz musicians did also suggest that there might be more than just these two broad preferred tempo ranges. We found statistical "bumps" at about MM 92, 117, 160, and 220–230. (MM 92 is a blues tempo, or medium ballad; MM 117 is common for a medium-tempo blues or a faster ballad; MM 160 is frequently used for a medium-tempo swinger; and MM 220 is typical of a fast dixieland number.) But we will need more information before we can be sure.

Of even greater concern to jazz musicians is stability of the beat. It is simply a given in jazz that the idea is to keep as even a tempo as possible, and the musician who routinely "rushes" or "drags" is likely to be castigated by his fellows and critics who recognize what is happening.[18]

There are exceptions: Gene Krupa once said that he did not believe it was crucial to keep metronomically exact time,[19] and some musicians have said that a beat can shift, provided the change is a consensus that everybody feels. But these statements have been made deliberately in face of the common rule: the beat should not deviate.

Given the efforts made to hold the tempo, we were not surprised to find that jazz musicians usually were able to do so within quite narrow margins: of the one hundred performances in our sample, it was rare to find tempo ranges of ten percent from fastest point to slowest point. The bulk of our sample showed tempo shifts of less than five percent. Typically, tempo movement was confined to a range of three percent.

But tempos did shift. In very few cases was the tempo held within the margin of experimental error, and included in our sample were some of the most illustrious groups in jazz history—the Oliver Creole Jazz Band, the Armstrong Hot Five, the Morton Red Hot Peppers, the Ellington, Basie, and Goodman orchestras, the Charlie Parker Quintet, the Brown-Roach Quintet, and others, using drummers as admired as Jo Jones, Baby Dodds, Sid Catlett, and Max Roach.

Nor were the tempo shifts consistent: in some instances there was a broad tendency for the piece to speed up, in others, to slow down. But what we saw most frequently was a constant succession of tempo shifts, both faster and slower over brief segments of each piece, even within the span of four measures, which might take five or six seconds to play. Indeed, we found it to be rare for any two successive sixteen-measure segments of a performance to be played at precisely the same tempo, and very often we discovered tempo shifts of two percent from one eight-measure segment to another.

Why, if these musicians are equipped with natural internal timing mechanisms, which they have honed to a knifelike edge from thousands of hours of playing experience, should there be any deviation from exact tempo at all? There is, of course, the possibility of the mechanical error we spoke of earlier, and other human factors—a lapse of concentration, an unusual rhythmic figure that throws people, and the like; undoubtedly such more or less chance factors played a role in creating the rhythmic shifts we have observed.

But we think there is more to it than that. We first began to suspect that something was going on when we compared three takes of Duke Ellington's 1930 "Ring Dem Bells," and discovered that the band slows down in all three cases when Johnny Hodges plays his solo, and speeds up at Barney Bigard's chorus. Again, across all four takes of Parker's classic "Donna Lee," the tempo slows during the opening bars of Parker's chorus, and then proceeds to speed up through the chorus. On all four takes, the tempo continues to rise during the Miles Davis solo that follows, slows again on three of the four takes (in the third take the tempo remains steady), and then slows again in all four takes during the closing ensemble "head." Yet again, in two takes of the Wolverines' "Lazy Daddy," with Beiderbecke playing lead, the tempo consistently slows throughout, until the final ensemble, when it picks up.

These tempo shifts are slight, in some cases of less than one percent, but the consistency with which they occur strongly suggests that chance is not the only factor at work. To test this hypothesis, we systematically timed a group of Teddy Wilson solos (some of them with rhythm accompaniment), which a number of alternate takes were available for—as many as seven takes in one case. In all cases the performances were timed in their entirety in eight-bar segments, except for tags, which were often played deliberately rubato.

The results were subjected to rigorous statistical analysis, and we were able to conclude that many of these shifts occurred at the same points in a sequence of takes at a level of statistical significance. What this indicates is that at certain points in his performances, Wilson was deliberately either slowing or speeding up the tempo for musical purposes. These tempo shifts were small, and would be, I think, imperceptible to most experienced listeners, in part because they were disguised in a good deal of the rhythmic complexity characteristic of any jazz performance. We suspect that Wilson himself was unaware of what he was doing. Nonetheless, the effect is there, and it suggests that despite what jazz musicians claim about the requirement for an unvaried tempo, they do in fact—at least in some cases—use tempo shifts, however unconsciously, for musical purposes.

How far this effect will be found in other jazz performances is a question we cannot answer at this point. Teddy Wilson was trained in classical music, where tempo shifts for expressive purposes are routine, and he was growing up at a time when the concert orchestras, which he played in as a youth, used tempo shifts in the Sousa and other marches they featured. It may be that younger players, with different musical experiences, would not employ this effect.

As we might expect, the tempo shifts in the Wilson performances tend to come at structural divisions in the pieces—typically, he speeds up slightly at the bridge. Wilson was a very even player, using few changes in dynamics, and did not frequently build to crescendos and climaxes, and we would expect him to be guided by the tune's structure. But in the cases of the Ellington "Ring Dem Bells" and the Parker "Donna Lee," it is apparent that other factors, perhaps having to do with the way a given soloist phrased, or "swung," affected the tempo.

Perhaps the most interesting of our findings has been in respect to the jazz practice of doubling, or halving, the tempo.

This device was particularly popular from the late 1920s through the swing period, as a way of adding a little variety to the music. Usually, the tempo shift was made by one instrumentalist in the course of the break, of at least two or more, usually four, bars. (Actually, the break itself would necessarily be out of tempo, and thus without bar lines, but it would as a rule replace a given number of bars in the chorus just played.)

The idea of doubling or halving is absolutely central, not merely to jazz, but to all Western music, since "imperfect" duple time began to come into favor in the fourteenth century. Music is built around whole, half, quarter, eighth, sixteenth, and even thirty-second notes, although of course there has always been a lot of triple time played. Structures very frequently are made up of two-, four-, and eight-measure units. Indeed, the popular song, which has been so much a vehicle for jazz improvisation, was based on two-measure phrases repeated to make up four measures, to which a four-bar variation was added, and then the whole repeated to make up sixteen measures.

Given the critical nature of the doubling process, the results of the Collier, Rose, Ellis, and other studies showing that the tendency, even with musicians, not to accurately halve a beat is striking. And we wondered, if jazz musicians divide beats on something like a 1.8 to 1 ratio, would they do the same thing when doubling up the tempo as a whole?

Putting together a representative sample of tempo doublings or halvings was difficult, because the practice has become rare, and in the main we had to depend upon older recordings. We expect to add to our sample over time, but at the moment it is small.

But even though our sample was small, the results were so remarkably consistent as to be highly suggestive: in every case the supposed doubled tempo was significantly more than twice as fast, in many cases substantially so. What we also discovered was that the slower the initial tempo, the bigger the jump above a mathematically true doubling. Obviously, the 1.8 to 1 ratio we saw in beat division did not manifest itself here.

But that was not all. In twelve instances the bands eventually returned to what appeared to be the original, slow tempo. In all twelve cases the final tempo was somewhat faster than the original one. Once again there was remarkable consistency: in only one case was the difference negligible. In all the remaining instances, the final slow tempo was between 4 percent and 18 percent faster than the original one, with seven out of eleven falling into the 5 percent to 10 percent range.

This cannot have been consciously intentional. Experience makes it quite clear that few people, however well trained, will be able to select a tempo just slightly faster than a given one when another tempo has intervened.

We also found two examples of tempo "halving"—where the performance started at a swift tempo, and then shifted down. Remarkably, the fast-slow ratio held firm, so that the procedure was reversed: the new tempo was distinctly slower than a mathematical halving would have produced.

In a few cases we had alternate takes of these performances where doubling and halving of tempos took place. One very interesting example was a pair of recordings made by a group called Lavere's Chicago Loopers in 1944. The two recordings were cut on different days, and in each case three takes were made. We were surprised, for one thing, by how close the initial tempos were on each take, generally within the range of two or three percent. Even more interesting was how similar the fast–slow tempo ratios were, in all six cases ranging between 2.37 and 2.53. Especially startling was the comparison of the final slow tempos the band returned to after the doubling. In the case of the Lavere cuts for all six takes on two different tunes made on different days, they ranged between MM 91 and MM 100, with all three cuts of "Up a Lazy River" ranging between MM 96 and MM 94, and two of three takes of "Baby Won't You Please Come Home" coming within one beat per minute of each other.

We saw a similar result on three different versions of "Peg O' My Heart" by an Eddie Condon group, which featured trombonist Miff Mole. One cut was a studio version, another was made of a live radio broadcast not long afterward. For the studio version there was also an alternate take for further comparison. To begin with, the original tempos for both the issued studio take and the radio broadcast were virtually identical; the two up-tempo portions were within about two percent of each other, and in all three cases the returns to the final slow tempo were within the same range.

It appears to us, at this early point in our investigations, that jazz musicians are not really doubling or halving tempos. Instead, they have in mind specific fast and slow tempos they wish to arrive at, and they are able to do so with remarkable accuracy. A case in point is the three takes of "Peg O' My Heart" by the Condon group. The initial tempo of the alternate take is about ten percent faster than the issued take. A tempo shift of ten percent is perceptible to musicians, and we suspect that this new tempo was chosen deliberately for some purpose or other. Nonetheless, the up-tempo portion and the final slow tempo are closer on both takes—indeed, the final tempos of both takes are for practical purposes identical. In this case, at least, the controlling factor was not ratios between slow-fast-slow tempos, but preset ideas about what the tempos ought to be in each case. And this, Collier thinks, can be explained by the tempo gap in the MM 160 to MM 190 range: in order to arrive at a "fast" tempo, the players have to jump over the gap, regardless of how slow the original tempo was. And this was what happened: the doubled tempos landed above the "slow" range far more frequently than a true doubling would have brought them to.

What the experimental psychologists will make of all of this is something that Collier, Ellis, and their colleagues will have to determine. For the musicologist, the message is that we know a lot less about rhythm than we think we do. Much of the foregoing, obviously, is only suggestive. Most of the work is yet to be done, for jazz musicians are performing a formidable array of rhythmic operations to produce their effects, which are still only faintly understood. But it is already clear that for a jazz musician, tempo is not a mechanical thing that can be hammered out by a drum machine—but flexible, a living, breathing component of jazz.

5

The

Embrace of

Show

Business

In twentieth-century America, the terms "art" and "commerce" have come to be seen as so antithetical as almost to preclude any one person's pursuing both. "Going commercial" is precisely the abandonment of art: What is art cannot be commerce, and what is commercial cannot be artistic. No matter where people stand in respect to either, they are invariably suspicious of the other. There have always been doubts about Robert Frost in the poetry establishment, because too many ordinary readers could quote from "Mending Wall" and "Stopping by Woods on a Snowy Evening." On the other side of the coin, movie makers, radio and television producers, and the like have been almost pathologically afraid of anything that smelled of "art." The view was, "If you want to send a message, get Western Union."

When jazz was in its earliest stages, from, let us say,

the beginning until the mid-1920s, there was not much concern about whether or not it was commercial. It was clearly popular, both in the early dixieland form and then in the symphonic style, which came forward after 1921, and few people saw this as a defect. But by 1925 there was a growing feeling in some of the musicians, commentators, and close fans that a distinction ought to be made between a "purer" form of the music and a more commercial type. Initially this distinction revolved around the issue of "blackness": the more Negroid a performance seemd to be, the less commercial and therefore purer it was. In 1925, Carl Van Vechten was complaining that too many black Broadway productions were merely slavish imitations of the white style, and was urging "some more sapient manager" to put on Bessie Smith or Clara Smith "to sing Blues, not Blues written by Sissle and Blake or Irving Berlin, but honest-to-God Blues, full of trouble and pain and misery and heartache and tribulations. . . ."[1] (Why Van Vechten, and others who have taken this view, are so eager to hear about other people's miseries, has not been explained.) And in 1930, Charles Edward Smith, who would be one of the most significant jazz writers of his time, wrote, "Louis Armstrong, at present the only outstanding figure in jazz, succumbs more and more to the white man's notion of Harlem jazz."[2] At this moment Armstrong was being guided by the highly commercial Tommy Rockwell, who was moving him away from the old New Orleans style into the show business mainstream. This seemed to Smith, and other jazz writers, a sellout. The attitude was in part a product of the left-wing ideology of the time, which saw show business as of a piece with entrepreneurial capitalism, which of course it was.[3] But it also reflected notions, drawn from the Romantic movement, of the artist as outsider, which a popular show business star obviously was not. Very quickly the problem of going commercial was generalized beyond the question of blackness: anybody could prove to be impure.

From that day to the present, jazz fans and critics have remained suspicious of too much commercial success by a musician. They have always felt happier with the musicians who did not become rich and famous, like Pee Wee Russell, Clifford Brown, and Lester Young, than with those who made a lot of money, because their artistic purity was assured. Armstrong was not the only jazz musician to be chastised for selling out: Benny Goodman, Stan Kenton,[4] and Cannonball Adderley[5] were likewise held in suspicion. Bing Crosby's enormous popular success has even today kept him from being treated seriously as the first-rate jazz singer he was in the early days.[6] And there can be no doubt that a good deal of the criticism of Wynton Marsalis was a direct consequence of the Grammy award and the publicity campaign mounted on his behalf by his record company and others. In jazz, as in the other arts, it is felt by many that a musician who makes a lot of money cannot have been wholly honest.

Yet the truth is that jazz began its life, and grew to maturity, not as a form of art, but cocooned in the enormous entertainment industry that has been a primary feature of American life in the twentieth century. For the early players, there was nothing wrong with going commercial: that was the whole idea. However much they enjoyed their music, and however firm they were in their concept of how it should be played, people like Morton, Oliver, Keppard, James P. Johnson, and the rest were entirely aware that they were in show business, and that their job was to entertain audiences. Making a lot of money and getting their names up in lights may not have been the only point of playing jazz, but they were major considerations, and musicians took it for granted that if audiences did not like your music, why, you had better do something about it. Jazz was, at first, a part of show business, and in order to understand how it developed, we need to understand the entertainment industry it grew up in.

As we have seen, twentieth-century show business was a byproduct of the city that grew on the flood of immigrants and people from the farms, and the technological explosion that made moving pictures, phonograph records, radio, and eventually television, possible. Huge numbers of people were now gathered within easy reach by train and trolley car of baseball fields, vaudeville houses, museums, concert halls, cabarets. At the same time, the industrial system, with its defined workday, produced for millions, if not for everybody, a certain amount of free time that needed to be filled.

The new city created both the possibility of, and the need for, the industrial entertainment machine that today so preoccupies us. And by the time jazz was becoming popular, there existed in the United States a huge system of theater chains, moving-picture houses, dance halls, cabarets, radio stations, and saloons, which required a constant flood of performances of all kinds. Jazz was there to help fill the empty moments.

Claims have been made that at least in the early days, jazz was a folk music. Sidney Finkelstein specifically called his early book *Jazz: A People's Music*, and said flatly that jazz was "a folk art and a people's art."[7] Otis Ferguson, who wrote about jazz for the *New Republic* and other periodicals, said, "Jazz is folk music."[8]

It is probably true that in the very early days in New Orleans, the music was mainly made by nonprofessional part-timers primarily for the use of their own community, at parties, dances, picnics, funerals. But the tradition of the black entertainer antedated jazz, and it is clear from the reminiscences of Jelly Roll Morton and others of the first generation of jazz musicians that at least some of them were working as professional entertainers in the New Orleans vice district, at expensive white restaurants like Tranchina's, where there was also gambling, and fairly early in the day, at dances at Tulane University and elsewhere.[9]

The minute these early black musicians started playing for white audiences, the line between folk music and professional entertainment was crossed. These whites, many of them well-to-do, hardly belonged to the black folk culture. The musicians as a general thing enjoyed playing, of course, but they were working in locations like Tranchina's and Mahogany Hall, not out of love of the music, but because they could make what seemed to many blacks living in poverty like a lot of money. Morton, in discussing his mentor Tony Jackson, has made it clear that Jackson was an all-purpose entertainer who could play anything, from operatic arias to the blues.[10]

In fact, it is probable that jazz evolved out of ragtime at least in part in the show business embrace. Most of the jazz pioneers began their musical lives as ragtimers. Buddy Bolden was listed as a professional musician in the New Orleans city records as early as 1901, when jazz, if it existed at all, was still at an incipient stage.[11] Morton, too, was initially a ragtimer (indeed, he claims it was he who made the leap from ragtime to jazz).[12] It is clear, then, that while jazz did contain some folk elements, it had always, from the beginning, had at least one foot in show business.

Jazz musicians began spreading out from New Orleans almost before the music was really formed, or had a name. Sorting out the movements of these early jazz musicians is not easy, for there is very little written record—although there is some—and we are heavily dependent upon the memories of old men and women recalling events that took place fifty—or in some cases sixty or seventy—years earlier. Reb Spikes, a West Coast musician working in the early years of the century, said, "A bunch of those Creoles came out . . . about a year or so apart. . . . They all came through here . . . 1907 or '08, or '09, like that, you know."[13]

The key figure appears to have been Bill Johnson, primarily a bassist, who also played guitar and banjo. Very early, Johnson formed a band in New Orleans called the Original Creole Orchestra, which included George Baquet on clarinet and Ernest Coycault on cornet, and made "a hustlin' trip all over Dixie, just like the German bands used to do at the time."[14] The Johnson group, with some changes in personnel, was on the West Coast by 1907.[15] At some point (sources differ), cornetist Freddie Keppard joined the group, and it began to work around the Coast playing black and tans and jitney dance halls. In 1914 it joined a vaudeville circuit, reaching New York in 1915, where it played the prestigious Winter Garden. According to one of the group's members, it worked incessantly through these years, a good deal of the time in vaudeville. So popular was it that by 1917, there were "six Creole bands out" touring the country.[16]

Other musicians quickly followed the example of the Original Creole Orchestra, among them Jelly Roll Morton, who may have been on the West Coast by 1912. The local musicians began to learn the New Orleans style, and by the time of World War I, there were several local bands playing jazz on the West Coast, the best-known today probably being Sid Le-Protti's So Different Jazz Band.

Somewhat later there was a similar movement north to Chicago by the New Orleans jazz players. Once again it is difficult to be sure of the details, but it appears that the first group to reach Chicago was led by trombonist Tom Brown. As early as 1913 the band was "discovered" by the dancer Frisco, who wanted to bring them north. It was 1915, however, before they actually went north to open at Lamb's Cafe, where they played an extended engagement. As Tom Brown's Dixieland Jazz

Band, they went on to New York, where they played the Century Theater.[17]

Another band, led by comedian Bert Kelly, arrived in Chicago in 1915,[18] and finally, in 1916 drummer Johnny Stein brought north the group that would become the Original Dixieland Jazz Band, with some personnel changes, where it opened at the Schiller Cafe.[19] These were white groups, but the blacks were coming, too: Bechet in 1916, Oliver in 1918, and others.[20]

These musicians were being drawn out of New Orleans to the big cities of the North and West because pay was substantially higher. Where they might be paid a dollar and a half a night back home, they could make fifty dollars a week or more in Chicago. But for blacks there was more to it, for the period saw a tremendous movement of blacks out of the South into the Northern cities where conditions were better and the ever-expanding industrial machine was creating a demand for labor.[21] The movement of jazz out of New Orleans must be seen in the context of this general migration of blacks from the rural South to the industrial North.

Nonetheless, it is abundantly clear that these emigrating jazz musicians were not coming north to play solely for their own people in the bars and dance halls of the black enclaves. Roy Palmer, Sugar Johnny Smith, Lawrence Duhé, the Oliver group, Jelly Roll Morton, the Original Creole Orchestra, the Original Dixieland Jazz Band, and the Memphis Five all played vaudeville.[22] And these were only a few. In September 1916, months before the Original Dixieland Jazz Band's splashy success at Reisenweber's, *Billboard* reported that "The Jazz Band" was "vaudeville's newest craze."[23]

But it was not just in vaudeville. New Orleans trombonist Zue Robertson had a band with the Kit Carson Wild West Show.[24] Virtually every jazz group of any kind worked frequently in dance halls, both the "open" halls where anyone could enter for a fee, like Lincoln Gardens or Freiberg's in Chicago, or the dime-a-dance halls, like the Pagoda and Purcell's on the Barbary Coast.[25]

The more fortunate of these jazz bands were also playing big cabarets and the cabaret-like restaurants of the time, which offered a lot of entertainment. The Original Dixieland Jazz Band opened at Reisenweber's in January 1917, and after it left, the restaurant was ready to sign the Tom Brown group for an extraordinary sixty weeks, although the deal collapsed when New York City's mayor instituted a one o'clock closing. (The action at Reisenweber's ran from midnight until as late as six in the morning.[26]) In Chicago the Casino was "noted for two kinds of jazz band—one for dancing and the other a colored organization with several of the men playing on jugs (known as jug jazz)."[27] Another Chicago place that would become an important location for jazz was the Dreamland, a black and tan, which, according to *Variety*, opened in May 1917 specifically to present jazz. Oliver and Bechet both worked there in 1918.[28] Shortly after, the paper reported that in Coney Island, an entertainment center, "every place down there has its band of the jazzing type"—Nemo Rothe's band at the College Arms, Frank Ross and his Jazz Band at the Harvard Inn, Roy King and his Jazz Band at Gallagher's, and more.[29]

This activity was taking place, for the most part, before 1920, which was very early in the game. That year, however, saw the first regularly scheduled radio broadcast. The radio boom was explosive; sales of radio equipment more than doubled from 1922 to 1923.[30] The demand for programming was enormous, and very quickly radio producers reached out for jazz. Fletcher Henderson made a radio broadcast in 1921. According to William Randle, Jr., in 1924 the show from the Club Alabam in Times Square, with the Henderson or Sam Wooding orchestra, was broadcast forty-seven times. Clarence Williams was on radio in 1922 and 1924. When the Savoy Ballroom in Harlem opened in 1926, a remote line was immediately installed, and thereafter the bands from there were on the radio as frequently as eight times a week. Henderson regularly broadcast from Roseland after he opened there, and Ellington broadcast at least 210 times from the Cotton Club from 1927 to 1930.[31]

Similarly, the phonograph industry began bringing jazz bands into the studios in 1917 when Columbia made the first Original Dixieland Jazz Band recording,[32] and on the heels of the great success of the group's Victor records, jazz quickly became a staple element in the phonograph industry. Indeed, it has been claimed that Bessie Smith's 1923 recordings helped save Columbia, hurt by the economic slump of the postwar years, from bankruptcy.[33] In retrospect we can see that virtually every jazz musician of consequence in the period was well recorded.

It is clear that, contrary to what has been widely believed, jazz, far from being anathematized, by as early as 1917 had become a fad, a craze. Performers everywhere were slapping the word "jazz"—or "jaz," "jasz," or "jass" as it was variously spelled—on any kind of production that would even vaguely support the title. In May of 1917, Reisenweber's announced the opening of an annex to be called the Jazz Kitchen. (It failed, due to the early-closing law.[34]) There were jazz revues, jazz cabarets. A spate of songs hoping to capitalize on the jazz craze erupted onto the market in 1917, among them "Jass a Yankee Doodle Tune," "Jazebo Johnson's Hokum Band," "Mr. Jazz Himself," "Jazz It Up," "Everybody's Jazzin' It," "Everybody Loves a 'Jazz' Band," "When I Hear that 'Jaz' Band Play," which was used as a "closer" at the Ziegfeld Midnight Frolic. All of these songs were published by mid-1917.[35]

Inevitably, bands everywhere were adding the word "jazz" into their titles: the Banjo Jazz Boys, at the Martinique in

Atlantic City, Fischelli's Jazz Band at the Vogue restaurant in New York, Armand Hand's Rathskeller Jass Band at Riverside Park, the Tokio Jazz Band at the famous Tokio restaurant in New York, Hum Red Payne's jazz orchestra with the Johnny J. Jones America Show, Walter Jackson's jazz band playing clubs and fraternities in Indiana, the Western Jazz Band at the Pemberton Inn in Hull, Massachusetts, Sophie Tucker and Her Jazz Band on the Orpheum circuit, and a Symphonic Jazz Band, using the title before Whiteman did, which may explain why his band was billed as Paul Whiteman's Jazz Classique when it came east in 1920 to make its mark. Once again, all of these bands were in operation in 1917.[36]

It should not be thought that everybody was in love with the new jazz music. Teddy Morse, in his "Sharps and Flats" column in the *New York Clipper*, a show business paper, announced in March 1917, only six weeks after the Original Dixieland Jazz Band had opened at Reisenweber's, "Those celebrated 'Jazz's' didn't set us on fire in the East, after all. Many a silent prayer, hitherto unused, went heavenward when the 'flop' became known."[37]

By June, however, Morse was beginning to feel a little uneasily that his prediction of the demise of jazz had been premature, and he offered his readers this verse:

I have an ear for music,

Most everybody has;

But what is there that's Beautiful,

In a howling band of jazz?[38]

(Morse's assessment of his ear might have seemed more convincing had his verse scanned a little better.)

Billboard's music reviewer was no happier with the jazz craze than Morse was. He happened to be the black actor Clarence Muse, who had complained about the erotic element in black entertainment, and my supposition is that he did not like the idea of blacks being associated with this vulgar new music, either—a position taken somewhat later by the *Chicago Defender* columnist and bandleader Dave Peyton, who, among other things, complained that Louis Armstrong's group at the Blackhawk was too noisy and would give black bands a bad name.[39] Muse said, "What is jazz? Any sound utterly devoid of harmony." In another column he ran a lengthy letter from a reader that read in part, "The jazz band craze is an empty-headed fad. It emerged from the dives and night orgies of jig revelry. It permeated the San Francisco Barbary Coast and underworld haunts, spread to the cabarets and dance halls and finally frivoled into the glittering palaces of American society, and, like ships that pass in the night, we may well exclaim, 'What new next!'"[40]

There was also plenty of opposition to jazz outside of show business. Civic leaders, churchmen, government officials railed against it. To them, it was particularly the so-called jazz dances that offended because of the sexual implications in them, but they did not like the music, either. As Ron Welburn has said in his exhaustive examination of jazz writing, "Americans were divided about the worth of jazz" in these early years.[41]

Yet there can be no doubt that despite the opposition from some quarters, jazz was being swept into show business at an explosive rate: in 1916 it was known to a considerable number of Americans who regularly visited dance halls and cabarets, especially in the vice districts; a year later there were hundreds of dance bands in the United States claiming they were playing jazz; and a year after that, there were several hundred jazz records on the market, and jazz bands were routinely playing college dances for the children of the wealthy and being booked into prestigious restaurants and theaters.

We must bear it in mind that a great many of these early

"jazz" bands were not playing what most critics today would call jazz. Prime examples of these were the putative jazz bands of Earl Fuller, Wilbur Sweatman, and Ted Lewis, among the best-known bands of the time. (Sweatman was black, the others white.) These three leaders were already established when the jazz craze hit, and hoped to cash in on it by imitating the Original Dixieland Jazz Band, and possibly other groups they may have heard earlier in Chicago and on the West Coast. Their groups were presented as jazz bands, written about as jazz bands, and recorded as jazz bands. At the time, few people would have distinguished between these groups and the New Orleans groups then recording, primarily the Original Dixieland Jazz Band and the Louisiana Five. Indeed, it is probable that jazz fans today unfamiliar with this early music would also have trouble making the distinction. The key point is that the attempt to create an aesthetic of jazz that would allow interested people to determine what was jazz and what was not did not come until the arrival of symphonic jazz, in the years after 1921, forced the issue. All of these early bands, ranging from the Creole Orchestra to the Earl Fuller Jazz Band, appeared to have in common certain musical practices—perhaps "propensities" would be a better term—mainly a novel rhythmic swing and an exuberant polyphony, along with two others drawn from the ragtime it developed out of—an abundance both of syncopation and countermetrics. In these terms they all counted as jazz.

Later, when the dust had settled and jazz was better understood, the musicians committed to jazz and their fans began to feel that there was something superior in the music played by the New Orleanians, and it was this that they tried to capture. To some extent this distinction was fostered by the belief that, as played by blacks, the music was more authentic, a view that persists today. Nonetheless, most specialists in this early jazz would agree that the difference between the jazz of, say, the

Oliver and the Sweatman groups, was substantial. Perhaps the fairest comment on the Fuller and similar groups, was made by Wilder Hobson, who was a youth when the band was playing. He said that the Fuller group was "in reality a ragtime outfit, though a good one. Its abrupt syncopations are markedly different from the flowing rhythms of the Dixieland [Jazz Band]."[42] As such, there is no reason to denigrate these groups as any more commercial than the real jazz bands.

The full acceptance of jazz was slowed somewhat by the entrance of the United States into World War I and the economic recession that followed. To a lot of people it seemed unpatriotic to go out dancing when American soldiers were being shot in France. In the fall of 1918, when the war was winding down, *The Literary Digest*, an important middlebrow weekly of the time, reported, "The usual public dances in the halls have, in a large measure, been abandoned for the duration of the war."[43] The postwar recession hurt the record industry along with everything else. But by 1923, recovery was complete, and jazz established itself in the entertainment mainstream. In that year a band of youngsters, with Duke Ellington at the piano, was brought down from Harlem to provide music for a new nightclub in the Broadway area meant to attract tourists, sports, gangsters, and the general run of New York night-lifers.[44] Late in the same year, or early in 1924, Fletcher Henderson was brought into another club in the area, the Club Alabam.[45] In 1924, Claude Hopkins, a pal of Ellington's from Washington, D.C., took a band into the Smile-a-While Cafe in the resort town of Asbury Park, New Jersey.[46] In 1924, the Wolverines, with Beiderbecke, were booked into Doyle's Dance Hall in Cincinnati.[47] In 1923, a fourteen-year-old Chicagoan named Benny Goodman dropped out of school and began working the dance halls and cabarets, like Gunyon's Paradise and the Green Mill Gardens.[48] By 1924, virtually every one of the best jazz musicians of the time was in show business: Armstrong and Coleman Hawkins with Henderson at the Roseland Ballroom; Bubber Miley and Bechet, briefly, at the Hollywood Club with what would become the Ellington orchestra; Bix with the Wolverines at Doyle's; Morton and Oliver in various locations in Chicago.

Furthermore, 1923 was the year when the record industry, recovering along with the rest of the nation, turned to jazz in earnest. That year saw the first records by Oliver, Morton, and Bessie Smith; Ellington and Beiderbecke began recording the next year. From then until the stock market crash in 1929, the freshet became a flood. At the end of the Roaring Twenties, Beiderbecke was the featured soloist with the most famous dance orchestra in the world, the Whiteman group; Armstrong was performing in a fancy nightclub and working in a Broadway musical with Fats Waller; Henderson was still at Roseland, the best-known dance hall in the country; Ellington was at the nation's most famous nightclub, the Cotton Club; Oliver would have turned the Cotton Club job down because the pay was too low, and was working at prestigious restaurants like the Quoque Inn on suburban Long Island.

When we examine the early history of jazz, then, we cannot see it as developing the way an art form might, out of a dynamic of its own. For example, French art of the nineteenth century, from, say, Ingres to the Fauves, was frequently without a significant popular audience, and therefore could be tugged and hauled whichever way the artists (whatever their reasoning) thought best. Key to the process were the private philosophies of art of Corot, Manet, Seurat, Cézanne, Gauguin, or Picasso, not pressure from an audience that, for many of these painters, hardly existed.[49]

Jazz, on the contrary, had a considerable audience, which was giving many of the musicians substantial incomes and a good deal of prestige, and this was particularly true of the blacks, most of whom would have been working at pick-and-shovel jobs had it not been for music. Pressure from the audience was always there.

I do not mean that these early jazz musicians constantly trimmed their sails to suit the vagrant breezes of every new fashion. It is important for us to keep in mind that these musicians were excited by jazz—they were *interested* in it—and most of them had, or were developing, clear ideas of how it ought to be played. They were not simply vaudevillians reaching out for the largest possible audience. Nonetheless, they had to reconcile what they wanted the music to be with the demands of the audience. There is a good parallel in the nineteenth-century novel. Writers like Dickens, Twain, Dostoyevsky, and Balzac certainly had ideas about their cultures and the nature of human life they wished to get across, and they had their theories of how novels ought to be put together. But they were thoroughly alive to the fact that their books had to sell in fairly large quantities. This did not necessarily mean that they had to bend their beliefs; but it did mean that they had to shape their work so that they could express these beliefs in terms that would grip their readers.

Jazz musicians of the early period were in the same position. Many of them, barely out of their teens, were making incomes that would have seemed unreal to them a few years earlier. They were buying fancy clothes and expensive cars, even investing in the stock market. So they enlisted in show business, and thereafter they found themselves constrained by the wishes of the entrepreneurs who were doggedly pursuing public favor. The results were immediate and decisive, for hardly had jazz moved into the mainstream than the public made clear its preference for the big dance band playing arranged music, to the rough five-piece dixieland group playing New Orleans polyphony. This fickleness was extraordinary: the old style had captured the public fancy in 1917; as late as 1924, dixieland bands like the Wolverines, the Memphis Five, and the

Clarence Williams Blue Five were still popular. By 1925, the need for change was apparent, and by 1926, Ellington, Henderson, Armstrong, Beiderbecke and Oliver were all working with bands playing in the new manner. The black show-band leader Sam Wooding said, "When I was in Barron's, and when I left Atlantic City, it was dixieland style. But now, dixieland was giving way, and such bands like, you know, some of the fellows from Ohio, and Fletcher Henderson and my bands and some of the other bands. . . . It all happened in the early 'twenties."[50]

The switch in taste can probably be attributed to the fact that dixieland, while unquestionably popular, as the success of the Sweatman, Lewis, and Fuller orchestras attests, was never the preference of the majority. But by 1926 the big dance band playing some sort of jazz-based music was the dominant form in popular music. You could still sell dixieland: Morton, Beiderbecke, Nichols, and others went on recording a fair amount of it into the late 1920s. But it was becoming a specialized taste. If you wanted to play the best-paying locations and sell lots of records, you had to play in the new manner.

It is not clear that it mattered very much to all of the musicians. Jelly Roll Morton went doggedly on in the old way long after it was obvious that dixieland was dead, and Beiderbecke recorded as much as possible in the small band context, even recording "At the Jazz Band Ball" and "Clarinet Marmalade" ten years after they had been hits for the Original Dixieland Jazz Band. Furthermore, I suspect that Oliver, who was getting on in years, would have preferred to play in the New Orleans style he had worked in for nearly thirty years. The white Chicagoans, like Goodman and McPartland, also tended to play in a freewheeling small band context when they could. But Ellington and Henderson had never been dixielanders; Armstrong had become a featured soloist, and had no reason to return to the more confining role of the New Orleans cornet lead.

Whatever they felt about it, they had no choice, as the case of Morton makes clear: he went on working in the old manner, and in 1931 his company, Victor, stopped recording him, while it went on recording Armstrong and Ellington, who were leading big bands, in abundance.

One immediate effect of the change in popular taste was to bring the saxophone forward as a principal instrument in jazz. It had become faddish after World War I, and had been brought into the dixieland bands as a sop to public taste, used by them mainly as a novelty to solo from time to time.[51] But it did not have the power to compete with the brass and, depending upon which of the family was used, it collided with one of the other winds, and existed on sufferance.

The new dance band built on the Hickman-Grofé design had saxophones at its heart. The instrument was also ideal for the little trios that still provided a great deal of music for dancing, because it could be played in a quieter and more legato fashion than brass instruments, and was therefore more suitable for private dances and parties in homes and small clubs. Very quickly there grew a mystique about the instrument. It came to be seen in the popular mind as the quintessential jazz instrument. Magazine illustrations, book jackets, and cartoons depicting jazz almost invariably featured a saxophone, and novels and stories about the new, freer lifestyle were filled with descriptions of "throbbing," "wailing," or "moaning" saxophones. By the end of the 1920s, saxophonists like Coleman Hawkins, Jimmy Dorsey, Frankie Trumbauer, Benny Carter, and Bud Freeman were seen as major figures in the music. In time it would be the saxophonists, not the trumpet players, who were the kings of jazz, such as, for example, Hawkins, Hodges, Lester Young, Charlie Parker, John Coltrane, and Ornette Coleman. Today the idea of jazz without the saxophone is unthinkable; in 1924 it was not; and it was audience pressure, in part, that forced the change.

Perhaps more important, the show-business embrace jazz was caught in had a considerable effect on the careers of a number of critically important musicians. It was particularly marked in the case of Ellington and Armstrong. Ellington, we remember, did not begin his professional career as a jazz musician.[52] There is no indication in anything he ever said or wrote about his apprenticeship to suggest that he was enraptured by the new music. His interest was in making money and being popular with the crowd, as he explicitly said himself. He came to New York with a group called the Washingtonians, which was led (insofar as anyone actually led) by the banjoist Elmer Snowden, as a journeyman pianist trying to catch hold of the popular, and difficult, stride style.

The group turned to jazz for the same reasons that millions of young Americans turned to it—because it was interesting, exciting, the up-to-date thing. But they would have been forced into it willy-nilly when they were booked into a Broadway club, the Hollywood—later the Kentucky Club—because jazz was what the job called for. They hired the very hot Bubber Miley and, briefly, Sidney Bechet to juice up the band, and by 1925 they had become a rather rough-and-ready dance-cum-jazz orchestra.

In 1927, the Cotton Club needed a new band. The well-known King Oliver group was offered the job, but turned it down because the money was not good enough, and the Ellington group, almost by chance, got the opening. The band was not really up to the job. Most of the musicians were poor sight readers, accustomed to working from rough head arrangements, and were not prepared to play the more polished, professional kind of music a place like the Cotton Club required. Ned Williams, later Ellington's publicist, said, "I can't say I was too much impressed with the Ellington crew [at first]. It definitely didn't have the form and polish it acquired later on."[53]

But the Cotton Club was an important opportunity for Ellington, and he was determined to succeed. He borrowed Louis Metcalfe, a good professional trumpet player, from Sam Wooding, a fellow bandleader;[54] and through a lot of rehearsal, a good deal of musical genius, and a certain amount of what Ellington called "skillipooping"—that is to say, the use of flashy effects to obscure a lack of substance—he pulled the band through.

As it happened, in 1926 and 1927, national radio "chains"—the forerunners of the great television networks of today—were being put together. These chains needed an immense amount of program material. One simple way to get it was to install a "wire" in a nightclub and broadcast the entertainment live across the nation. It was assumed that the club's entertainers would perform free for the publicity in it. The expense of a location broadcast was therefore minimal.

The celebrated Cotton Club was an obvious place to put a wire, and for over three years the Ellington band was heard nationwide several times a week, not merely late at night, but sometimes at suppertime in the East when mainstream families were listening. These radio broadcasts were critical in making Ellington famous; so famous indeed that in 1931 he was invited to visit President Hoover at the White House as one of a group of "Negro leaders."

Ellington thus was deeply enmeshed in the entertainment industry, and the symbiosis had a direct and dramatic effect on his career as a composer. Ellington admitted that he was more prone to look for good times than sit at the piano and write. "Without a deadline, baby, I can't finish nothing,"[55] he once said. For Cotton Club audiences it was possible to dish up more or less the same program night after night, because the audience was constantly changing. In fact, Cotton Club shows were quite elaborate, carefully rehearsed, and ran for six months at a time; there was a limit to how much variety

Ellington could have introduced even if he had been so minded.

But radio was different. The same fans were likely to listen to every broadcast, which meant that he had to have at least some new material for them as often as several times a week. By itself the existence of the radio wire in the Cotton Club forced Ellington to create.

So did his records. In the early days of jazz the big money in the music business was from the sales of sheet music. Records were seen by music publishers as a good way of getting new tunes publicized, especially after vaudeville began to falter during the 1920s. This fact of Tin Pan Alley life had enormous consequences not only for Ellington, but for jazz as a whole. In about 1925, a song publisher named Irving Mills was looking for a group to record some of his new tunes. He lit upon the Ellington group, still a more-or-less cooperative band known as the Washingtonians, because the group was inexpensive and out of work often enough to be happy for any kind of a paycheck. Mills and Ellington quickly realized they could be useful to each other, and soon they struck up a deal by which Mills agreed to manage the band—his connections were of considerable value—in exchange for fifty percent of the stock in the orchestra. This agreement, which was with Ellington and not the other members of the Washingtonians, instantly made Duke the boss. By 1926 he was fully in control, with his own ideas shaping the music. Without Mills this might not have happened.

It is certainly true that without Mills, Ellington would have recorded a lot less than he did. Mills needed tunes to publish and needed to get the tunes he published recorded. Ellington was also eager to establish himself as a songwriter, because there was far more money in writing hit tunes than there was in leading a dance orchestra. The system was circular: it was not economical to go into the studio to cut one tune. You needed at least two to make up a recording, and in fact it was the usual practice to record four or even more at a session.

The consequence was that Ellington was forced to produce a steady freshet of new works. In 1926 and 1927, Ellington had only a hazy grasp of music theory. But, with his great, if untrained, musical intelligence, he began to work out his own methods of composition, in which he would enter the studio with scraps and pieces of music in hand, and develop something on the spot. And in this way he produced the first masterpieces that made him famous—"Black and Tan Fantasy," "East St. Louis Toodle-Oo," and the rest.

In sum, a great deal of Ellington's music, including many of the treasures we revere today, was produced solely to meet the demands of the entertainment industry the Ellington orchestra was part of. A major side effect was that along the way Ellington got a great deal of experience, not merely in writing tunes, which does not necessarily involve much musical knowledge—Irving Berlin could not even harmonize his own melodies[56]—but in composing for a jazz orchestra, which does require an understanding, if only instinctive, of a good deal of music theory. Ellington learned by doing; by 1940, when he was turning out some of the greatest works in jazz history, like "Mainstem," "Cotton Tail," "Harlem Airshaft," and "Ko-ko," he was the undisputed master of the short jazz composition. And he had learned his craft because show business had forced him to work at it.

But there was more to it than that. By the early 1930s, Ellington was coming to be seen by intellectuals, both in the United States and abroad, especially England, as something more than just a dance band leader. In particular, a critic named Robert Donaldson Darrell, whom we shall hear more about later, was comparing Ellington to Stravinsky, Bartok, and Delius. In England, jazz writers were reading Darrell, and alerted to Ellington, began to take a serious interest in his work.

Darrell, who interviewed Ellington in 1931, was thoroughly aware of the role show business played in shaping Ellington's work. He wrote:

> As a purveyor and composer of music that must be danced to (if he is to earn his living), Ellington's composition is narrowly limited to dance exigencies, while he is allowed a wide range of expession in the way of instrumental performance. It is hardly remarkable that the latter experimentation has borne fruit; what is remarkable is that working within constricted walls he has yet been able to give rein to his creative imagination and racial urge for expression. Perhaps the very handicaps, permitting no high-flown excursions into Negro Rhapsodies and tone poems, allowing no escape from the fundamental beat of dance rhythm, have enabled Ellington to concentrate his musical virility, draw out its full juice, dissipating none of his forces in vain heaven-storming.[57]

The English critics, however, saw matters differently. When Ellington visited England in 1933, they impressed upon him the fact that he was a musical genius, and urged him to write precisely those tone poems Darrell hoped he would eschew. Throughout the remainder of his career, Ellington more and more put his energies into writing suites, tone poems, and the like, at the expense of the purely jazz pieces, motivated in part by the belief that these larger, at times grandiose, works reflecting the masterpieces of the European composers would earn him more status as an artist than the jazz pieces his reputation had been built on. The earliest of these works—"Creole Rhapsody," "Reminiscing in Tempo," and "Black, Brown, and Beige"—were disliked by the critics, including the same Englishmen who had urged him to compose them. Later on, serious critics simply ignored these extended works. The *New*

York Times, for example, reviewed virtually none of them after "Black, Brown, and Beige."

In recent years there has been an attempt by some jazz writers to raise the general opinion of these pieces, in part triggered by my criticisms of them.[58] It is my view—and I am not alone in this[59]—that the original criticism of these works is correct, and that the revisionists are primarily concerned with keeping Ellington's image well-polished rather than with the musical value in these pieces.

But whatever one thinks of these works, few responsible jazz critics would trade them for Ellington's regular jazz pieces. Nobody with any sort of ear would take "The New Orleans Suite" over "Cotton Tail," or "The Three Kings" over "Harlem Airshaft." It seems quite clear that R. D. Darrell was right: Ellington created his best work when he was constrained by show business considerations than when he went vainly heaven-storming.

The effects of show business on the work of Duke Ellington were therefore substantial. Suppose that in the 1930s and 'forties when Ellington was producing the bulk of his enduring masterpieces jazz had been academicized, as it eventually would be. Suppose there had been available to Ellington foundation grants, visiting professorships, chairs, lecture series, wealthy sponsors. With this kind of economic security and the prestige that goes with being associated with a university, it is almost certain that Ellington would have written far fewer of the short jazz pieces he needed for his record dates and radio broadcasts, in order to work on the extended pieces. Ellington disliked the word "jazz," and again and again insisted that he was not composing it, but rather writing "Ellington" music, or "the music of my people." Given this attitude, would he have written "Cotton Tail" if he had not needed a tune for a recording session?

The great body of work Duke Ellington left us, then, did not simply grow out of his musical imagination. It was, instead, forced out of him by the entertainment industry it was created for. I am not saying that Ellington cold-bloodedly ground out commercial works for the immediate market, although some of his pieces were certainly made in haste without much concern for artistry. He was mainly guided by his sense of the kind of music he wanted to produce—the music he wanted to hear— and his work was thoroughly individual, personal, and immediately identifiable as his. But it is as Darrell said: the very limitations of the dance band form kept Ellington's weakness for lushness and grandiosity in check. They forced him, as athletes sometimes put it, to "stay within himself"—that is, to do what he did best, perhaps did better than any other jazz musician who ever lived.

The effects of show business on Ellington were almost wholly salubrious. In the case of Louis Armstrong they were not.[60] Like Ellington, Armstrong was guided through most of his career by tough, experienced show business professionals with gangland connections who were interested only in money. Both Irving Mills and Armstrong's most important manager, Joe Glaser, had a shrewd sense of what the public wanted, and both urged their clients, who happened to be two of the greatest jazz artists of the first half of the music's history, to produce products that would sell fast, and to hell with posterity. Neither Armstrong nor Ellington objected. Despite the considerable differences in their characters, both wanted badly, for different reasons, to find popular success—to become stars. It has to be kept in mind, as we shall see in more detail shortly, that in the 1920s and 1930s, when Armstrong and Ellington were finding their first fame, that only the most ardent fans and a handful of intellectuals thought that jazz might have enduring value. To the entertainment industry, the bulk of the dancers, the popular press, most academics, and even many of the musicians, jazz was seen as all of a piece with the rest of show business, a music made for the taste of the moment, which changed to match the shifts in popular taste, and was no more likely to be seriously considered ten years later—or even ten months later—than was the daily comic strip.

The musicians, of course, wanted to play it, and hoped to get paid for doing so. For the blacks and the children of the immigrants coming out of the slums and the cotton fields, music of any kind was a way out of the packing plants and the coal mines, and would have been worth reaching out for, even if they could not play the kind they liked. There was, in this early day, then, nothing in the value systems of Ellington and Armstrong to caution them about the dangers of tainting their art with commerce. As a consequence, they judged the advice being given them by their managers in pragmatic terms: were the records selling, the band being booked, the fees going up?

To Louis Armstrong, it came as something of a surprise to find himself acclaimed. Shy as a young man, he was clever about ingratiating himself with people who could help him, but he was not the sort to push himself forward. He was nervous about leaving his home ground, and stayed behind in New Orleans long after most of the best players had left. He came north only when King Oliver, whom he trusted to protect him, summoned him, and he was careful to play second cornet behind Oliver's lead, only stepping forward when he was told to. It was clear to musicians that he was something special, however, and in 1924, Fletcher Henderson brought him to New York as a jazz specialist, to give the band the hot touches the public seemed to want. This was purely a commercial decision: Henderson may well have appreciated Armstrong's tremendous gifts, which were apparent even then, but if the public had not been demanding a certain measure of jazz in its music, he would not have reached out for Armstrong.

The solos Armstrong played and recorded with Henderson

gave him wider fame among musicians and some of the more astute fans of the new dance music. In 1925, mainly for personal reasons, Armstrong went back to Chicago, where he immediately began to make the famous Hot Five records, one of the seminal series in jazz history. He was able to do so because OKeh, which recorded the series, had decided to find itself a niche in the black record market. Armstrong had been a featured soloist with a band that was having a considerable success in an important New York location, and the records he had soloed on, some of them major labels, were selling well. It seemed clear from all of this that Armstrong had some sort of popular appeal. The decision to make the Hot Fives, then, was a purely commercial one.

OKeh's judgement proved to be correct. Blacks, and increasingly, whites, especially college students, began buying the Hot Five records. Charles Black, a retired Columbia University law professor, said:

> In Austin [Texas], as soon as I "discovered" Louis, I found out that all the young musicians in Austin knew all about him, and knew every note on the "Hot Fives." They referred to him, moreover, as to someone they had long known about. He was already an idol. He had a very considerable non-musician following, too, at the University. I think that, in addition to printed material that can now be researched, there must have been quite a word-of-mouth grapevine; this can't all have been something found in Austin alone.[61]

Armstrong, clearly, had a foot in the mainstream of the entertainment industry quite early on.

By this time Armstrong, who had begun his musical career as a boy in a street-corner vocal quartet, and who liked to sing, was occasionally singing in the Sunset Cafe where he was working. It occurred to OKeh's executives, possibly either E. A. Fearn or Myknee Jones, to record an Armstrong vocal. The second one, "Heebie-Jeebies," sold a reported 40,000 copies, which made it a considerable hit for a small company, and from then on, OKeh increasingly asked Armstrong to sing.

By 1926 it was clear to everybody that it was Armstrong, not dixieland jazz, that was selling the Hot Five records. Step by step OKeh brought Armstrong forward, until by 1928, when he was making masterpieces like "West End Blues" and "Tight Like This," the New Orleans musicians had been replaced by journeymen whose only function was to support Louis, sometimes with written arrangements. And as we have seen, the emergence of Armstrong as a soloist was a factor in turning jazz from an ensemble into a solo music.

To this point, then, the commercial decisions made by OKeh were all to the good, if we allow that the abandonment of the New Orleans style was desirable. But by this time Armstrong had fallen under the wing of one of the tough, gang-connected people who would guide his career for much of his life—Tommy Rockwell, eventually a force in popular music. The vogue for black entertainment was reaching a peak.[62] All-black shows were regularly being mounted on Broadway, and black entertainers like Florence Mills, Bill "Bojangles" Robinson, and Paul Robeson had become stars. Armstrong was already attracting white fans; and it was clear to Rockwell that there was a lot of money to be made with Armstrong if he could be moved out of the black and tans of the Chicago South Side, and into the show business mainstream.

In 1929, Rockwell set about repackaging Armstrong. He backed him with an ordinary dance band modeled as much as anything on the Guy Lombardo Orchestra, which was coming into prominence at the moment. He also moved Armstrong from OKeh to Victor, a major label, and began having him sing pop tunes, like "Ain't Misbehavin'" and "I Can't Give You Anything but Love, Baby," instead of the blues and hot numbers with comic lyrics that had been the basic repertory of the Hot Fives. Armstrong even tried to produce a dulcet sound in imitation of the manner of Bing Crosby, who had become very popular through his vocals with Paul Whiteman. (Armstrong was unable to sing in this way for very long, due to growths on his vocal cords that afflicted him all his life, and quickly reverted to his natural rasp.)

The die was now cast. From this point on, commercial considerations would come first in Armstrong's career. Through the 1930s and into the 1940s, to the end of the swing band period, Armstrong's singing, rather than his trumpet playing, came increasingly to be the point of his performances. He worked more and more from hit tunes, many of them, like "Red Nose," of the most ephemeral kind. Onstage he played the genial clown, grinning and mugging and telling bad jokes.

He continued to play trumpet, of course, and along the way, almost by accident, made a number of superb pieces, like "Sweethearts on Parade," "Ev'ntide," "Mahogany Hall Stomp," and more. But his success was built more on his singing and his genial presence than it was on his trumpet playing. The great moments were becoming increasingly scarce.

They became scarcer still after 1945, when the big bands collapsed. For a while it appeared that Armstrong was finished, a relic of a time gone by, as indeed was the case with many of the swing band leaders. But once again his manager, in this case Joe Glaser, was able to reposition him. There was, at the time, a revival of interest in the old dixieland style, which was being cried up by certain jazz writers as the only authentic form of the music. Sidney Bechet was finding a new audience, including many people who had not been born when he made the Clarence Williams records.[63] Others, like Eddie Condon, were recording for major labels and broadcasting regularly.[64]

Furthermore, the popular taste, for a variety of reasons, had shifted away from the swing bands to vocalists singing romantic songs in a light, easy manner: Sinatra, Vic Damone, Eddie

Fisher, Perry Como. Armstrong was both a vocalist, and the greatest of New Orleans players. Glaser reasoned that if Armstrong returned to the old style of the early Hot Fives, he would draw the serious jazz fans back to him. He put Armstrong in front of an all-star dixieland band, which included some of the finest of the older players, among them Earl Hines and Jack Teagarden. Glaser was right, in that the fans of the older music turned out to see their hero return to the old faith. He had not expected, however, that Armstrong would find a brand new audience of people who loved him for his singing and winning manner. He very quickly found himself a major international star, whose name was known all over the world.

Once this was clear, Glaser began to drop the expensive jazz stars and increasingly hired competent journeymen. Armstrong was playing less and less, and singing the most egregious sort of pop tunes—"Kiss of Fire," "April in Portugal," "I Get Ideas." He tended to play the same tunes in the same way night after night—he must have played "Indiana" literally thousands of times during this period—and in general became wholly unadventurous in his playing. He was determined to give the people exactly what they wanted, neither more nor less.

It must be admitted that Armstrong, through poor technique acquired at the beginning of his career, and overwork, had severely damaged his lip, and with the best will in the world would have had to do a lot of singing in the course of an evening in order to spare his lip. And it also must be admitted that on occasion Armstrong produced brilliant music. In particular, a multirecord set called "A Musical Biography," organized by Milton Gabler, a very knowledgeable jazz producer, contains some playing that at times approaches the level of the Hot Fives. But these were rare: commerce had taken over.

It is important for us to keep in mind the fact that Armstrong was not acting under duress. It is true that he was not always able to assert himself against authority figures; it is true that he let Glaser and others choose his sidemen for him, and frequently decide what, where and when he would perform. But it is also true that Armstrong did not take easily to being told how to behave once he was on the stand, and he was quite capable of making a fuss when he felt he was being challenged. Furthermore, the mugging, the joking, the clowning around that he did was not a contrivance, but his natural style, a way of behaving he had developed as a small boy in New Orleans to ingratiate himself with the people he needed at times to provide him with the necessities.

Nonetheless, if Armstrong had wanted to play more straight-ahead jazz, he could have. After 1935, the great success of the swing bands was making it clear that the American public would tolerate a good deal of hot music. Indeed, Benny Goodman, Woody Herman, Artie Shaw, and a number of other leaders began presenting small groups drawn from the orchestras playing straight-ahead jazz once or twice an evening. They were recording these groups, too, and the Goodman Trios and Quartets in particular were hits. The opportunity was there for Armstrong to play a lot of jazz, but he went in the opposite direction instead, tending more and more to sing and play the pop songs that seemed to him surefire.

The same was true of the postwar All-Star groups. Admittedly, by the late 1950s, health and embouchure problems were limiting his playing. But the Gabler "Musical Biography" set demonstrates that he could still play brilliant jazz when he wanted to. He was by this time wealthy, and in any case could always book a high-paying tour if he needed money. Over a twenty-year period, from say 1935 to 1955, there was nothing standing in the way of his devoting a substantial portion of his energies to playing good jazz. And yet he did not.

Louis Armstrong was given to writing things down on paper. He turned out thousands of letters, some handwritten, others pecked out on a typewriter; apparently he wrote a good deal of his second autobiography, *Satchmo*, himself, and he has left behind chunks of other personal writing. There is virtually nothing in this fairly bulky body of writing to suggest that he considered what he was doing was art; even more surprising, he rarely applied the word "jazz" to his music. It was always just "music."

As we have seen, Duke Ellington struggled against the constraints of show business, using his income from his songs to keep his band going so he could write those extended pieces, for which there was only a modest audience. Armstrong did not; he embraced the entertainment industry, using it not so much to become rich, as for the vast audience it was able to bring him. And he put himself in the hands of the Glasers and the Rockwells because they were the ones who knew how to turn the trick.

The cases of Armstrong and Ellington stand out, because they had long and prolific careers in jazz, but most other musicians were similarly affected. Benny Goodman liked playing in the small band style he had started out on, but when he set about forming a band of his own it was modeled on the hot dance bands of Ben Pollack, Red Nichols, Fletcher Henderson, and others. And when it was suggested that he record in the small band style with a trio, he was reluctant, and chose for its first records, safe popular standards. Much to his surprise the trios and later small groups proved to be popular, and in the end with them Goodman produced a major body of work in jazz. Like Ellington, Goodman had found a way to play excellent music within the parameters established by the marketplace. Conversely, Bechet, Oliver, and Morton did not: they hewed closely to the old New Orleans style, and fell into obscurity. Had any of them been willing, or able, to find the right compromises, they might have gone on working in music, and perhaps altered jazz history.

The case of the swing bands is instructive. They simply took over popular music after Goodman's sudden success in 1935. They were not merely part of the music business; by the late 1930s, they *were* popular music. Song writers were utterly dependent upon acceptance by the swing bands for the exposure their songs needed; if the swing bands would not play your tune, it was dead.

But the swing bands themselves were the captives of public fancy. And it quickly became clear that the tolerance of the venturesome was limited. The music was initially quite simple, built on triads and sevenths chords, but by the early 1940s some of the bandleaders, bored with playing the same simple harmonies every night, began reaching out for something more interesting. Benny Goodman was using Eddie Sauter, who had substantial theoretical training, to write complex pieces like "Superman" and "Clarinet à la King." Charlie Barnet was deliberately looking to Ellington as an example, and Ellington himself was producing pieces like "Ko-ko" and "Harlem Airshaft," which were several strides beyond anything in the history of American popular music.

But the public stubbornly refused to follow. Goodman recorded the Sauter pieces, but played them only rarely. Ellington found it necessary to play the more complicated pieces sparingly, and depended on simpler pieces, like "I Let a Song Go Out of My Heart" and "Don't Get Around Much Anymore" for the bulk of his repertory. Barnett counted on "Cherokee" and "Redskin Rhumba," not "The Duke's Idea," to please his audiences.

The final effect was that the musicians could not develop the sort of big jazz band they wanted to. Public taste, through the entertainment media, was calling the shots. To most Americans jazz was not art, not a serious music. It was supposed to be fun, not homework.

What would have happened to jazz when the swing band era ended had things remained the same is difficult to know. A portion of the general public was still willing to follow the Kenton, Herman, and Raeburn bands into a more experimental, thornier music, at least up to a point. But there were sharp limits; the Raeburn band did not last, and eventually both Kenton and Herman bands were operating on an occasional basis.

The bands of the dixieland revival also continued to show life, hanging on to a loyal if relatively small audience up until the present day. It seems to me that as long as jazz remained essentially a wing of show business, it would have continued to attract a following, but it would have been sharply limited, probably to the dixieland and swing band forms that had always had audience appeal.

But change was coming, for in the 1950s, jazz went to school.

6

Art

and the

Academy

The concept of the artist as a special creature with an almost religious calling has a long history in Western culture. It may actually have existed in prehistoric times among the European peoples who created the famous cave paintings, played flutes, and decorated their tools and weapons with incised sketches and symbols. It certainly was operating among the Greeks of classical antiquity, when sculptors, dramatists, and poets were held in high esteem by their fellows. People frequently have had a sense that there was something magical about the ability to create a poem or piece of music that could summon up the emotions, make the hair of the neck stand on end.[1] From this there followed the idea that the artist who could turn this trick was being guided by a godlike spirit—his "muse" or "genius," as the term often was. Surely there was something special about somebody who possessed this "gift."

With the rise of Christianity, the Greek idea of the artist as a special being died out. Art was now to be at the service of the church, and the artist was to be its anonymous servant. "The aesthetic consciousness was gone: the arts were justified as sermons," says one writer.[2] The names of the sculptors, architects, and stained-glass workers who created the great Gothic cathedrals of medieval times are lost to us. So are the names of the composers of the Ambrosian and Gregorian chants, and even much of the organum into the twelfth century, when we can begin to assign names to some of the compositions. These creators were seen as craftsmen, on the social level of the artisan.[3] Sculptors and painters were listed in public records alongside bakers and parchment makers, and an artist was expected to paint decorations on hearses as well as create altarpieces. Indeed, according to art historian Andrew Martindale, "there is, in fact, little evidence for an informed interest in the arts by non-artists"[4] in the Middle Ages. A wealthy churchman or princeling might hire a musician or painter to entertain or amuse him, but there was little serious discussion of aesthetic principles.

124

The emergence of the modern concept of the artist came, not surprisingly, with the Renaissance. The revived interest in classical antiquity awakened the old notion of art as an ennobler of life and the artist as somebody special. As the Renaissance rolled north across Europe, the reputation of the artist grew. Says Frank P. Chambers, another art historian, "Magistracies and knighthoods were awarded to artists in the fifteenth century. . . . Raphael at the height of his fame lived more like a prince than a painter and was always attended by a retinue of servants and pupils. . . . Titian, Fortana, Bernini, Borromini, were all but noblemen."[5] There was, at that time, no sense that the artist was, or ought to be, poor; no idea that he should be an outsider or outcast.

That idea was a product of the romantic imagination of the

eighteenth and nineteenth century. Precisely why artists decided to see themselves as outsiders is hard to know. Arnold Hauser has suggested that artists came to feel they were outside the social system during the early part of the eighteenth century, when the old patronage system in which the aristocracy sponsored writers came to an end, and the new publishing scheme by which writers earned their livings from the sale of books had not yet come into being.[6] Whatever the case, according to Chambers, one of the first artists to affect the posture of outsiders was Denis Diderot, the French encyclopedist, who was born in 1713. The first of the "literary 'originals' of Paris, self-conscious of his genius and in the unconventionality of his manners," he was "fascinated by the aspect of wild, uncultivated scenery and by 'the sweet melancholy . . . of ruins and solitude.'"[7]

Romanticism "prescribed no laws and regulations, but expected rather the lawlessness and individuality of genius. . . . The romantic cried out continually against obedience to academic codes and against the imitation of models. Genius, they said, is above prescription and above criticism."[8]

Futhermore, "Romanticism insisted upon the absolute antithesis of reason and imagination. . . . The Romantics therefore conceived of an art of no intellectual content, an art whose element was the pure spirit of man." Typical was the view of Goethe, who said, "I am rather of the opinion that the more incommensurable and the more incomprehensible to the intellect the poetic production is, so much the better it is."[9]

By the late eighteenth century the Romantic movement, headed by Wordsworth and Coleridge, was gathering steam in England, to which Americans frequently looked for art and ideas. But romanticism did not penetrate the colonies immediately. Americans were pragmatic and adhered to the ideal of "plainness," exemplified by the hard-working, God-fearing farmers who constituted the bulk of the country's population.[10]

There was little room in this ideal for the half-crazed poet spouting verse about daffodils and the west wind. In fact, the democratic notion that in America no man was better than another led many Americans to treat art with contempt. Actors were routinely hooted down, laughed off stage, or pelted with aged fruit and vetetables and at times more dangerous objects.

Theater managers frequently had to come on stage to beg drunken audiences to stop throwing things and let the show proceed. In Rochester, New York, in about 1830, one newspaper editor complained that when a show was on in a theater near his home the uproar was so great he could not sleep at night.[11] Lawrence Levine, in his study of attitudes toward art in the nineteenth century, has pointed out that during the early part of the century, not even the august William Shakespeare was immune from attack.

> Hamlet was a favorite target in numerous travesties imported from England or crafted at home. Audiences roared at the sight of Hamlet dressed in fur cap and collar, snowshoes, and mittens; they listened with amused surprise to his profanity when ordered by his father's ghost to "swear" and to his commanding Ophelia, "Get thee to a brewery"; they heard him recite his lines in black dialect or Irish brogue and sing his most famous soliloquy, "To be, or not to be," to the tune of "Three Blind Mice."[12]

This attitude was not, of course, universal. The United States of the day had its serious readers who were buying the books of Hawthorne and Irving, and were attending the concerts of opera companies brought over from Europe. But in general, Americans were suspicious of art lovers, who they suspected were putting on airs.

A change came with the rise of Victorianism through the middle years of the nineteenth century. The new call was for order and decency. This new ethic could not condone drunken audiences flinging withered cabbages at some wretched actor attempting to put over the pathos of Lear howling on the heath. Opera was similarly tempered. Charles Hamm, the authority on popular music, says, "Popular support of opera, which had largely sustained it since the eighteenth century—through ballad opera and English comic opera to adapted versions of the great works of Rossini, Mozart, Bellini, and Donizetti—gradually eroded in the middle years of the nineteenth. Slowly but inexorably, opera became class entertainment, produced chiefly for the cultural and social aristocracy of America."[13]

Art, it was now believed, had a power to uplift and improve. Leslie Stephen, father of Virginia Woolf and Vanessa Bell and himself an important critic, said flatly that a novel should "purify and sustain"—that is, help people resist temptation.[14] A child who was exposed to good literature and spent his daily hour drearily practicing his Czerny exercises would be less likely to fall to the temptations of sex and drink. Art had a lofty mission, and it followed logically that art itself must be lofty.

The final result was what Levine has called the "sacralization" of art. Art was to be seen as almost as holy as scripture. Efforts, which we now take for granted, were made to see that Shakespeare was performed as written, that musicians preserved the intent of the composers whose works they were playing.

Now that art was holy, questions inevitably arose about who was fit to handle it. There was a growing view that the great unwashed were not capable of following Shakespeare's language, could not grasp the beauties of Verdi's music. Leave the common people to their saloon comedians and dance hall jingles, and reserve art to those who could appreciate it. A debate arose over whether the common people ought to be encouraged to visit museums. There were those who believed that since the inferior orders could gain nothing from art, it was just as well to discourage them from impeding those who could benefit from the exhibits. Not everybody agreed: there were those who disliked the antidemocratic principle in this idea. But it was widespread nonetheless.[15]

The consequence was that what would eventually be called "culture" was increasingly seen as the property of wealthier classes. The well-to-do, through contributions and purchase of season tickets, became the primary supporters of the opera and the symphony. The middle class was the heart of the audience for the novel, as it always had been. Only the well-off could afford to commission paintings, and only the very rich could buy the European master paintings that many seemed willing to spend their fortunes on.

One consequence of the new attitude toward art was that it became academicized. This had not previously been the case. American colleges were designed primarily to educate people for the pulpit. Later, they were expanded to train people for the law and other professions. At the heart of college education were classical studies—the learning of Latin and Greek; the study of Plato, Aristotle, Cicero, and the rest; along, of course, with some professional courses in mathematics and, eventually, the sciences. The study of art, except as it related to the classical languages, was considered frivolous. As late as the 1830s, at Harvard, modern languages were "not quite considered academically respectable," although they were offered as electives.[16] Art, in the modern sense, was not taught at all.

But by the post–Civil War period, the Victorian belief that art was uplifting was taking hold. English literature was being set up as a separate course of study in the 1870s;[17] modern-language courses became standard in the 1870s and 1880s; philosophy emerged as an important discipline in the 1880s; and at about the same time, "the fine arts also began to be promoted as academic studies."[18]

In fact, as far as the fine arts were concerned it was more theoretical than real for some years. In 1900 hardly anything like "creative writing" existed in the colleges, and according to one writer, Laurence R. Veysey, as late as 1900, "professors of English would even 'lose caste' if they wrote a novel and the fact became known."[19]

The movement towards fine arts was growing, however, and by the 1890s there were courses in music at Yale, Columbia (where Edward McDowell was head of the program), and elsewhere.[20] The ideal of education was now, according to one professor at Columbia University's Teachers' College, "culture" and the "discovery of the individual." Taken together this meant that the well-educated person knew the fine arts as well as ancient languages and mathematics.[21] Thereafter, courses in literature, music appreciation, the history of painting, creative writing, and all the rest, began to proliferate in college catalogues, until by the 1920s the main point of education for many appeared to be the acquisition of a knowledge of philosophy and the arts. It was a change of considerable magnitude in the American system of education.

By the early part of the twentieth century, then, the activities that we subsume under the name of art—painting, the dance, opera, the symphony, the theater, literature—had come to be seen as both virtuous and prestigious. The artist had status (although paradoxically many continued to see themselves as outsiders, even when they were on college faculties, or held federal grants), and through the twentieth century art increasingly attracted the attention of Americans. Young children were encouraged to paint, write poems, and bang on bells and triangles from early ages. There were symphony orchestras in every major American city, and in many smaller ones as well. Lines formed at museums to see pictures by masters long dead—there were certainly more people in the Metropolitan Museum of Art in New York or the Art Institute of Chicago on Sunday than in any number of cathedrals. Most significantly, today the number of young Americans choosing careers in painting, the dance, writing, and music is staggering. In recent years, 40,000 people *annually* earned college degrees in the visual and performing arts, and almost the same number took degrees in literature.[22] Needless to say, the social system can accommodate only a tiny fraction of these people with careers even in the commercial arts, to say nothing of the high arts. For example, it is doubtful that the more important symphony orchestras, the ones capable of paying their members a living wage, hire more than a few dozen new people a year, out of the several thousand who graduate from conservatories annually.[23] Similarly, it has been estimated that ninety percent of ordinary "trade" books do not pay for the time it took to write them, even by the most niggardly standard.[24] It is, in truth, impossible for more than a tiny fraction of the horde of aspirants to the title of "artist" to actually publish even one book, much less a substantial body of work; to work professionally in the theater or film; to regularly exhibit and sell their paintings; to earn their living playing music, even of the most commercial sort. Yet so prestigious is the calling of the artist today that young people pour into the conservatories and art school anyway.

The fact that art had become prestigious inevitably led people to apply the term, where they could, to classes of work they happened to be interested in. One of the earliest manifestations of this was the appearance of the concept of folk "art," which was in existence by the middle of the nineteenth century: the *Journal of American Folklore* was publishing articles on folk music as early as the 1890s.[25]

More significant for jazz was the concept of the "popular arts," which arose in the early decades of the century. This idea followed logically from the concept of primitivism, as a parallel to the idea of folk art. By the turn of the century, it was clear that "the folk" were not merely Appalachian farmers carving figurines or black sharecroppers singing in the cornfields; the term, if it meant anything, also had to include the mobs of immigrants swarming in the slums of the great industrial cities of the Northeast. For these people, folk painting was the comic strip; folk music, Tin Pan Alley tunes they sang, danced to, and frequently created; folk drama, the movies for which they provided the first audience, and quickly came to dominate as producers and exhibitors.

It was all of a piece with the new spirit of the age. If these people were worth painting, worth photographing, worth chronicling in novels and plays, surely their entertainment must also be worthy of consideration. The first to make a significant study of the phenomenon was Gilbert Seldes, who in his 1924 book *The Seven Lively Arts* and a number of magazine and newspaper articles, made precisely this point, that what had hitherto been considered mere entertainment could be taken more seriously.

In a 1924 piece in the widely circulating *Literary Digest* Seldes wrote:

> Among the lively arts, jazz is at present the most promising. It is hard, precise, and unsentimental. . . . Here the breath of life is definite, even if it is not always a great wind; here sharp minds and simple souls are expressing something gay and light, with simplicity and a certain carelessness of conventional pedantry which is near to courage. Jazz is roaring and stamping and vulgar, you may say; but you can not say that it is pale and polite and dying.

In the same piece the magazine reported the observations of "the musical critic of the *London Times*" who saw a movement among young Americans to take jazz seriously. "'Jazz,' they say, is, indeed, something which has sprung from our soil; let us accept it and enjoy it."[26]

It should be pointed out that many of these writers included the symphonic jazz of Whiteman and others, as well as the earlier dixieland, under the rubric of "jazz." But many of them did not, and defined jazz as we would today. Thus a state of mind was created, at least among artists and intellectuals, for the acceptance of jazz as an art form—the only original art form created in America, as people began saying very early.[27]

The first such reference to jazz as an art that I have been able to find appeared in an article in the *Musical Courier* in 1922.[28] A little later in the year, a writer in *The Nation* referred to it as "an industrialized folk music."[29] In 1924, Olin Downes routinely applied the word "art" to jazz in his review of the famous Whiteman Aeolian Hall Concert,[30] and in 1926, Don Knowlton, writing in *Harper's*, said, "Five years ago it was proper to loathe jazz. Today it is the smart thing to hail it as the only truly American contribution to music, and to acclaim it as Art."[31]

But still there were doubts. Many of the intellectuals of the time were a little uneasy about shoving a Duke Ellington or an Irving Berlin into the pantheon with Bach or Beethoven. A certain distinction had to be kept. Jazz—however defined—might be art, but it was not high art. There was a tendency to think of it as folk music, an "industrialized folk music," perhaps, not quite on the level of the Fifth Symphony.

This view continued to be held into the 1940s. Sidney Finkelstein in his 1948 book *Jazz: A People's Music* called it "a folk and a people's art."[32] Rudi Blesh in his 1946 book called it "an African art form."[33] Thus, as late as this, even writers whose devotion to the music was not in question were reluctant to classify jazz as a high art. And it was this attitude, that jazz was not high art, that for a long time kept it from being accepted by the academy.

There were a few scattered exceptions. As early as 1919, Len Bowden, a student at Tuskegee Institute, organized a "Syncopated Band," for the purpose of introducing his fellow students to the new music, and Alabama State Normal College for a number of years in the 1930s and 1940s gave credit for membership in the 'Bama State Collegians, a dance band.[34] In 1932 the composer Percy Grainger invited Duke Ellington to speak at Columbia, and the same year he was given the New York School of Music annual award for his first extended piece, "Creole Rhapsody."[35] But Ellington was always seen as a special case, and it was little enough.

As a consequence, jazz studies, such as they were, were done entirely outside of the academy. The first impetus came from the development of a passion for hot record collecting. In the early days, of course, jazz records were seen as a popular commodity meant to sell quickly and disappear. They were issued haphazardly and casually withdrawn when the label decided they had run their course. There was, furthermore, no way to duplicate a recording in the home. As a consequence, jazz fans were endlessly scrambling to get hold of the records of their favorites, hunting them down in record shops, trading with other collectors.

This all became somewhat easier after the stock market crash in 1929. With the Depression, people increasingly turned to radio for entertainment, which was free once you owned a set. Phonographs became dispensable, and many people sold theirs because they were going broke, because they were moving to smaller quarters or going back home. Secondhand dealers were usually asked to take the records as part of the deal when they bought a phonograph, and millions of them piled up in secondhand shops across the country. There were other millions of them in attics, garages, and cellars. These used records rarely cost more than a nickel, and sometimes went for a penny each.

It has been claimed that the first serious record collectors were a group of jazz fans at Princeton.[36] By the mid-1930s there were hundreds of jazz fans out there, avidly collecting the Morton, Henderson, Beiderbecke, Oliver, and Armstrong records they needed to fill out their collections. The passion for record collecting was by 1934 a sufficiently widespread phenomenon for *Esquire* to run an article on the subject. The writer, Charles Edward Smith, said, "Today, a check-up reveals collectors of *hot* in almost every college and preparatory school in the country. The substantial following enjoyed by Louis Armstrong is due largely to jazz enthusiasts at prominent universities—Yale, Princeton, etc.—who began collecting his records five or six years ago."[37]

It was, however, not enough to own the records. It was also necessary to know all about them: the personnel, the issue date, the take and master number, the studio where it was made. These young jazz fans were constantly bombarding musicians for details of record sessions they had frequently long forgotten. Some were able to worm their way into the files of record companies, many of them killed by the Depression, where they found treasure troves of data. And of course they did a lot of close listening, arguing for this or that identification.

The work of these hot collectors proved to be critical for jazz history. For one, they were responsible for preserving this early jazz, much of which would otherwise have simply disappeared as record companies discarded aging files. They also provided the basis for modern discography. (Actually, the first full-dress jazz discography was put together by a Frenchman, Charles Delaunay, and discography has ever since been a European specialty. But in fact, Delaunay and subsequent European discographers were heavily dependent on these American collectors.[38])

Hot collecting was particularly a hobby of college students. Groups at Yale and Princeton were especially active, but there were many others elsewhere. Among the ones at Yale was Marshall W. Stearns, who was at the college when Hammond was there.[39] Stearns was born in 1908, and thus was around when the jazz boom of the 1920s began. He played various instruments in high school, became a leading member of the Yale Hot Club, and eventually went on to earn a doctorate in

English literature, with a specialty in Chaucer. He thus had scholarly training, which he applied to the study of jazz. He later said that from the late 1920s he was "trying to read all the writings on jazz, listen to all the recordings of jazz, and talk to all the musicians who play jazz" he could.[40] Stearns was not alone in investigating jazz history; others, like Rudi Blesh, William Russell, and Charles Edward Smith, were also scrambling around for data. But Stearns, as a professional scholar, was better equipped to deal with the material he was collecting, and in 1936 he began a series of pieces for *Down Beat* on the history of jazz, which ran into 1938.[41] He was impelled to do so by the appearance in America of the Frenchman Hugues Panassié's book, *Jazz Hot*, which jazz experts in the United States considered badly flawed.[42]

Meanwhile, Stearns and Hammond had founded the United Hot Clubs of America (UHCA), which joined the New York, New Haven, Chicago, Cleveland, Boston, and Los Angeles Hot Clubs under a single roof. It occurred to somebody that the UHCA could make a little money by reissuing some of the rare items Hot Club members were interested in. Milt Gabler proprietor of the Commodore Record Shop, which specialized in jazz and was a hangout for musicians and fans, told the UHCA he would guarantee sales of 1,000 copies if the club could persuade the major recording companies to license reissues. The program was very quickly put into effect. In 1937 a second club, the Hot Record Society, also began a reissue program.[43]

Nobody got rich from these reissues, but they showed that there was a certain amount of money to be made from these older recordings, and in 1940 the major labels stopped licensing the hot clubs and embarked on their own reissue programs. These reissue series were given a tremendous boost in 1942 when a dispute between the musicians' union and the record companies resulted in a ban on recording, which lasted until

1944. It was now wartime, and the companies could only produce a limited number of records in any case. They needed product nonetheless, and one way to get it was to reissue material they already had in their files. The result for jazz lovers was a bonanza, and three and four record "album" sets of Beiderbecke, Armstrong, Bessie Smith, Red Nichols, Jelly Roll Morton, and more came onto the market.

But perhaps more important, the reissuance of these older records in artfully designed packages with what seemed to be scholarly brochures on the musicians involved, resembling very much the album sets of classical music that had been long familiar, suggested that the music had some sort of lasting value. [44] Many young people—high school and even junior high school students—heard the Hot Fives and Bix and His Gang first through these reissues. To these young people the new spirit of the 1920s that had enlisted so many of their parents in the jazz cause meant nothing. The music had to have an appeal of its own, and the sober way the reissues were presented encouraged them to believe that the music might be worth trying to understand. Jazz was, for these young people, a serious business right from the start, and the idea that it might be an art was not difficult for them to accept.

They were abetted in this view by a fairly considerable body of writing just beginning to appear. By 1937 or so, *Down Beat* had become a pretty good jazz magazine, carrying articles on discographic arcana, interviews with various of the legendary figures that have always hung from jazz like ornaments on a Christmas tree, Stearns' historical pieces, and workshops by instrumentalists, the most important of which were the transcriptions and analyses of piano solos by Sharon Pease, which appeared in the magazine from 1937 to 1941.

In 1936, *Metronome*, which had basically covered classical music, switched to swing, and in time became a true jazz periodical. Very quickly the first of the "little" jazz magazines appeared,[45] produced to some extent as antidote to what was seen as the commercialism of *Down Beat* and *Metronome*. The *HRS Society Rag*, under Steven Smith, dated its first issue July 1938. The competing *Jazz Information* appeared in September 1939. Where *Society Rag* was fairly catholic in its tastes, *Jazz Information* was partisan to the older, New Orleans style, and there was a good deal of rather acerbic byplay between the staffs of these magazines.

In the late 1930s there also appeared the first sensible books on jazz: Winthrop Sargent's *Jazz: Hot and Hybrid*, Wilder Hobson's *American Jazz Music*, and Frederic Ramsey and C. E. Smith's *Jazzmen*.[46] These books had their weaknesses, but they were excellent efforts for the time. Like the reissue programs, the very existence of these books and periodicals suggested that the music could be treated seriously. Futhermore, they worked together: the reissue programs allowed young jazz lovers to hear the music they were reading about; the books and magazines allowed them to read about the music they were hearing.

It cannot be said, however, that this flurry of activity in jazz during the late 1930s constituted a real discipline of "jazz studies" in the sense that scholars use the term. It was informal, unsystematic; much of it in the hands of very young and often inexperienced people whose enthusiasm outdistanced their objectivity. This was the period of the dixieland revival—indeed, the revival was in considerable part created by the purists—when a great deal of heat went into the battle between those who insisted that only the older music was the real thing, and those who also admitted into jazz the newer swing style. This writing was rarely analytic, but ran heavily to attacking or defending this or that musician, style, or critical position.

Nor was it yet possible to teach jazz in high school and college music departments. These were staffed almost entirely by people who were committed to classical music. In fact, the older, senior people in music departments had in the main been trained in classical music before they had heard a note of jazz, and they had seen it from the beginning as an enemy competing for the attention of their students. They did not merely feel that jazz was unworthy of academic attention; they actively hated the stuff.[47]

But if resistance to jazz was still there, by the 1940s it was growing weaker. As early as 1940, a Professor J. T. H. Mize, not surprisingly only twenty-nine, was teaching at Ellisville Junior College in Missouri, "a regularly scheduled course in jazz requiring extensive preparation, research, reading, field trips and even laboratory work," with the cooperation of his administration.[48] In 1943, Rudi Blesh gave a series of lectures at the San Francisco Institute of Art. In the same year, Rye High School, in fashionable Westchester County north of New York City, was carrying "classes in Appreciation of Contemporary American Popular Music."[49] By 1946, the Grosvernor Library in Buffalo, New York, had a collection of a hundred good hot jazz records, built by the library's public relations man, Harold Hacker.[50] In the late 1940s Stearns lectured on jazz at New York University.[51]

The 1940s also saw the beginning of what academics would consider real jazz scholarship. As far as I can discover, the first such article was Morroe Berger's sociological discussion of the acceptance of jazz in America.[52] Then, in 1948, Richard Alan Waterman, the ethnomusicologist and jazz bass player, published in the *Journal of the American Musicological Society* an article called "'Hot' Rhythm in Negro Music," in which he looked at certain relationships between jazz and tribal music.[53] More significant was Waterman's "metronome sense" article, discussed earlier, which was read in 1949 and published in 1952. In 1949 also, one of his students, Alan Merriam, wrote a master's thesis on jazz. Merriam went on to publish a bibliography of jazz, which is still considered a basic work.[54] In 1951,

A. M. Jones, at the time one of the leading authorities on African tribal music, whose work still remains of value, published a piece in the *African Music Society Newsletter*, called "Blue Notes and Hot Rhythm," locating the source of both jazz rhythm and blue notes in African music.[55] These pieces, few as they were, constituted the beginnings of a discipline of jazz studies.

Unfortunately, Marshall Stearns died of a heart attack in 1966, Richard Waterman died relatively young, and Alan Merriam was killed in a car accident in 1978. If these men had lived longer, it is fairly sure that they would have gotten jazz studies on firmer ground than it is now.

Meanwhile, in 1946, at North Texas State University, M. Eugene Hall persuaded the authorities that the school ought to offer a "dance band" major, on the sensible grounds that whatever music students were studying, as a practical matter they would earn their livings playing in dance bands—or so it seemed at the time. In fact, as Hall later admitted, "From the program's inception, jazz experimentation, rather than dance music *per se* has been the byword."[56] That is to say, the real point of the program was to allow young jazz students to compose, arrange, and improvise. Hall's course became the model for the scores of university jazz courses that have proliferated since.

But this activity was very thin. In 1949, Merriam wrote, "The average legitimate music school has little, if any, interest in jazz, and often is violently opposed to it in any forms, although these barriers are slowly being lifted."[57] An important factor in breeding acceptance of jazz in the universities was the death of the swing band right after the war. The end of swing threw out of work several hundred musicians, many of them very well trained. At the same time, school and college enrollments soared, in part due to the returning war veterans who were flooding into the schools under the G.I. Bill. Music departments were necessarily expanding, and many of the former swing band players sought shelter in school and college music departments, where they began campaigning for jazz courses and "stage" bands, a term developed to avoid the still-suspect word "jazz."

Because many of these early jazz teachers were primarily musicians, and not scholars, they inevitably focused on practical musicianship. The result was that composing and playing programs substantially outpaced the development of jazz scholarship. In 1949, Stearns, then at Cornell, announced his plan for a United States Jazz Institute, which, however, was several years in coming.[58] At a few colleges, including Ohio State University and the University of Illinois, there were jazz clubs of one kind or another, with weekly record sessions, discussion groups, and lectures. *Down Beat* saw a "recent trend in colleges of recognizing jazz, swing, and popular music as 'legitimate' . . ." and in the spring of 1949 announced that it was increasing its coverage of campus music.[59]

But again, this activity was sporadic and limited. Four years later, *Down Beat* made a story out of the fact that Brandeis University was instituting a course in jazz, suggesting that such courses were still uncommon.[60]

Furthermore, while record sessions and lectures undoubtedly stimulated interest in jazz on campuses, they hardly constituted formal jazz scholarship, which remained very thin on the ground. The number of formal jazz papers published during the decade of the 1950s can be counted on the fingers of two hands. The first doctoral dissertation in jazz that I have been able to discover was Hugh L. Smith, Jr.'s, "The Literary Manifestations of a Liberal Romanticism in American Jazz," given at the University of New Mexico in 1955. Somewhat better known is Chadwick Clarke Hansen's 1956 thesis, "The Ages of Jazz: A Study of Jazz in Its Cultural Context." Then, in 1960, came Neil Leonard's "The Acceptance of Jazz by

Whites in the United States, 1918–1942,"[61] which resulted in his influential book, *Jazz and the White Americans.*[62]

The critical year for the academization of jazz was 1956, when the dam, if it did not exactly burst, at least sprang a serious leak. It is probable that the establishment of the Newport Jazz Festival two years earlier was important in encouraging institutional acceptance of the music. Newport, as a summer enclave of the very rich, was the epitome of propriety, and the sponsors of the event, the wealthy and very social Louis Lorillards, were precisely the sort of people who had become, in the twentieth century, the guardians of culture. The festival's great, and immediate, success, also encouraged sponsors of the classical music festivals the Newport event had been modeled on to reach out for jazz musicians and critics, in part excited by the crowds of people Newport was drawing every year. In 1956 the famous open-air concert series at Lewisohn Stadium in New York for the first time in its thirty-nine year history included a jazz concert, which featured the Armstrong and Dave Brubeck groups.[63] Jazz people began turning up at music festivals along with famous conductors, composers, and virtuosos, and the jazz festival itself became common. *Down Beat* said, "In no summer [1956] in American music history have so many jazz festivals and appearances by jazz musicians at other festivals been scheduled."[64]

A second factor was the plans announced in 1956 for State Department tours of jazz musicians to foreign parts. The ostensible purpose of the tours was to counter the successful effort the Russians were making to sell Communism through cultural exports. The real reason for it was that the racial upheaval in the South was giving the United States a fat black eye abroad, especially in Third World nations, which, it was felt, were at risk of falling to Communism. A tour by a black jazz musician would demonstrate that not all American blacks were unhappy, downtrodden, or angry.[65] Eventually Armstrong, Dizzy Gillespie, and Benny Goodman went on well-publicized tours.

This acceptance of jazz by the wealthy Lorillards of fashionable Newport and by the American government undoubtedly helped give jazz respectability. But fundamentally I think it was sheer momentum. By 1956 a lot of the older music teachers, who had hated jazz out of gut feelings, were retiring. Their places were being taken by people who had danced to the swing bands, or even played in them. The resistance was simply wearing away.

The key event occurred in the spring of 1956 when Dean Robert A. Choate of Boston University announced that for the first time jazz would be taken up at the annual national conference of music educators three months later. According to Choate, the conference had "never discussed jazz in any phase before. But we have discovered that you cannot discuss music in America without bringing in jazz. . . . We cannot stay within the little tower of the classroom."[66] This was the academic establishment speaking, and the imprimatur of this heavyweight organization was high-velocity ammunition for young jazz instructors trying to persuade department chairmen to put in jazz courses.

Less significant, but certainly symptomatic, was the decision of the editors of the profoundly scholarly *Dictionary of American Biography* to include jazz musicians. In 1956 it issued a supplement to cover eminent Americans who had died between 1936 and 1940. King Oliver, who died in 1938, was included.[67]

Perhaps the most significant development of all in the academicizing of jazz was the institutionalizing of the college jazz concert. Colleges had always been major buyers of jazz music. Students were hiring jazz bands for their dances right from the beginning:[68] the Ory and Oliver bands, and probably others, played at Tulane before most of the rest of America had heard of jazz, and the Original Dixieland Jazz Band was regularly booked at proms and fraternity dances from at least 1918. During the 1920s the Ellington, Henderson, Goldkette, and many other groups routinely played college dances. The swing bands, too, were highly popular on campuses, and most of them counted on playing proms, dances, and house parties. As late as 1953, when the swing bands were dead elsewhere, the campuses were still booking them: in that year Ray Anthony played over seventy college dates.[69]

Booking a band for a dance, however, was one thing; hiring one to play a concert was another. A dance was frivolity, an occasion apart from education, an "extracurricular" activity. A concert was not. Among other things, dance bands were generally paid for by the students as part of the house party or prom fee; an officially recognized concert could be paid for out of the same fund that brought in lecturers and string quartets.

143

A jazz *concert* thus was serious business—educational, uplifting. And in the middle of the 1950s there came a surge in them that really amounted to something of a fad. *Down Beat* editor Jack Tracy wrote that in the past, music educators had "looked at jazz with disdain. . . . Then, a couple of years ago, the atmosphere began to change. A lot of it began with the exploratory work Gene Hall began to do in Texas. . . . Bookers began to find that the college and high school market was becoming a fruitful one for jazz concerts. Dave Brubeck was a powerful force in opening up school after school to jazz. The Modern Jazz Quartet, Gerry Mulligan and many other groups found not only a friendly atmosphere in which to purvey their music, but an intense interest on the part of students in it."[70]

It was important to the acceptance of the jazz concert that the music was at the moment dominated by the relatively accessible West Coast, or "cool" school. Its proponents were mainly young, good-looking musicians, most of whom had studied classical music seriously, and were bringing to jazz procedures that they had found in it. Dave Brubeck had studied with Darius Milhaud, had introduced novel time signatures with his famous "Take Five," and was attempting to play contrapuntally with his saxophonist Paul Desmond. John Lewis, leader of the Modern Jazz Quartet, had a master's degree in music from the famous Manhattan School of Music and drew heavily on European forms for the Quartet's repertory. Gerry Mulligan had been involved with the experimental "birth of the cool" group fronted by Miles Davis, and like Brubeck was playing contrapuntally with Chet Baker in a pianoless quartet, which suggested a chamber group.

These musicians and their somewhat introspective music, with its suggestions of the chamber ensemble, were exactly tailored to suit the academy. At a reception following a concert, a Brubeck or a John Lewis could talk intelligently to faculty and music students about Poulenc and tone rows. Theirs was an easy music to academicize, because they had already carried it halfway into the academy beforehand.

But jazz studies, as a discipline, still languished. Attempts to publish scholarly journals devoted to jazz usually failed very quickly. The trickle of dissertations on jazz became a thin stream, averaging about one a year through the 1960s and 1970s. One problem was that few universities had senior people in music departments likely to encourage graduate students to work in jazz studies, or who were competent to supervise jazz dissertations. Jazz dissertations tended—and still do—to run to descriptive analyses of this or that player's solos. Historiography especially was neglected.

Jazz education got a second boost in the late 1970s, when college enrollments, for a variety of reasons, began to fall. College music departments, along with everybody else, were faced with cutbacks, which could cost jobs. In order to bring enrollments up, music departments that had not covered jazz before began offering jazz courses, and those that already had jazz programs attempted to expand them. Some of these were general courses in American popular music, which allowed the professor to spend a lot of time on rock, which students were particularly willing to study. But jazz especially benefitted because it had already been established in the academy as an appropriate field of study.

Jazz was, by the 1980s, a part of the academy. It is true that in 1990 only about a hundred colleges and universities had degree programs in jazz.[71] But according to William McFarlin, Director of the International Association of Jazz Educators, it is now very rare for a college or university not to have some sort of jazz activity, usually a history course, a course in jazz improvisation, and perhaps, in music schools, a course in jazz pedagogy.

McFarlin also estimates that some 15,000 of America's 28,000 secondary schools have jazz programs.[72] Jazz could be studied the same way that English literature or classical music could be studied. It was even possible to get a doctorate in it and make the study of the music a lifetime's work. Enshrined in the academy, it was, *ipso facto*, a form of art.

Jazz was still to some extent attached to the entertainment industry. A lot of jazz musicians were earning portions of their incomes as they had always done, by playing in clubs and restaurants, working at weddings and parties, making recordings, and playing for dancing. Jazz continued to draw a popular audience in a way that poetry or the classical ballet could not. But, increasingly, jazz musicians and composers were getting their livings in the same way that poets and choreographers were—through faculty posts, grants, academic residencies, or subsidized performances. In one recent year, the National Endowment for the Arts gave seventy-one jazz fellowships for a total of $450,000 and gave another fifty-four institutional grants in jazz for $752,500.[73]

In the forty years from the mid-1940s to the mid-1980s, jazz had undergone an interesting process. The route it had traveled, from the world of show business to the arms of the academy, had been traveled by other art forms before. Again and again, what has come to be seen as the high art of an earlier age was at the time of its creation exactly the sort of popular art that jazz was taken to be in the early days. The English novel, as devised by Fielding, Richardson, Defoe, Sterne, and Smollett, was meant to be light amusement for a rising middle class that was largely literate and had a good deal of spare time to fill. These early novelists were careful to ensure good sales by filling their books with sexual allusions, often meant to be comical, built around the battle of the sexes. Plots boiled with coincidences and misunderstandings, virtuous heroes struggled with rogues and won out in the end. But by the late nineteenth century, novelists like Conrad, James, and Woolf were treating their craft with high seriousness; critics were brooding over them; and it had become possible to get academic degrees studying the works that Defoe and Smollett had designed to achieve quick popularity and vast sales.

The same process took place in classical music. According to Donald Jay Grout, "A feature of the eighteenth century which is hard for us nowadays to appreciate, yet which was incalculably important, was the constant public demand for new music. There were no 'classics,' and few works of any kind survived more than two or three seasons. Bach had to provide new cantatas for Leipzig and Handel, a new opera every year for London; and Vivaldi was expected to furnish new oratorios and concertos for every recurring festival at the Pietà." It is said that he composed his opera *Tito Manlio* in five days. [74]

Arnold Hauser adds, "Anything in the nature of useless music had not existed at all before this time, and pure concert music, the only purpose of which was to express feelings, only existed from the eighteenth century onward." And he continues, "Art and craft, which are not wholly divorced in [Mozart], are completely separate in Beethoven, and the idea of the unique, unrepeatable, utterly individual work of art is realized even more purely in music than in painting, although the latter had made itself independent of craft work centuries ago. In literature, as well, the emancipation of the artistic purpose from the practical task had already been perfectly accomplished by Beethoven's day."[75]

There was a time when poetry, too, was an art for the masses. "Beowulf" and the epics of Greece and Rome were intended to be recited aloud for mass consumption. In medieval Europe, the courts commanded verses from the *trouvères* and troubadours, and in the Renaissance, gentlemen and ladies often composed verses for the amusement of their friends. Even as late as the nineteenth century, poems were printed in what were for the time large editions, poets like Browning and Tennyson could live from their work, and all around the United States there were "Browning Circles" made up of the middle class, which were essentially fan clubs. But by early in the twentieth century, poetry had disappeared into the academy.

In the mid-nineteenth century the ballet was seen as a somewhat salacious entertainment, which attracted a great many upper-class, even aristocratic, gentlemen, who were there mainly to prey upon the working-class girls who made up the corps de ballet. The art historian Robert L. Herbert, writing about Paris, says:

A proper bourgeois girl would literally be descending to the working class were she to become a ballet dancer. These divisions began to break down in the 1880s and were largely dissolved by the turn of the century, owing to the rapid alteration of class structure in Paris. The glamour of the star dancer made her envied and therefore increasingly respectable (some achieved distinguished marriages and then moved into upper-class circles). In the 1860s and 1870s, signs of the coming breakdown of the old class lines were found in the growing number of daughters of Opéra personnel who joined the ballet.[76]

But in the twentieth century, the ballet had become an amusement for an educated elite, and had to be subsidized to survive.

As still another example, as late as the eighteenth century in Europe, painters were seen in part as craftsmen, who would do whatever work they were called upon to do. Boucher accepted commissions to paint Easter eggs for the French king, and according to art historian Dore Ashton, "While there is no indication that Fragonard produced occasional artifacts on demand, he certainly made many drawings, prints, and paintings to satisfy the patrons who offered the material support he needed."[77] Today most painters make their livings by teaching, and would not be very willing to accept commissions to paint Easter eggs.

By the nineteenth century, art, to use Levine's term, had become "sacralized," securely lodged in the academy, where it had to exist on charity. Inevitably, the artistic process changed. Hauser says:

> The fundamental difference between composing for a nobleman or a personal patron in general and working for the anonymous public is that the commissioned work is usually intended for a single performance, whereas the concert piece is written for as many repeats as possible. That explains not only the greater degree of care with which it is composed, but also the more exacting way in which the composer presents it. Now it is possible to create works which would not be consigned to oblivion so quickly as commissioned works, he sets out to create "immortal" works. Haydn already composes much more cautiously and slowly than his predecessors. But even he writes over a hundred symphonies; Mozart writes only half as many and Beethoven only nine.[78]

The single most important consequence of the academizing of art was very quickly to make it increasingly incomprehensible to a mass audience. This was not inevitable: there is no reason why novelists could not have gone on telling good stories in the manner of Fielding and Twain; painters turning out anecdotal canvases like all those endless crucifixions, rapes, and battle scenes that figure so largely in painting from the Renaissance into the nineteenth century. But they did not. By the twentieth century, Joyce, Eliot, Proust, Picasso, Nolde, and Schoenberg were creating artworks that required a good deal of training to comprehend.

I do not mean to imply that prior to recent times art was always created for a mass audience. In some cases it was, in some it was not. The early liturgical chants were intended for the edification of the generality of worshippers, but by the time of the Ars Nova of the fourteenth century, music had gotten so complicated, sometimes sung in two languages at once, that the pope ordered a return to the simpler style so that ordinary worshippers could grasp it.[79] And, of course, for centuries the most significant literature was written in a language that only an elite could understand. Nonetheless, the bulk of what we today term "art" was created, if not always for the masses, at least with a specific audience of nonspecialists in view.

The movement from *Moll Flanders* to *Ulysses*, from *The Magic Flute* to *Sacre du Printemps*, was paralleled in jazz by a movement from "Tiger Rag" to "Ascension." In the 1920s and 1930s, jazz was highly democratic, enjoyed by working people—most of the musicians came out of the working class—in dives and dance halls, as well as by wealthy slummers going uptown to the Cotton Club. By the late 1950s, jazz musicians had discovered that they could earn their livings playing concerts, rather than working in restaurants, nightclubs, and dance halls. No longer hedged in by show business, they began to experiment, to deliberately academize the music. Coltrane studied Slonimsky's arcane system of modes and scales; Cecil Taylor was at the New England Conservatory;

others were dipping into the musics of Africa, India, and the East for ideas. And just had been the case with the novel, painting, and poetry, so it was with jazz: the general public turned its back on it in favor of rock. The change came because the musicians were always looking for something new to do, in part out of boredom with the old, in part for the challenge, and in part simply because they suspected it was expected of them. The very idea that they were experimenting, thinking, and analyzing by itself helped make jazz academically acceptable. In a certain sense, an art form cannot be academized until it has an intellectual base.

So jazz was to a substantial degree removed from show business and established in the academy. The way an artifact is embedded in a society must have its effects. For jazz, the first of them was to insulate the music, to an extent anyway, from the pressures of the marketplace. Avant-garde jazz had a better reception on college campuses than it did outside them, and a number of the avant-gardists became attached to colleges: Anthony Braxton at Mills, Archie Shepp at the University of Massachusetts, Bill Dixon and Milford Graves at Bennington, and others elsewhere. A far higher proportion of the jazz performed and taught at colleges is avant-garde than is the case in clubs and at concerts elsewhere.

Second, the freeing of jazz from the marketplace permitted the development of repertory programs of various kinds, for which there is only a small general audience. Lincoln Center has regularly recreated the recordings of older players, including King Oliver, Johnny Dodds, Jelly Roll Morton, and James P. Johnson.

The academization of jazz certainly, to an extent in any case, made it possible to expose the music in all its variety. And this, of course, is as it should be; students of classical music are expected to be familiar with organum and *musique concrète* as well as the more familiar classical and romantic repertories.

But the movement into the academy had other, subtler effects. For one, the old system of trial-and-error learning was eliminated. Not all of the early jazz musicians were wholly self-taught: many of the black players like Armstrong and Jabbo Smith had come out of homes and orphanages where music tuition, good or bad, was routine. The stride pianists frequently had formal piano training as kids, and many of them could play some of the classical repertory. A few instrumentalists also had "legitimate" training: in Chicago, Goodman, Jimmy Noone, and Buster Bailey all studied with the famous classical teacher Franz Schoepp.

But in the main, jazz musicians taught themselves by copying local players, and most especially, the solos of their heroes engraved in the grooves of recordings. They began, not by learning a system for playing, but by trying to recreate certain sounds and effects they liked. They were not learning hand positions, fingering, an embouchure. They were instead teaching themselves how to achieve a particular tone, a type of vibrato, certain chord movements that happened to appeal to them. They searched, they experimented, until they got what they wanted.

And they had to do it on their own. It is exceedingly rare to find in the reminiscences of the earlier generations of jazz musicians of their having been aided as apprentices by an established player. Both Jess Stacy and Teddy Wilson said that Art Tatum had been helpful in showing them things;[80] Dizzy Gillespie taught the young beboppers the new chords, and Armstrong always credited King Oliver with being his mentor, although it has never been clear what, exactly, Oliver showed him; and as Armstrong's playing was very different from Oliver's, it is probably that Armstrong was simply grateful for the older man's emotional support. These few examples aside, you simply do not see in the literature statements like, "So and so showed me how he got his lip trill, how she phrased the blues, how he made the turnaround in such and such a tune." And this is still frequently the case. While musicians are likely to be supportive of one another, cheering each other on, and complimenting them afterwards, it is not usual for them to take a fellow player aside and advise them to, say, use the third valve in a certain passage, or employ a different hand position for a given chord. And even when a player asks directly for advice he is likely to be given an evasive answer, along the lines of "I never figured out how I do it myself."

In part, jazz musicians are reluctant to offer advice because it might seem presumptuous. But, at bottom, it has to do with the fact that jazz is a highly competitive business, simply because there have always been far more people interested in playing it than the system can accommodate. Jobs, prestige, record dates, money, are all hard to come by, and the musician who has through a good deal of hard work reached a certain level of skill is not eager to share his secrets with potential competitors.

So jazz musicians, in an earlier day, had to learn for themselves. Bix Beiderbecke, studying the records of the Original Dixieland Jazz Band, worked out a system of cornet fingering that remains unique; Jack Teagarden developed an unorthodox trombone technique that is almost inimitable; Rex Stewart took the half-valve effect that Armstrong frequently employed, and made a whole system of playing out of it.

This way of learning was inevitably limiting: some brass players, like Armstrong, damaged their lips through bad technique; many were never able to read well enough to work in the big bands or the studios; and few of them were able to produce the legitimate sound called for in symphony, pit, and movie orchestras. They could do, often, only what they set out to do, which was to play jazz in a certain way.

But self-teaching gave them something else, and that was a distinctive, individual quality that made their work instantly identifiable. Each musician was guided in his choice of tone, sharpness of attack, selection of notes, and all the rest of it, by his own taste—by what he wanted to hear coming out of his instrument. And because taste is always individual, something that springs from deep inside the personality, their work was bound to be distinctive. It was this approach that gave jazz its enormous variety.

In academic circumstances it is otherwise. Young players are taught as they have always been taught, to aim for a long-standing performance ideal, using methods developed over decades, even centuries. This is not to accuse jazz instructors of artistic fascism. Most of them are well aware of the dangers of over-rigid training, of squelching the musical instincts of their students. But nonetheless, most of them feel duty-bound to give their students the same rudiments, exercises, and études that music students in any field will get. They are being told how the instrument ought to be played, how it ought to sound. It could, in fact, hardly be otherwise: a teacher who told his students to "go home and work it out for yourself" would soon be out of work. But while this kind of rigorous training is necessary to produce musicians who play with good intonation, clean tone, speed, and flexibility, it can inhibit the development of an individual sound.

This kind of training is going on in the secondary schools more than in the colleges. Students who are accepted into college jazz programs will for the most part already have gained a certain level of instrumental skill, and in these cases instructors will—or at any rate should—encourage them to seek the individual manner that is critical to good jazz playing.

But there is another factor in jazz education that works against individualism even at the college level. Jazz education in colleges began as courses in "dance band" playing, and that meant in the style of the big bands most popular at the moment—those of Basie, Kenton, and Herman. By the late

1940s, when jazz education was cranking up, these groups were the most interesting big bands still working. They were playing an extension of the swing style of the 1935–1945 period, which had its roots in the dance bands of the 1920s, but they were larger, harmonically more advanced, and open to experimentation in the use of novel instruments and elements drawn from twentieth-century classical composers, in particular, Stravinsky, who actually wrote pieces for these bands. Moreover, although some junior high and high school bands draw from the Glenn Miller and other swing repertories, the lab band repertory is basically 1950s-Basie in flavor. In a 1981 survey of jazz courses in seventy colleges and universities, jazz educator J. F. Gould concluded that "bop and the aftermath through the 1950s" is emphasized.[81]

This focus on the playing of written arrangements has, if anything, increased. In a 1990 article, another jazz educator, Jeff Jarvis, wrote, "As more and more school jazz bands become competition-oriented, the natural tendency of the director is to disguise or eliminate problem areas. . . . Some directors only buy charts that don't require improvisation. If a solo section is included, it is often eliminated or the student is encouraged to play the written solo."[82]

Jarvis is speaking of secondary schools, but the effect is felt in colleges as well. To be sure, any responsible jazz educator teaches improvisation, or at least attempts to teach it. But many have concluded that improvisation is almost impossible to teach, and it is obviously much easier, and much more effective, to drill students in lab bands, which, in many cases, the students find more enjoyable than struggling with the chord changes.

And even when improvisation is taught, it is often done in a way that is limiting. The problem is the old one—how do you teach a student to be imaginative, to develop a feeling for musical relationships, to swing? What the jazz instructor can do, however, is give the student a harmonic basis for improvisation—the chord changes, to put no fine point on it. The result is that a great deal of instruction in improvising comes down to showing students chords, chord relationships, substitutions—where, for example, the Mixolydian mode can be slipped in, and so forth.

With students all over the United States being taught more or less the same harmonic principles, it is hardly surprising that their solos tend to sound much the same. It is important for us to understand that many of the most influential jazz players developed their own personal harmonic schemes, very frequently because they had little training in theory and were forced to find their own way. The work of players like Young, Beiderbecke, Ellington, Parker, Coltrane, and Coleman is filled with notes, phrases, and in the case of the avant-gardists, whole solos that cannot be explained by reference to textbook harmony. This is obvious in the case of the work of Coltrane and Coleman, and of course the boppers made a dramatic harmonic break with their predecessors; but it is also true of Beiderbecke and Young, if in a subtler way. The effect has been to some degree disguised by academically trained analysts, who are usually able to explain odd notes by rooting them in an extension of a more basic chord—a minor ninth, a raised fourth, and so on. In my view this was not the way these players saw it. We remember that Lee Young said that his famous brother did not like anyone to call the chords for him, because he would "start thinking of the only notes that will go in that chord, and he would say that's not what he would hear." Players like Beiderbecke and Young, and many others, thought melodically, not harmonically; a note that escapes ready explanation is there for its function in the melodic line, rather than as part of a vertical harmonic structure, or even as a passing tone.

Young jazz musicians, I think, do not always understand

this. They tend to think vertically when they are playing a horizontal line, and this once again tends to homogenize their work.

This homogenizing process is not peculiar to jazz. Although professors of painting and creative writing do see students individually, much of the teaching of art goes on in the classroom where a dozen or a score of students are all being given the same advice, all being pointed toward the same models; and the result is vogues for one or another style—as, for example, the recent tendency toward minimalism in the short story. When an art form enters the academy, despite the best efforts of teachers, a certain homogenizing tendency is inevitable, and I think that jazz educators have done no worse in this respect than teachers of writing, painting, and dance.

But it does seem to me that there are certain things that might be done. For one, we need a more rigorous approach to jazz history. I am going to have a good deal more to say about jazz studies later in this book. For the moment I will only point out that it is not *possible* to write a good jazz history, simply because huge areas of it have never been studied with the care that, for example, the history of art or literature is usually studied. Furthermore, there is tendency for jazz history curricula to overemphasize recent developments at the expense of early ones. One widely used jazz text, Mark Gridley's *Jazz Styles: History and Analysis*, devotes eleven pages to John Coltrane, almost four pages to Sun Ra, just over three pages to Louis Armstrong, and a paragraph to King Oliver.[83] It is usual to devote more time to recent developments than to earlier ones in art courses because they are more immediate and significant to students and teachers alike. But imbalances as large as this tend once again to force students into a common mold. Readers of this particular text are bound to come away from it with the idea that all of jazz, from the beginning until the mid–1930s—nearly half of the music's history—is merely precursory to bebop. Many jazz educators, whose expertise is in music rather than jazz history, take a similar approach. How many jazz students are given any experience at playing dixieland in the manner of Morton or the Chicagoans, small-band swing on the model of the Goodman sextets or the Kansas City Six, or the minimalism of the Gerry Mulligan groups, none of which is beyond the ability of advanced jazz students to play? To be well grounded in jazz, students ought to have had some experience with the music in all its forms, especially if they are going on to teach it, as many of today's students inevitably will. And I think that if some effort were made to broaden the scope of jazz teaching, it would help to give the music the richness, variety, and individualism that is clearly potentially there.

Yet beyond the homogenizing effect that the movement into the academy has brought to jazz, there is another consequence that may in the long run prove to be more profound. As I have tried to show, what comes to be seen as the great art of an earlier period, in its own time usually stood in some functional relationship to the society that spawned it. The artists may have been anonymous and unregarded, as were the medieval church-builders; they may have been treated like princes, as was frequently the case during the Renaissance; they may have been seen as outsiders, as the romantics were. Nonetheless, the art itself in general had an immediate appeal to its own culture. Greek drama had grown out of religious ceremonies and had the semi-religious function of explaining the behavior of gods and humans. The music and art of the earlier Christian church were meant to inspire religious feeling, and still have the power to do so. Even the poems of the putative outcasts, the romantics, were widely read: Byron's "Don Juan" was a best-seller. These works were created for specific audiences, for whom it was expected that they would have significance, or "meaning."

The sacralization of art has created in America, and I think the rest of the Western world, the strange phenomenon of the artwork that has no function other than to be art. As a consequence, everywhere people are writing novels, painting pictures, or composing tone poems for which there is no significant audience—which, in many instances, are not even *intended* for an audience. That is to say, the poet or the painter assumes at the start that the work will be of interest only to a small group of professionals in the field who will sit in judgement on it, rather than simply responding to it as an audience ordinarily does. What matters to the artist is to earn points: good reviews in appropriate media, fellowships, prizes. A startling amount of art today is produced primarily for the reviewer. Indeed, the very fact that a piece of work gains a significant audience is by itself enough, in the eyes of many critics, to make it suspect. If the ordinary American can understand it, surely it must lack the subtlety and depth that a work of art must possess. That is why, today, reviews and reviewers—"the critics"—have so much power: a piece can be deemed a "success" only if it gets a good report card from the important review media, academic journals, and important elders in the field.

A consequence of this system is that it is more important for the artist to follow prescribed lines in making the work than to make it move people. The system is thus circular: the less the artist is concerned with an audience, the smaller the audience becomes, until it reaches the vanishing point.

This whole question was addressed directly by the avant-garde composer Milton Babbitt in a now-famous 1958 article for *High Fidelity* called "Who Cares If You Listen?" Babbitt's position was that, like modern philosophy and modern physics, the discipline of composing music has become so arcane that there is no hope that even a fairly well-educated public can understand it. "At best, the music would appear to be for, of, and by specialists. . . . It is my contention that

. . . this condition is not only inevitable, but potentially advantageous for the composer and his music."[84]

Babbitt's position is unassailable. In a democracy we allow anyone to write whatever he wants for whatever audience—or none at all—that he chooses. This is precisely what a great many artists, including many famous ones, have chosen to do: create for the specialists in their fields, and forget broad public acceptance. As a consequence, the majority of "serious" novelists, poets, composers, actors, and painters survive economically through some attachment to colleges, universities, and other institutions as teachers, artists-in-residence, lecturers, holders of fellowships, and recipients of grants. Their works are published in small-circulation magazines, and presented at local repertory theaters, in college concert halls. Their audiences are likely to consist of college students, teachers in their own fields, and their competitors. Without the academy the bulk of contemporary art would disappear, and their creators would have to find other work.

There are, of course, exceptions, always exceptions: some good novels have substantial sales, some first-rate plays have long runs, some fine recordings are profitable. But how many composers, how many poets, how many actors, can live by their work? There was a time when they could, and they could because they saw to it that their work had some relevance to their societies. This is no longer the idea in art.

It is inevitable that the academizing of jazz will affect it in the same way. Indeed, it already has. For one thing, the big jazz band that so many jazz students are being trained to write for and to play in is as dead as the brontosaurus. This may be regrettable, but it is the case. Players schooled in big-band music will find themselves making their living by recycling their educations in a moribund form of music at the schools and colleges where most of them will find jobs. The same is true of the avant-garde jazz, which is now thirty years old and has still failed to find an audience outside of the academy. This once again may be regrettable: jazz is badly in need of new ideas, which the avant-garde might provide. But it remains true that so far the avant-garde has not been able to capture a significant audience for its work.

And this, at last, brings us back to the whole question of commercialism—of "selling out," to use the common phrase. It seems to me that framing the question this way, setting art in *opposition* to commerce, obscures an important point. Most of the artists we today consider "great" did not simply make an object that resembles a play or a symphony. Instead, even if they were not very conscious of it, they achieved their effects by working on the feelings of normal human beings. They were manipulators, magicians, performing sleight-of-hand. They knew how to build suspense, to create climaxes and resolutions. They knew what sort of devices would inspire awe and pity, produce tears and laughter. This, essentially, is the business the artist is in. David, Wagner, Sophocles, Shakespeare, Dickens—these people knew what they were about when they chose the themes, devices, and procedures they did. They took it for granted that they could not make an object in the abstract, but had to make one that awoke thoughts and feelings in their audiences.

As far as jazz is concerned, it should be clear that I believe a particular set of attitudes present in America around 1915 to 1925 made its widespread acceptance possible: it exactly suited the new cry for a freer, more expressive life. But I also think that it commanded a wide audience because its practitioners understood that they were in show business. There was no doubt in the mind of the Ellingtons, Armstrongs, Teagardens, and the rest that they had to "make the people happy." They had to engage the minds and the emotions of the dancers and cabaret-goers who were paying their salaries. They had to make them feel something, make them want to dance and sing.

Even those, like the members of the Austin High Gang, who saw the jazz musician as a point of light in a world of Philistine darkness were in fact producing music that got a lot of people excited. These musicians chose as vehicles popular tunes, some of them execrable, which they knew their audience liked. They set tempos that people could dance to, they used harmonies that ordinary popular music fans could grasp, they tried always to capture that infectious swing that was basic to the music's appeal.

The show business constraints were of course limiting. Change had to come by easy stages, experiments introduced at intervals. But the demands of the marketplace kept the musicians aware of the audience—aware of the fact that there were real people out there whose feelings had to be engaged.

In attempting to awaken feelings in people, there is of course always the risk that the artist will reach for the easy effect. Louis Armstrong used the showy, high-note ending of questionable musical value to excite audiences; Duke Ellington felt it was necessary to give his fans his old hits long after they were worn to death; Benny Goodman did the same; the players in the Jazz at the Philharmonic troupe were prone to instrumental shrieking and screaming, which they knew got audiences stomping and cheering.

But this problem of finding a center point between the purely meretricious and the art devised only for specialists, it seems to me, is a problem the artist should not *avoid, but confront*. Trying to understand what effect a given device, tactic, or procedure has is, I believe, a part of the artist's work, part of what he does. Indeed, it may be the critical part. The artist must understand the difference between the showy display and the effect that strikes at the heart of people; it is his business to make this distinction. He must avoid the cheap device, but he must also be constantly aware that few people are going to be interested in his work if he does not do what is necessary to engage them.

It is not easy to maintain this balance. Artists again and again miss the center point, sometimes avoiding the easy effect, but failing to awaken much in the audience; at other times getting a large response, based on an appeal to a superficial excitement. And it is precisely because the middle ground is so difficult to find that we turn up so few Mozarts, so few Michelangelos, so few Duke Ellingtons and Charlie Parkers. But there lies the challenge for the artist.

It may be that I am wrong about this idea that the artist ought to keep one foot in show business. It may be that jazz should follow the route taken by poetry, contemporary music, and modern dance—that is to say, to become a field for specialists. But that is not how the works that made jazz significant in the first place were made. Armstrong's "Hotter Than That," Ellington's "Mainstem," Goodman's "Gone with What Draft," Parker's "Just Friends," Coltrane's "Giant Steps"—these and so many more grew out of the desires and wishes of the musicians who made them, but they did so within the confines of the commercial entertainment industry. I think this is a fact contemporary jazz musicians ought to keep in mind.

7

Jazz and Pop

One of the problems that confronts the art historian and the aesthetician is determining what should and what should not be included under the rubric of any particular art form. Should we treat the Viennese waltz as serious music? What about the vast nudes drawn from classical mythology of Bouguereau and Cabanel, so admired by the Victorians, which we now see only as the established art the Impressionists were in reaction to? Literary critics agree that *The Adventures of Huckleberry Finn* is a masterpiece; but what about *The Adventures of Tom Sawyer*, which uses many of the same characters in the same setting?

The problem has particularly bedeviled jazz. Almost from the beginning, critics, musicians, and fans were arguing over what should and should not be classified as jazz. The problem arose when, on the heels of the commercial success of the Original Dixieland Jazz Band, bandleaders around the country began slapping the word "jazz" on their product, a good deal of which could not by any definition qualify as jazz. (In view of some sixty years of grousing over the fact that a white group had the honor of making the first jazz record, it is worth noting that a black group, Borbee's "Jass" Orchestra, was the first to *issue* a record with the word "jazz" on it; the Borbee group, however, was by no means a jazz band.[1]) Only six weeks after the famous opening at Reisenweber's, *Variety's* cabaret columnist was differentiating between "the genuine 'Jazz Band' at Reisenweber's" and other groups that were trying to get a handle on "legitimate 'jazz stuff.'"[2]

The arrival of the symphonic jazz bands further confused the issue: the musicians and the close fans scorned them, but a lot of the intellectuals who were interested in jazz did not. R. D. Darrell, writing in the July 1927 issue of *Phonograph Monthly Review*, said, "Jazz receives its apotheosis in the works of George Gershwin on the one hand, and the more Negroid 'hot' or 'blue' jazz on the other. The latter types . . . are best when played by Negro orchestras."[3] Darrell would eventually come to what is now the orthodox view, that symphonic jazz did not qualify; but at the moment he, like a good many others, was prepared to house a great deal of popular music in the jazz tent.

The problem was an issue once again during the swing band era when the popular music of the time was suspiciously jazz-like. It was clear enough that the very popular Goodman, Ellington, Crosby, Basie, Barnet, and Herman bands were playing a lot of music that was very hot stuff indeed; but it was clear as well that they were also playing a lot of music that was almost wholly commercial. Today most jazz histories include a chapter on the swing bands, but at the time the jazz fans were by no means sure. Wilder Hobson opened his 1939 book with the statement that "most of the so-called 'jazz' or 'swing' heard on the radio is what the players themselves call 'commercial' music, dance arrangements of popular tunes designed with a sharp eye to the market," and he goes on to say that this is not jazz. But he added, "However it may be mixed with commercial music, there is as much genuine jazz played today, at least in public, than there has ever been before."[4] What troubled Hobson, and has troubled a great many in the jazz community since, is the simple fact that Armstrong's "Heebie Jeebies," Ellington's "Take the A Train," Henderson's "Sugar Foot Stomp," Goodman's trio and quartet recordings, Coleman Hawkins' "Body and Soul," Bechet's "Summertime," Brubeck's "Take Five," Coltrane's " A Love Supreme," and Davis' "Bitches Brew" were all, in terms of their time, "best sellers," or something on that order; and all of them are considered today to be at the very heart of the jazz canon.

The critical lesson here is not that it is hard to separate jazz from pop, but that we may have got hold of the wrong end of the stick. I think we can make better sense of the problem if we stop seeing jazz as a kind of poor relative running alongside its gross and vulgar popular cousin, but instead as the spring at the mountaintop that starts down the slope, gathering water as it tumbles over the rocks to become the broad river in the plain below. For the truth is that jazz is the wellhead from which American popular music in the twentieth century has sprung.

Two major forms have dominated in that period. The first was the big dance band playing arranged music interspersed with jazz soloing, best known in the big swing bands of the 1935 to 1945 period, but with roots going back to perhaps 1915. The second is rock in its various forms—rock-and-roll, acid rock, folk rock, heavy metal, and the rest. Neither could have come into being without jazz, and both have continued to draw on jazz for new ideas throughout their existences.

The first of these, the big dance band, was not an invention of the twentieth century. Large orchestras, some of them of thirty pieces or more, playing arranged music, had performed for the elaborate balls of the rich in the nineteenth century.[5] But in the main, prior to about 1920, music for dancing in America was supplied by small groups of anonymous musicians, usually in some combination of piano, drum, banjo, violin, and one or two winds.[6] Two-piece groups of, say, piano and violin or wind instrument; or piano, drums, or banjo, were common; and certainly thousands of dances were played by a pianist alone.

In about 1910 in San Francisco and the West Coast generally, and soon afterwards in Chicago, the five- or six-piece New Orleans jazz band arrived, and was quickly taken up for dancing. Local musicians began to imitate the New Orleanians, and by 1915 or so these dixieland bands, of varying worth as jazz bands, were providing an increasing amount of music for dancing, principally in low-class cabarets and saloons, and taxi dance halls.

Among them in San Francisco was a well-trained young musician named Ferde Grofé, who would in time compose some semi-classical pieces, one of which, the *Grand Canyon Suite*, containing the popular "On the Trail," would become a standard American work. I have written elsewhere about Grofé's role in the development of the modern dance band, and I will only summarize here.[7] What we know about him, in any case, is limited. Grofé was the son of German immigrants. His father, who disappeared early, is reported to have been a singer. It is known that his mother, his grandfather, and an uncle were accomplished musicians: the grandfather played with the Metropolitan Opera in New York, and the uncle with the Los Angeles symphony. Grofé was trained in music from childhood—he later said that he was writing music from as early as he could remember—and he went to play with his uncle in the Los Angeles Symphony.

A job like this, however, could not support a musician. Grofé was also working in the dance bands that were proliferating in response to the dance craze of the time. He was aware of the new music coming out of New Orleans, and although he was by no means a fine jazz musician, he could play the music well enough by the standards of the day; *vide* his solo on Whiteman's 1922 "Chicago" and his accompaniment to the trumpet solo on "Way Down Yonder in New Orleans," recorded the next year.

In 1915 or thereabouts, Ferde Grofé was probably the only person anywhere who was well versed in both jazz and classical music. At some point it occurred to him that he could improve on the very limited dance music being offered if he brought to it some of the ordinary devices of formal music, such as grouping instruments in choirs to provide harmonized melody lines, adding counter-voices, alternating solo voices with polyphony, and so forth. None of this was very complicated: the very popular military and concert bands of the day had been utilizing these devices as a matter of course for decades. The significance was that Grofé was applying these more interesting and musically sophisticated devices to dance music, hitherto a stepchild in the world of music. He began, then, in a rather haphazard fashion, arranging dance music for the groups he was working in, using what was called the "huddle system." The term derived from the huddle used by sandlot football players in which the team captain would improvise each play, saying, "Charlie, you cut over toward the maple tree, and Frank'll fake a run toward the barn and lateral back to you," a system still in use among American kids who have not been driven into formal teams and leagues. In Grofé's case, he would play on the piano a line of music for each of the members of the group, many of whom could not read music, and bit by bit put together a complete arrangement, a scheme Duke Ellington would use to great effect ten years later.

Also working around San Francisco at the same time was a drummer named Art Hickman, who played some piano as well. In 1913, according to Bert Kelly, who led early jazz bands on the West Coast and in Chicago, Hickman put together a small dance band to accompany the San Francisco Seals, a minor league baseball team, to their spring training camp at Boyes Hot Springs. There were newspaper men along, a good deal of drinking, and a visit by Hickman and the sportswriters to Jack London, who was living in the area.[8] One of the writers did a little story on the group, which he called a "jazz" band, and went on to describe jazz as "pep" or "enthusiasm." This is the first use of the word "jazz" in print that anyone has discovered to date. (This definition of jazz as "pep" fits with what I take to be the most convincing hypothesis for the derivation of the word. At that time, and even today I think, athletic coaches frequently exhorted their troops to better effort by crying, "Put a little gism in it," meaning, fire, drive, masculine force. The step to "jis it up," was small; and to Northern ears a Southern pronunciation of "jis" would be remarkably close to "jas." Support for this theory comes from a 1917 *Variety* article that said, "Negro bands were the original jazz bands, and their expressions of 'jazzing it' and 'put a little jazz on it' are still very popular at their picturesque balls."[9] Philologist Peter Tamony, who has studied the Hickman band, agrees, and points out that the word was often "jasm" in the nineteenth century.[10])

Presumably because of the publicity the Boyes Hot Springs jaunt engendered, Hickman was asked by James Woods, manager of the prestigious St. Francis Hotel, to bring a band into the Rose Room for dancing. (The standard "Rose Room" was written by Hickman to celebrate the room.) What kind of music the group was playing is difficult to know, but by 1913, New Orleans blacks had been playing in San Francisco for at least five years, and it is probable that the Hickman people were playing some sort of raggy version of New Orleans jazz.

At some point Hickman became aware of Grofé's new approach to dance music, and brought Grofé into the group as pianist and arranger. Exactly what sort of arrangements Grofé was giving the band and how it sounded at this point is, once again, difficult to say. The critical moment came in 1918 when somebody heard a vaudeville saxophone team, Bert Ralton and Clyde Doerr. To this point, the saxophone had been seen as an unusual or even eccentric instrument, and it was mainly used in vaudeville for its novelty effect. Hickman no doubt was aware of the novelty value of the saxophone, but Grofé saw that saxophones could be used as a small "choir" in the dance band. Doerr and Ralton were hired. This was the beginning of the saxophone section, which would become the heart of the modern dance orchestra. Wilder Hobson, who was young when the Hickman band was becoming celebrated, said that Doerr and Ralton "were among the first to demonstrate the fine tone-possibilities of their instrument," and added that their playing was "the distinctive feature" of Hickman's music.[11]

The Hickman orchestra, with its saxophones, made a sensation in dance music circles in San Francisco. In 1919 the band was brought to the Biltmore Hotel in New York, where it also created a minor sensation, and a boom for the saxophone began. According to Abel Green, dance band correspondent for the *New York Clipper*, Hickman, with his New York exposure, was the start of the new dance band.[12] Joe Laurie, in his memoir of vaudeville, said, "the guy who started all the dance bands" was Hickman.[13] The jazz writer Charles Edward Smith, who had been a teenager when the Hickman band made its first splash, said, "Contrary to the widespread misconception, inspiration in swing bands was inspired not by jazz, but by popular dance bands, such as that of Art Hickman."[14] And James T. Maher, an authority on early dance bands, said that Bob Haring, Jr., whose father arranged for Hickman for a time, said, "Everybody—all the players, and the arrangers, and even the band leaders—the saxophone playing . . . Bert Ralton and Clyde Doerr . . . completely changed the way the New York musicians thought about the saxophone."[15]

The great success of the Hickman orchestra encouraged others to follow his lead. One of the first to jump in was another classically trained musician who was working around San Francisco, Paul Whiteman.[16] He was something of a fast liver, and like Grofé and Hickman, he spent a lot of time in the Barbary Coast, where he heard the new jazz music. Whiteman's first step was to hire away Ferde Grofé to play piano and arrange for his group. The Whiteman band, with Grofé's arrangements, was an even greater success than the Hickman group. By 1920 it was playing in New York, and soon its Victor records were selling in the millions. By 1923 it had become the most famous popular music organization in the United States, and probably the world.

Paul Whiteman had a keen sense for publicity. He also had yearnings for the respectability he had lost when he had fled his parents' home to take up the wayward life of the gigging musician. He announced that he was going to make a lady out of jazz and dubbed his music "Paul Whiteman's Jazz Classique,"[17] and eventually "symphonic jazz." In fact, at least two other bandleaders of the time, Paul Specht and Vincent Lopez, claimed to have invented symphonic jazz. (The term had been used by someone as early as 1917.[18])

Specht's claim is particularly interesting.[19] In 1915 he was working at the Fowler Hotel in Lafayette, Indiana, home of Purdue University, where he was heard by literary celebrities George Ade, James Whitcombe Reilly, and others. He made what he claims was the first dance band radio broadcast in 1920, and in 1922 he was brought to New York by the show business entrepreneur Gus Edwards. As early as 1923, Specht began featuring a little dixieland band drawn from the men in his orchestra, which he called The Georgians. This group included drummer Chauncey Morehouse, who would play with many jazz bands through the 1920s; trombonist Russ Morgan, who would eventually have a well-known dance band; and Frank Guarente, today forgotten but in the early 1920s considered a major figure in the new jazz music. Guarente, an immigrant from Corsica, eventually wound up playing in New Orleans in 1914, where, so he claims, he hired the King Oliver band to play for his twenty-first birthday. Guarente also says he played the famous Tom Anderson cabaret on Rampart Street in 1915, and heard what became the Original Dixieland Jazz Band in a "cat house" on Iberville.[20] A good deal of this is suspect, but the outlines are correct.

What is important about all of this is the fact that Don Redman, later to be Fletcher Henderson's musical director, was for a period a factotum in the Specht office.[21] (Even today popular commercial bandleaders will field several groups from their "offices.") Jazz writers have for decades been claiming, on the basis of little evidence, that Henderson and Redman together invented the formula for the swing band. It is clear, however, that the bigger dance band playing arranged jazz had been around for several years before the Henderson band began to make its mark. Henderson presumably brought Don Redman in as musical director precisely because of the dance band experience he had gotten with the Specht office. The Henderson band, of course, went on to become one of the preeminent hot dance bands of the time, while the Specht band is today forgotten—although it could play surprisingly hot when it wanted, as the records attest.

The point is that the great success of Hickman, and especially Whiteman, drew all the other bands in after them. The dixieland group playing unwritten music began to fade away. As we have seen, after 1923, the Henderson, Ellington, Armstrong, Oliver, and Nichols groups were reshaped to conform to the new "symphonic" style of the jazz, and the most popular bands that appered thereafter, like the Goldkette, Casa Loma, and Pollack groups, were cut to the same pattern. For the next several years it appeared that jazz would continue on this path, with increasingly larger bands playing ever more complicated arrangements, albeit with the rhythmic feeling of jazz.

But it did not turn out that way. Through the latter years of the 1920s it became clearer and clearer that a substantial proportion of the dancing public, especially the young, wanted a hot version of dance music. Henderson brought in Armstrong, Ellington brought in Bechet and Bubber Miley, Whiteman hired Beiderbecke and Trumbauer away from Goldkette. By 1926 even Paul Specht was playing a boiling hot version of "Static Strut." And by the end of the 1920s many of the most popular dance orchestras were playing a great deal of straightforward jazz, among them the Pollack Orchestra with Goodman and Jack Teagarden; the Henderson band with Hawkins, Jimmy Harrison, and Benny Carter; the Casa Loma Orchestra with Clarence Hutchinrider and Sonny Dunham; and of course the Ellington group with its cadre of great soloists. Although Hickman, Whiteman, and Specht, among others, had created the formula for the arranged jazz band, it was these later groups who discovered what to do with it, and it is their records that have become central to the jazz canon.

There was, of course, a great deal of very ordinary dance music being played. But even the most commercial of these bands kept on hand a musician or two who could turn out an occasional hot jazz solo. Benny Goodman was frequently hired for this purpose, because he was a superb musician who could sit in the saxophone section sight-reading the arrangement, and then pick up his clarinet and blow the requisite hot chorus. Bud Freeman said that he was brought into the Roger Wolfe Kahn Orchestra for the same purpose. "It was dance music, and I was just a soloist in the band," meaning that he was there primarily to add a jazz touch from time to time.[22]

But more singificantly, even the corniest of these popular dance bands were undergirding their music with the $\frac{4}{4}$ "swing" beat that had been a critical factor in turning the $\frac{2}{4}$ dance music of the earlier day into jazz. Many of them did not swing very much, but they were expected by dancers to swing a little—to provide a polite touch of the rhythmic lift that was central to jazz. They were, if not exactly jazz, of the genre.

The big dance band that took over popular music in the late 1920s was jazz-driven. It could not have been what it was without jazz; indeed, it is difficult to see how it could have come into being at all had jazz not existed.

In 1935 a new version of the big dance band appeared, which quickly came to be called the "swing" band. The explosion of swing was triggered by the enormous success of the Benny Goodman band in 1935 and the years that followed.[23] Goodman based his band on the big dance bands of the late 1920s, some of which, like Casa Loma, Henderson, and Ellington, had carried over into the 1930s. His own particular mix, however, featured a lighter swing than the earlier bands had displayed, tightly drilled ensembles, and an easygoing, swinging approach to ballads, which sounded fresh to young people looking for something of their own. Numbers of other musicians formed bands in hopes of following in Goodman's wake, and by the late 1930s there were scores of swing bands, of greater or lesser celebrity, working all over the United States.

The swing boom was once again a product of the conflation of art and commerce that has been so much a part of jazz history. On one hand there were a lot of musicians around who wanted to play hot music; on the other there were people out there who wanted some sort of lively music to dance to, or simply listen to, provided that it was not too complicated, not too dense, not too harmonically advanced. A compromise had to be struck: the swing audience would accept—indeed demanded—a certain number of hot swingers in a program, but they also wanted sentimental ballads sung by sexually appealing young men and women. In the 1940s Goodman commissioned various people with considerable training in music theory, especially Eddie Sauter, to write arrangements that were more complex and harmonically advanced than the run of dance band scores, but he tended to edit out the more difficult parts, and did not break them out more than occasionally.[24] Duke Ellington, who by 1940 was at a peak of creativity, could play his thorny "Ko-ko" in places like Fargo, North Dakota, but he was careful to surround it with a lot of his popular hits like "I Let a Song Go Out of My Heart," and "Don't Get Around Much Anymore," played by Johnny Hodges in a tone dripping honey.[25]

The question that remains is, was the music of the swing bands jazz? As I have said, many jazz writers today assume that it was, and jazz histories generally include a chapter on the swing bands along with everything else. But during the swing period itself, the jazz critics tended to be scornful of the swing bands. Few of them would have admitted the bands of Glenn Miller, Tommy Dorsey, or Artie Shaw to any discussion of jazz; and many even ruled out the Goodman, Ellington, and Luncefore bands.[26] The critics would usually admit that a hot solo by Berigan with the Dorsey band or Bobby Hackett with Glenn Miller was indeed jazz, but they saw these vagrant moments as rare gems in a vast dross of commerce.

Our best conclusion, I think, then, is that whether swing is jazz or not depends upon one's individual definition of jazz; but however we write the definition, it is undeniable that swing rests solidly on a jazz foundation. The superstructure may rise a long way from the foundation; but remove the foundation and the rest sinks into the ground and disappears.

The big band movement collapsed after World War II for reasons we have seen, although the style continued to be important to popular music for some years: many of the singers who took over popular music for a decade or so after 1945 had started as band singers—Frank Sinatra with Harry James and Tommy Dorsey, Perry Como with Ted Weems, Jo Stafford with Dorsey, Peggy Lee with Goodman, Ella Fitzgerald with Chick Webb—and for a long time afterwards they were usually accompanied by orchestras out of the swing band tradition.

But a dramatic change was coming. Rock was, in many respects, the antithesis of swing: rough, rather than carefully crafted, harmonically rudimentary as opposed to the advanced chords of the late swing bands, relentlessly individualistic rather than cooperative, driven by a jackhammer rhythm, rather than the extraordinarily subtle swing beat. It arrived with a speed that surprised—indeed shocked—older pop music fans and the music industry, which had grown fat on swing. Many people with established tastes were convinced that rock would be a short-lived fad, and they kept waiting for its demise. It did not come, however, and in retrospect we can see that it should not have been as much of a surprise as it was, for its relationship to jazz was much closer than it first appeared.

It is very rare in the history of anything that we can pinpoint a moment when a large phenomenon begins. But in the case of rock, we can. It was the deliberate creation in 1936 of a Chicago group called the Harlem Hamfats.[27] The midwife was a black musical entrepreneur named J. Mayo Williams, known as Ink Williams for his penchant for signing people to contracts. According to Paige Van Vorst, the authority on the group, Williams had under contract Joe and Charlie McCoy, brothers who had grown up in the Mississippi blues tradition. Joe played guitar and sang; Charlie played guitar and mandolin. This was a time before the boom in the Chicago blues style, when swing was beginning to blossom, and jazz still had a substantial black audience. The blues vogue of the 1920s had ebbed to some extent, and in order to supply a more contemporary sound, Williams decided to back the McCoys with a small jazz band he found rehearsing afternoons in a tavern. The group was typical of the small swing bands playing in bars and clubs in black neighborhoods all over the United States, not much different from the small groups working along New York's Fifty-second Street and similar locations.

The group was led by a trumpet player and singer named Herb Morand. He was a New Orleans Creole and inevitably had swallowed the Armstrong style whole, to the point where he could sing in an uncanny imitation of his idol. The clarinetist was a dwarf named Odell Rand, who played the smaller E♭ clarinet, which in any case had always been used occasionally by New Orleanians. One of the group's regular bass players, John Lindsay, was a New Orleanian who had recently worked with the Armstrong orchestra. The other bassist, Ransom Knowling, was also a New Orleanian, and one of the busy bluesmen in Chicago at the time. Pianist Horace Malcolm was a typical self-taught blues player who worked the rent party circuit around Chicago, and the two drummers who were with the Hamfats at various times were both jazz-trained: Freddie Flynn modeled himself on Vic Berton of the Wolverines and Jimmy Bertrand, considered the leading black show drummer in Chicago in the 1920s; Pearlis Williams later was with Cootie Williams and Miles Davis.

The Morand group, then, was an out-and-out jazz band, deeply rooted in the New Orleans tradition, still struggling to survive in the flood of big dance bands washing around them. None of the players was an improvising genius, but Pearlis Williams and Lindsay had worked in fast company, and the others were, if limited, hard swingers.

The Harlem Hamfats were looking back a few years to the "evolved" dixieland band of the late 1920s, working in what came to be called the "Chicago" style: a small, hot, blues-driven jazz band that featured one or two horns and frequently a vocalist. In this evolved, or perhaps decadent, form, the ensemble horns did not play according to the formal dixieland formula, but ripped along side by side shouting at each other. Classic examples of the genre were the Billy Banks Rhythm-maker sides, which were about as ferociously hot as jazz gets, but many other jazzmen from the later 1920s through the 1930s were recording in this form, among them Bix Beider-becke, Coleman Hawkins, Jimmy Noone, and various members of the Austin High Gang.

Many of the records cut by such groups were aimed at the black market, although there certainly was some white audience for them. The music was not meant for dancing. It was essentially good-time "party music," simple and strong, the sort of thing people would play Saturday night over a bottle of whiskey.

What distinguished the Harlem Hamfats from similar groups was its strong blues character, supplied by the McCoy brothers. Ink Williams' hunch proved to be astute. The Hamfats' first record, "Oh Red," came off so well that Williams had it in the jukeboxes within a week. The rough, hard-driving, but clean sounding and carefully rehearsed little band found an immediate audience among blacks, especially in jukeboxes, an innovation then only a couple of years old, which was replacing live bands in taverns and small clubs.[28] The music was melodically simple, rhythmically direct, and the lyrics, sung by Joe McCoy and occasionally Morand, were frequently humorous and usually erotic. One of the Hamfats' biggest hits was "Let's Get Drunk and Truck" ("trucking" was the name of a dance of the time), in which the initial consonant of the last word of the title became increasingly indistinct. There was in these recordings an element of hokum that had been present in jazz since its vaudeville days; but it was mainly the bluesy rhythm that drove the music.

The Hamfats were strictly a recording band and appear not to have worked together in public more than a few times, if that. They recorded some one hundred records between 1936 and 1939, when they began to sound old-fashioned against the musically far more sophisticated swing bands that were capturing the black as well as white audience.

The Hamfats were not alone in playing this sort of romping, blues-oriented jazz. As I have pointed out, the Billy Banks Rhythmmakers were working in this genre from 1932, and so was Frankie "Half-pint" Jaxon from 1933. (Later Jaxon was frequently accompanied by the Hamfats.) There were also various washboard and jug bands coming out of places like Memphis and elsewhere that enjoyed some success. And later, some well-known jazz musicians, among them Tommy Ladnier, Lee Collins, Chu Berry, and Edmond Hall attempted to cash in on this market with blues recordings.

But it was the Hamfats who had the great success with black audiences, and as a consequence the group became the primary model for similar groups coming along after.

The most important, by far, of the Hamfats' followers was a group led by an alto saxophone player named Louis Jordan. Like Morand, Jordan was a straightforward jazz musician who was a featured soloist and singer with the Chick Webb band from 1936 to 1938. Jordan worked briefly with Fats Waller, who was also purveying a lot of "good time" party music, and then formed his own group, which he called the Tympany Five. This group used the Hamfats' formula of jazz-based blues, with erotic content and a good dollop of hokum, all melodically simple and rhythmically hard-driving. The shuffle beat was a staple, as on "Reet, Petite, and Gone" and "Salt Pork, West Virginia." Jerry Wexler, an important producer at Atlantic during the rhythm-and-blues years, said, "Shuffle was the crucial rhythm—Texas Shuffle, Kansas City Shuffle. Back in 1934–35 [1936–39] you had the Harlem Hamfats on Decca. They were essentially a New Orleans transplant and the antecedents of Louis Jordan with their shuffle style."[29]

The Tympany Five quickly became successful with blacks and then began attracting a white audience. By the mid-1940s, it was among the most nationally popular of black bands, and had hits with "Is You Is or Is You Ain't (My Baby)?" and "Choo Choo Ch'boogie." When the swing bands collapsed, the Jordan group, which was playing a different kind of music, rose out of the rubble, and through the second half of the 1940s appeared in a half-dozen movies.

The great success of the Jordan group inspired a lot of imitators, especially among young blacks. Among other things, it did not require the relatively high level of musicianship the swing bands demanded, and a lot of young instrumentalists with show business yearnings were drawn to it. Fats Domino was an admirer of Jordan.[30] Other groups in the mold were led by King Kolax, Eddie "Cleanhead" Vinson, and T-Bone Walker. A number of young jazz musicians of the day found their first employment with such groups, among them John Coltrane, Clifford Brown, and Ornette Coleman.

But the key figure was Bill Haley, who, during the late 1940s was programming Jordan and other rhythm-and-blues musicians at a small radio where he was working. He thought, "Why shouldn't a country-and-western group sing rhythm-and-blues?" Milt Gabler, who produced both Jordan and Haley, said, "We'd begin with Jordan's shuffle rhythm. You know, dotted eighth notes and sixteenths and we'd build on it. I'd sing Jordan riffs to the group that would be picked up by the electric guitars and tenor sax Rudy Pompanelli. They got a sound that had the drive of The Tympany Five and the color of country and western. Rockabilly was what it was called back then."

It was not just Haley, however. Chuck Berry said flatly, "I identify myself with Louis Jordan more than any other artist. . . . If I had to work through eternity, it would be Louis Jordan." Arnold Shaw, in his study of rhythm and blues, says flatly that Jordan was "the pivotal figure" in the rise of the music.[31]

There was now a new genre. These groups were sometimes called "jump" bands, but by 1950, the term "rhythm and blues" had been coined for the style. Out of rhythm and blues there came the "doo-wop" sound of the Drifters, the Clovers, and all the rest. From there to rock-and-roll was just a step. There was in the mix also the influence of the very popular black vocal groups, like the Ink Spots and the Mills Brothers; but basic inspiration came from the descendants of the Harlem Hamfats.

The line from the jazz-based music of the Harlem Hamfats to Elvis Presley is astonishingly direct. The path thereafter to the rock of the 1960s is a little more wandering, with influences coming in from a number of sources. But without jazz it would never have happened. And on that combination of jazz and blues, the whole enormous international industry called "rock" was built.

Jazz thus was the basis for the two major forms of popular music to emerge in the United States, and spread around the world, in the twentieth century. But it has had other, subtler effects on popular music as well. For one thing, right from the beginning it began to inflect the product of Tin Pan Alley. Within days of the Original Dixieland Jazz Band's opening at Reisenweber's appeared all those tunes celebrating the new fad.[32]

More significantly, the songwriters who were creating what we now see as the golden age of popular song, which dates from about 1920 to 1950, were very consciously putting devices they had taken from jazz into their melodies. It was most obvious in tunes like "I Got Rhythm," "Fascinatin' Rhythm," and "Anything Goes," which played upon the metric shifts that were everywhere in jazz, but there were subtler effects.

Despite the influence of ragtime, the amount of syncopation

in Tin Pan Alley songs before the advent of jazz was slight. Such major hits as "Avalon," "By the Light of the Silvery Moon," "Cuddle Up a Little Closer," "As Time Goes By," and "The Bells of Saint Mary's" are virtually without syncopation or other rhythmic complexity. Even Irving Berlin's putative ragtime hit, "Alexander's Ragtime Band," contains little syncopation aside from the "Come on and Hear" phrase that opens the song.

But after the early 1920s, when jazz had taken hold, syncopation was everywhere in popular song, not just in tunes like "Crazy Rhythm," "Birth of the Blues," and "Blues in the Night," where it might be expected, but in sentimental ballads like "Can't We Talk It Over," in which the critical rhyming words "over" and "over," "together" and "weather" are syncopated; in "Can't We Be Friends," in which, again, the key words are syncopated to accentuate them; in "Please Don't Talk About Me When I'm Gone," in which most of the melodic interest comes from the steady reiteration of a syncopated figure; in "Someone to Watch Over Me," where again a scalar melody is given interest through syncopation. After the rise of jazz, syncopation was routinely employed by songwriters, and some of them, like Gershwin, made it an important element in their work.

For a second matter, there were the new approaches to note choice that jazz musicians were making. As we have seen, players like Beiderbecke, Young, Armstrong, and Ellington were throwing out the rules to permit the use of notes and harmonies that did not fit with standard theory. The songwriters of the day were well aware of what the jazz musicians were doing. Some of them, like Ellington, Hoagy Carmichael, and Fats Waller, were working jazz musicians. Others, like the team of Dorothy Fields and Jimmy McHugh, who wrote a number of shows for the Cotton Club, were in the thick of the jazz world. Still others, like Harold Arlen, had started out working in dance bands. Jazz was something most of the song-writers of the great age knew about, and they drew from it harmonically as well as rhythmically.

Finally, in the broadest sense, it is simply the case that the majority of Americans liked jazz in certain of its guises. This is by no means to say that Armstrong's Hot Fives or Davis' 1960s work will ever be a majority taste. But Americans have been utterly at home with the basic jazz beat for four generations; according to one study, thirty-two million Americans annually hear jazz at least once; sixteen million go to jazz performances at least once, and five million hear it in more than one context.[33] Americans have always favored music with a jazz flavor. The big dance bands of the 1920s had to have rhythmic bounce, if not bite; the swing bands had to swing; the rockers had to have that rhythmic drive they had taken from jazz, however transformed.

I think we can say finally that jazz has supplied the language in which popular music speaks. It is to pop what Anglo-Saxon is to English: the source. Few people can read Anglo-Saxon, much less speak it; but when they speak English, they are speaking Anglo-Saxon, however developed. And in the same way, when people listen to rock, a swing band, a show tune, or funk, they are listening to jazz as well. It is buried inside; but you cannot tear it out any more than you can tear the heart out of a living creature and expect it to survive.

8

Black,

White,

and

Blue

Of all areas in American life, the one in which the long-standing and fiercely defended barriers between black and white races began to break down was jazz. As far back as about 1908, when blacks could be lynched for talking to white women, the Streckfus riverboat line initiated its entertainment policy with a group consisting of the black pianist Fate Marable and the white violinist Emile Flindt.[1] Not long afterwards, a few light-skinned blacks, like Achille Baquet and Dave Perkins, at times worked in white bands.[2] By 1920 or so, when few whites would allow blacks to enter their homes except as servants, young white musicians were apprenticing themselves to black jazz players in San Francisco's vice district, Chicago's South Side, and elsewhere, and at times sitting in with black bands or joining blacks in jam sessions.[3] Jelly Roll Morton recorded with the New Orleans Rhythm Kings in

1923; Eddie Condon arranged for a racially mixed group to record with Armstrong in 1929; and in 1932 the Billy Banks Rhythmmakers, a recording group, was routinely using white and black players. By 1936, at a time when blacks and whites still could not mix on athletic fields, Benny Goodman was presenting a racially mixed group to white audiences every night, and through the decade black faces were increasingly seen in white swing bands. By the mid-1940s, when blacks still could not play for major league baseball teams and were being admitted into white colleges under stringent quotas, the wall between the races in jazz was down: in 1947, the year in which Jackie Robinson joined the Brooklyn Dodgers amid much furor, Joe Glaser as a matter of course threw whites and blacks together to form the Louis Armstrong All Stars. And it is the opinion of Lionel Hampton, one of the stars of the Goodman Quartet, that jazz opened the doors for Robinson and all that followed.[4]

Given this history, it is startling—and not a little disheartening—to observe the extent to which jazz has become racially polarized in the past thirty years. The claim that jazz is black (or African-American) music, and that whites are in it only on sufferance, has been pounded home so relentlessly and vociferously that it is today taken as a given. Gunther Schuller, in his recent *The Swing Era*, divides his discussion of the bands of the period into chapters called "The White Bands" and "The Great Black Bands," the implication being that only black bands can be great. Jazz scholar Scott DeVeaux recently wrote, "Jazz is strongly identified with African-American culture, both in the narrow sense that its particular techniques ultimately derive from black American folk traditions, and in the broader sense that it is expressive of, and uniquely rooted in, the experience of black Americans."[5] This point has been pushed to an extreme by Burton W. Peretti, in a 1992 book in which he virtually rules whites out of jazz altogether. He insists that the white New Orleanians did not play jazz at all, but "Dixieland"; that jazz was developed solely in black ghettos; and that in general, "white jazz history is an appendix to an African-American mainstream."[6]

This insistence that jazz is black music is by no means universal. The black pianist Billy Taylor, who has long been a spokesperson for jazz, has said, "Jazz is American music. It says something about who we are. It is not just black classical music, but American classical music."[7] And there are out there thousands of white jazz fans who have devoted lifetimes to the music, and bitterly resent being told that jazz is not theirs. Nonetheless, the official position, which obtains in college and university jazz programs, granting organizations, and scholarly institutions like Lincoln Center, is that jazz is black music.

But the official position begs several questions, most of them important, in my view. Is jazz actually "expressive of, and uniquely rooted in, the experience of black Americans?" Can we really describe such a thing as "the black experience?" If so, what does it mean to say that jazz is black music? How are we to deal with the fact that for decades the core audience for jazz has been middle-class white males? And finally, is it really possible to assign ethnicity to a cultural artifact like a poem, a dance, a musical performance?

The idea that jazz is black music was not always widely accepted. To be sure, Americans had always identified a body of black music in their midst, which surfaced in the mainstream as the plantation music of the minstrels, the spirituals, ragtime. In the post–Civil War period, a number of important collections of black songs, especially spirituals, were assembled;[8] by the 1890s folklorists were publishing occasional scholarly articles about black music;[9] and in 1914 the great musicologist Henry Edward Krehbiel published his *Afro-American Folksong: A Study in Racial and National Music.*[10]

Equally, right from the start it was widely recognized that blacks had had something to do with the creation of jazz. In 1923, Gilbert Seldes, who invented the phrase "the lively arts," wrote a long piece on jazz in which he took the black roots for granted.[11] A 1927 book called *Kings Jazz and David* attempted to locate the roots of jazz in Southern blacks of the nineteenth century.[12] Bert Ralton, one of the pioneer saxophonists with Hickman, in a 1926 article ascribed the invention of jazz specifically to New Orleans blacks.[13] Dr. Frank Damrosch, one of the powers in American classical music, said in *Étude* in 1924 that "jazz originated in the dance rhythms of the Negro."[14] And as we have seen, as early as 1917, *Variety* explained to its readers that "Negro bands were the original jazz bands. . . ."

But even though the genesis of jazz in the black subculture was widely accepted, by the middle of the 1920s it seemed clear to most people that it had washed through the society enough to have escaped the culture of its birth. In 1927, R. D. Darrell wrote, "In the number of works which have recently appeared on the subject of jazz, the part Negro music has played in its genesis has been debated at length; it is sufficient here to say that the jazz of today has succeeded in assimilating whatever Negro, minstrel, semi-folk music, or other influences which went to make it up, and is now a distinct musical form—American to the core."[15] At this time Darrell was seeing jazz as coming in two variants: the symphonic jazz of Whiteman *et al.*, and the hotter jazz of the blacks (a view he would eventually modify); certainly it would have been absurd to describe the music of the symphonic jazzers as "Negro music," when it had been so dramatically Europeanized.

This view was set forth even by Constant Lambert, who said, "The point is that jazz has long ago lost the simple gaiety and sadness of the charming savages to whom it owes its birth, and is now, for the most part, a reflection of nerves, sex-repressions and inferiority complexes and general dreariness of the modern world."[16]

Gilbert Seldes, in his 1923 article, when it was not yet clear that symphonic jazz would push forward as it did, expressed a widely accepted idea when he wrote: "In words and music the Negro side expresses something which underlies a great deal of America—our independence, our carelessness, our frankness and gaiety. In each of these the Negro is more intense than we are, and we surpass him when we combine a more varied and more intelligent life with his instinctive qualities."[17] This idea, that blacks could feel but not think, while whites could think but not feel, was the opinion of many American whites at the time.

Nonetheless, by the time jazz had come to maturity in the late 1920s, the view that blacks were in some deepseated way better jazz musicians than whites had become distinctly a minority opinion.[18] Many black musicians did take pride in the fact that they were as good as, and frequently better than, whites at playing jazz, as the example of Armstrong, Ellington, Hines, Morton, and many others made abundantly clear. But few black jazz musicians or black fans believed that whites were invariably inferior jazz musicians, struggling to gain a foothold in an art that did not come naturally to them: too many black players were taking whites as models for that idea to gain much ground.[19]

On their side, most whites, both musicians and fans, were willing to grant to black jazz musicians an edge in "hotness"— I can think of no better term—which fit with the idea that blacks were more emotional than whites, and they made a point of listening to black bands to see what might be learned. But most of them believed that their own version of the music was equally valid and did not have to be apologized for.[20]

Correct or not, this was the majority view until after World War II: although jazz had been created by blacks in the first instance, it had become the general property of Americans of all races, all classes. Writers like Rudi Blesh, who went as far as to define jazz as "an African art form" as late as the 1940s, were a distinct minority.[21]

The idea that jazz was black music arose as one consequence of the new militancy of blacks of the 1950s and 1960s. A particularly vocal spokesperson for this view was Amari Baraka, the exceedingly militant social critic, who insisted that jazz was not merely black music, but was the music of rebellion. He said specifically that jazz was "Negro music" which "drew its strength and beauty out of the depths of the black man's soul. . . ."[22] Another important spokesman for this point of view was saxophonist Archie Shepp, who said, "We are not angry men. We are enraged. . . . I can't see any separation between my music and my life. I play pretty much race music; it's about what happened to my father, to me, and what can happen to my kids."[23]

But, as the black critic Gerald Early has pointed out, blacks were not alone in holding this viewpoint. The Marxist critic Frank Kofsky said that jazz "is first and foremost a black art— an art created and nurtured by black people in this country out of the wealth of their historical experience."[24] Other critics, like Nat Hentoff and the late Martin Williams, also subscribed to the notion that jazz was essentially black music, although one that whites could also play. Indeed, Williams was so eager to credit blacks with whatever he could that he insisted that blacks devised American popular dance and American slang, an idea that must have come as something of a surprise to many Jews, Irish, and Italians.

It was a time when Ellington was increasingly seen as "America's greatest composer," when the influence of Parker and Gillespie on jazz was profound, when the music appeared to be in the hands of the black avant-gardists like Taylor and Coleman. It certainly did appear that jazz was essentially a black operation. The idea that jazz was black music became embedded in the social consciousness, and has been taken for granted by most Americans ever since.

What few have doubted is that jazz was originally created by blacks. This idea, that jazz sprung from the black community is, indeed, the rock jazz historiography is based on. It is therefore surprising—indeed astonishing—that the direct evidence for this belief is slim to nonexistent. We do have a good deal of anecdotal evidence about such early black New Orleans musicians as Buddy Bolden, Freddie Keppard, Frankie Dusen, and others. What we lack is a clear idea of the kind of music they were playing. Were these pioneers essentially ragtimers? If so, who were the first musicians to cross some arbitrary but quite real line into jazz, and when did it happen? Jelly Roll Morton said it was he, and that it happened in 1902;[25] and dates given by others tend to support the arrival of something that might be called jazz in the years 1900 to 1905.

But Jelly Roll Morton was not "black" in the ordinary sense of the word. Neither was Keppard, nor such other important jazz pioneers as Bechet, Ory, Duhé, and Bunk Johnson. They were Creoles; and with the introduction of this fascinating subculture, we come to one of the great imponderables of jazz history.

New Orleans was originally founded and settled by French, and later Spanish, colonists, who built a rough city in a swampy lowland, and began to cultivate the surrounding area. They imported slaves, and in time many of them became rich, and built lavish city homes and country plantations where they lived in a grand style.

The term "Creole" was applied to the slaves born in the New World, but eventually came to be used for whites born there as well. These were for the most part whites, but among them were a certain number of *gens du couleur*—mixed-blood people resulting from liaisons between whites, mainly males, and blacks, a few of whom may have been free but in the main were not.

But the black Creole community was founded elsewhere.[26] The French colony of Saint Domingue—now Haiti and the Dominican Republic—predated the Louisiana colony, and was "the busiest colony in the Western hemisphere." Mortality of slaves was high, and as a consequence they were imported in huge numbers—864,000 in the eighteenth century alone.[27] As a rule, the white plantation owners and overseers came, not to homestead, but to make quick fortunes and return to Paris as wealthy men. They tended to be young, single males, and they routinely had sex with female slaves. Very quickly there was created an extensive sub-caste of mixed-blood *gens de couleur*, who occupied a social niche well above the slaves, but a notch below the pure-blooded French.

By the end of the eighteenth century the slaves vastly outnumbered the whites, so much so that "there were insufficient whites to go around as plantation owners, and, as a result, a sizeable number of *gens de couleur* of mixed Caucasian-Negroid ancestry joined ranks with the white elites."[28]

This huge slave population was difficult for the much smaller number of whites to control, and a great many slaves escaped into the mountains, where they formed "maroon" bands that maintained a portion of the African culture intact.[29]

In 1789, the slaves, taking advantage of the upheaval occasioned in France by the French Revolution and the turmoil that followed for years afterwards, revolted, and by 1810 it was clear that what would be called Haiti would be a free, black nation. By this time substantial numbers of the elite, both white and *gens de couleur*, had fled from Saint Domingue.[30] Many of them had landed in Cuba, only a short boat trip away; and in 1809 and 1810, again as a consequence of events in Europe, some 10,000 of them were driven out and immigrated to Louisiana, where there was a French-speaking society very similar to the one they had left.[31]

According to one authority, Thomas Fiehrer, these people were divided into roughly equal numbers of whites, blacks, and *gens de couleur*—the blacks among them being in the main slaves.[32] Many of them, says Virginia Dominguez in her careful study of this culture, "were men and women of prominence and education."[33] They established in New Orleans and its environs two parallel societies—one white, one mixed-blood. Both were French-speaking, both looked to Paris for ideas and fashion. Both were libertarian in spirit, with a special fondness for music and dance; both had their rich, poor, and middling families, although it was clear that members of the white caste generally outranked the *gens de couleur*.[34]

There was a certain amount of movement from one group to the other: wealthy white Creoles frequently took the beautiful quadroons and octoroons of song and story for mistresses, and raised parallel white and mixed-blood families. On the other hand, white-skinned *gens de couleur* often passed into white society, and spent their lives avoiding recognition by their dark-skinned cousins who knew perfectly well who they were, and worrying lest a dark-skinned child with crinkled hair should appear down the line.[35]

At exactly the moment that these immigrants were establishing themselves in Louisiana, the territory was filling up with "Americans," now free to settle in the area as a result of the Louisiana Purchase. (They had been trading in New Orleans previously, both with whites and the *gens de couleur*.) The effect of these simultaneous immigrations from north and south was to double the population of New Orleans between 1805 and 1810.[36] The term "Creole" came to be applied fairly indiscriminately to any of the French- and Spanish-speaking population, regardless of their origins. The Creoles tended to live in or east of what is today called the French Quarter, the

"Americans," to the west of it, and very quickly, according to Dominquez, "Southern Louisiana society was polarized into Creoles and Americans," with the inevitable tension between the groups.[37] But the Americans, with their business and political connections to the United States, which now owned the area, had the real power, and by the 1860s they, along with Irish and German immigrants flooding in, were dominant. It was, really, a "ternary" society, for the black Creoles continued to constitute a not-insignificant minority with a separate status, and to some extent separate folkways.

Although Creole culture had already begun to decline in the face of the dominant American culture, it was the Civil War that broke its back. One aim of post-war Reconstruction was to put blacks into places of power. The black Creoles, far better educated than the masses of new freedmen released from the plantations, were elevated to high places. "White Creoles found themselves out of power, economically decimated, and a numerical minority."[38] They drew together with American whites in the face of the overthrow of social norms, and in the end it was the black Creoles who came out the losers. They were resented by the whites whom they now had power over; but they were equally resented by the mainstream blacks, who had always seen them as part of the power structure, rather than fellow sufferers under the yoke. Fiehrer says:

> During the debacle of Reconstruction (1865 to 1877) colored and white Creoles divided bitterly over their respective relationship to the Federal state. They joined opposing political parties, established antagonistic presses, and engaged in a long, wasteful dispute that ultimately and fatally debilitated the Francophone community. . . . Creole society was dealt a fatal blow, since the long-standing intimacy among the three 'castes' was never repaired.[39]

Inevitably, when Reconstruction ended and the whites fought their way back into power, they quickly moved to create a biracial system in which there were only blacks and whites.

The white Creoles, now "genteel, perhaps aristocratic, but totally impoverished,"[40] were equally keen to draw a strict line between black and white to insure what remained of their status. And by the end of the nineteenth century, when the people who would first play jazz were being born, the black Creoles had been pushed well down the ladder, only a step or two above laboring blacks.[41] These black Creoles attempted to set themselves apart as much as they could; they kept up their French; they worked at skilled jobs like cigar-making, plastering, and bricklaying; they encouraged their children to cling to some sort of culture, like playing the piano; they frequently owned their own homes, however small; and they tried to impose on themselves a certain gentility that would raise them above the rough, laboring blacks who worked as stevedores, domestics, and field hands. But the social reality was inescapable: they had little more real power and wealth than the laboring blacks around them.[42]

The crucial question is, what role did these black Creoles play in the making of jazz? Some writers believe that it was central. According to Thomas Fiehrer, "The prosopography of early jazz reveals at its core a tight-knit Creole establishment of classical orientation, descended from the *ancienne population*, at least two dozen performers of Caribbean and Mexican origins, and a small but influential contingent of Sicilians."[43]

It is certainly the case that many of the most important of the early pioneers came from the black Creole subculture, among them Jelly Roll Morton, Sidney Bechet, Bunk Johnson, Lawrence Duhé, and Kid Ory. Moreover, many others of these early musicians had originally had French names, including George Lewis, Don Albert, George Brunis, Lizzie Miles, Big Eye Louis Nelson, and Dee Dee Pierce.

How important is the mere fact of having a French name, or having had French-speaking ancestors? This leads us into the exceedingly difficult question of cultural residues, assimilation, and cultural synergism—that is to say, to what extent are cultural artifacts handed down, how do they change form, and how can they be recognized?

We might begin with the fact that the Haitian refugees did not head immediately for New Orleans, but settled all up and down the Mississippi Valley, and indeed even in such faraway places as Charleston and Savannah.[44] Wherever they landed, they "were bound together in a strange land by their Creole culture and by the harrowing violence in St. Domingue."[45] These people, both black and white, tended to be clannish, and as Louisiana was Americanized after the Louisiana Purchase in 1803, they found themselves more and more an outgroup of French-speaking Catholics in an increasingly Protestant, English-speaking world.

Nonetheless, those who lived in New Orleans, willy-nilly were becoming acculturated. If they wanted to do business, they had to speak the Parisian French that was standard in the city for decades after their arrival. The whites from Haiti of course spoke Parisian French in any case, but the *gens de couleur* were forced to abandon the *patois*. According to Virginia Dominguez, the patois was "predominantly a language of rural blacks in Southern Louisiana. It was neither the language of the white Creoles . . . nor the language of the New Orleans colored Creoles."[46]

In the countryside, then, where the descendants of the mixed-blood Haitian refugees made their livings mainly as artisans or planters, there was less need to speak good French, or to acquire European folkways of the city. It seems apparent, then, that the somewhat isolated Creoles on the plantations were able to maintain a good deal of the old culture—the language, the African-based voodoo religion, and, what concerns us here, their music.

According to the ethnomusicologist Richard A. Waterman, one of the earliest of jazz scholars, Haiti is one of the places in the New World where "African religious music has persisted almost unchanged, and African influence upon secular music has been strong."[47] Waterman was speaking of the twentieth century, which makes it nearly certain that a good deal of almost pure African music was still being played in Haiti when the refugees were departing a hundred years earlier. This was an inevitable result of the constant influx of new slaves—sometimes tens of thousands of them in a single year[48]—bringing with them their music. With so large a percentage of the population of the island African-born or the children of African-born folk, a lot of the old culture was retained; and the presence of thousands of escaped slaves living in gangs in the mountains helped insure such retentions.

This African legacy was carried to Louisiana, where it lasted through the nineteenth century, more or less. One eyewitness, writing early in the twentieth century, said that the Creole songs were meant to be danced to, and were accompanied by barrel drums, gourd rattles, and bone rattles.[49] These were all African instruments. Other witnesses claim that the famous dances at the Place Congo were not held by ordinary slaves, but by black Creole freedmen, and that the music was provided by keg drums, jawbone rattles, pebble-filled gourds, and hand-made marimbas—once again, all African instruments.[50]

Furthermore, according to one early student of the music, "There is a rhythmic sharpness in Creole music, but whoever has learned it will easily find that though complicated, they are not faulty. Complicated, yet precise, and the many syncopated rhythms difficult to play." The rhythmic examples provided by this author are, in some cases, formidable, including triplets tied to eighth notes, which, we should not be startled to discover, is one device jazz composers have used in attempting to approximate jazz rhythms.[51]

We can speculate, then, that out in the Louisiana countryside there continued to exist into the last decades of the nineteenth century a unique subculture of mixed-blood blacks, in the main, descendants of the Haitian refugees, who continued to carry along with them a good many African residuals in their language, religion, music, and other folkways. To be sure, this culture was probably to some extent reflected in New Orleans, due to the movement off the farms to the city that occurred generally in the United States during the period. But if the testimony of our observers is correct, the Haitian culture was most strongly in evidence on the plantations.

This appears to be the case, at any rate, for the music. Steve Brown, a white New Orleanian who went on to become one of the premier bassists in early jazz, once said that out on the plantations, blacks would "play mazurkas and schottisches and things like that in their style, but instead of playing it in the regular schottische or mazurka tempos, they'd go make a different tempo out of it, and play it a little bit differently, see? And that's what attracted attention, as it went along, it would build up and I think more of us . . . we took ideas from out in through the country . . . as through the darkies that we heard play. . . . We took ideas, the white people did—that's the poor white trash as we called ourselves in those days."[52]

All of this is supported by the fact that a substantial number of the pioneer jazz players came from the plantations. Edward "Kid" Ory was born in La Place, in St. John's Parish in about 1890; Ory would become leader of what is generally reported to have been the best jazz band in New Orleans in the early 'teens, and was a leading figure on the West Coast in the early 1920s, when he made the first real jazz recording by a black band. Wellman Braud was born in St. James Parish in 1891, played guitar with the famous A. J. Piron band, a society group, worked with leading bands in Chicago and elsewhere as a bass player, and spent eight years with Duke Ellington, appearing on dozens of Ellington classics. Pops Foster was born in Plaquemines in 1892, worked with leading bands around

New Orleans, and in the 1920s with Ory in California. Buddy Petit, born in White Castle in about 1897, was widely considered one of the two or three best hot cornetists in New Orleans in the early period, and was cited by several contemporaries as having been the leading model for Louis Armstrong.[53] Jimmy Noone was born in Cut Off, in 1895; he worked with the Keppard and Petit bands in New Orleans, with Oliver in Chicago, and went on to become one of the finest of all the New Orleanian clarinetists. Lawrence Duhé was born in La Place in 1887; he played with a band led by his homeboy, Kid Ory, had his own bands around New Orleans, and became one of the early jazzmen to establish himself in Chicago. Another important cornetist, Chris Kelly, came from Plaquemines Parish. And the mighty King Oliver was apparently born on a plantation, although the details are uncertain.[54]

All of these people were born in an area of about a hundred miles in diameter due west of New Orleans. They had been born in the ragtime era before jazz existed, but were playing the jazz as it was developing out of what had gone before. Almost all of them were black Creoles; almost all of them served their apprenticeships playing in little local "kid" bands upcountry in the small towns and plantations they grew up on. They constitute a roster of the finest of the jazz pioneers. Petit, Johnson, and Oliver were certainly the best of the New Orleans cornetists of the earliest day; Bechet was without question the finest of the clarinetists, and Noone was considered by some next in line.[55] Ory was the best jazz trombonist in the city and remained the best trombonist in jazz until the mid-1920s. Not all of the early jazz masters came out of the countryside: Morton, the Dodds brothers, and Freddie Keppard were all New Orleans–born. But both Keppard and Morton were Creoles, and it is possible that the Dodds were as well, and their families may have only recently left the rural areas in a migration into the city caused by the general economic dislocations of the 1890s. Steve Brown said flatly, "I think hot music originally started right down here in New Orleans, and it all drifted in here from the plantations."[56]

There was also an older group who have frequently been treated in the literature as jazz musicians. This group would include Buddy Bolden, born in 1877, who has traditionally been called the "first" jazz musician; Isadore Barbarin, born in 1872, who played with many of the early brass bands; John Robichaux, born in 1886, who led very popular dance bands around New Orleans from 1893; Papa Celestin, born in 1884, who worked in the brass bands, and formed his own group in 1910; and Papa Jack Laine, born in 1873, a white leader who for a period controlled much of the white band business of New Orleans.

It is not at all clear, however, that the bands these older players were working with were playing anything that can be termed "jazz." According to Peter Bocage, a member of the younger generation, the famous Excelsior played "nothing but marches, you understand, no jazz." But when Bocage took over, "We used to mix up a little jazz in there, too."[57]

In particular, there is firsthand testimony that the legendary Buddy Bolden was not really a jazz musician. According to Bocage, who heard Bolden frequently, he had power and could play the blues, "but as for anything else there wasn't nothin' to it."[58] Manuel Manetta, another of the younger musicians, said that Bolden could play the blues and was loud, but otherwise played straightforward melody.[59]

The contemporary evidence all seems to point to Freddy Keppard. Manetta said that Keppard was jazzier than Bolden: "That's where it started originating out from, around Freddy."[60] Ray Lopez, a white cornetist who would make a substantial mark in Chicago in the early days, said that Keppard "was hottest."[61] And we remember that it was Keppard whom Bill Johnson sent for when he established the Original

Creole Orchestra in Los Angeles, the first important jazz band to work outside of New Orleans.

Curt Jerde, an authority on New Orleans jazz, has pointed out that at least in part the heating up of the old brass band music by Keppard and the younger musicians was a consequence simply of an ancient condition, intergenerational warfare.[62] As has happened so often in jazz, the new generation wanted something more exciting than the old-fashioned stuff they had heard their fathers playing as they were growing up, and began adding the blue accents and hot rhythms to the music.

But the use of the word "Creole" in the names of orchestras is not irrelevant: Bocage, Ory, Oliver, and others all used "Creole" in their band names. This was partly because there was a certain exotic appeal to the New Orleans Creoles, who had been made famous by George Washington Cable in his popular stories, and by romantic stories of the "quadroon" balls at which wealthy males courted beautiful young women of mixed blood. (The reality was apparently more sordid than the stories had it.) But the appellation was also chosen because it had a basis in fact: Bill Johnson, Ory, Keppard, Bechet, and others *were* Creoles, and it was still important for them to mark themselves off from the rough black musicians working in the honky-tonks.[63]

I am by no means saying that the black Creoles by themselves created jazz. To begin with, as Jerde, former head of the Hogan Archive of Jazz in New Orleans, and his successor, Bruce Boyd Raeburn, have pointed out, New Orleans and its environs were, by 1900, so racially and culturally mixed that it is at points difficult to distinquish a separate Creole culture, or even to be sure who belonged to it. Raeburn has written, "with mixed-blood Creoles teamed with blacks and whites [in jazz bands], not to mention Latin Americans like Martin Abraham, who was known as 'Chink,' any attempt to assign racial connotations to style would be relative, at best."[64] All sorts of people contributed to the making of jazz. To quote Raeburn again, "In New Orleans nothing is pure."

Nonetheless, the Creole culture was a reality. As Jerde says, "Creoles of color conducted themselves in ways that other of the city's African Americans did not."[65] Their music was different, and it was different in ways that resembled what jazz would come to be.

What about the whites? This is a difficult problem, because racial attitudes have tended to bias reports. The pioneering New Orleans blacks and Creoles rarely credited whites with any contribution. On the other hand, many whites denied that blacks invented jazz. Nick LaRocca always insisted that he and members of the Original Dixieland Jazz Band invented jazz,[66] and one German researcher, Horst Lange, has supported this idea.[67] Furthermore, some white musicians insisted that they did not listen to the black bands. Arnold Loyacano, who was part of the early white movement to Chicago, said that he did not listen to black bands, particularly; and Papa Jack Laine said the same.[68] Such whites may simply have not wanted to admit to black influence, but it may also have been true that they had not had any particular reason to go to places where black bands were playing.

Nonetheless, it is clear that at least some white New Orleanians made a point of hearing black musicians. We have seen that Steve Brown frequently heard the black country bands, and it was not only that:

> The old Negroes out there—I used to many times, when I was a kid, go along the river and these Negro roustabouts would be sitting out on the cotton bales waiting for the boats, and they'd be singing. And they'd harmonize so beautifully, you know what I mean—Oh, you've never heard anything like it in your life; I'd just sit around there and listen at them for hours. And they'd just sing until the boat would begin to come to be loaded, and they

have to go to work then. But I'd sit around, and some of them would bring their instruments; and some of them would have a banjo or something, some of them would have a trumpet, an old battered trumpet . . . improvising and playing . . . in their way, their style . . . like I heard a Negro one time in one of the churches, playing an organ. Well instead of playing the organ like you would ordinarily play, he'd make a lot of arpeggio notes . . . on the basses. [This would have produced a boogie effect.] And he had a rhythm going of his own, it sounded just like an orchestra in those days, see . . .[69]

Ray Lopez certainly listened to enough black musicians to be able to differentiate between trumpeters Keppard and Perez. And Paul Mares, cornetist with the New Orleans Rhythm Kings group, which made a mark in Chicago, said, "We did our best to copy the colored music we'd heard at home. We did the best we could, but naturally we couldn't play real colored style."[70] These admissions by early white jazz musicians that they were influenced by blacks are fairly rare. But there are enough of them, I think, to make it clear that the New Orleans whites did not arrive at their playing styles independently. Nonetheless, however the white pioneers picked up their jazz, by 1910 or so they were bringing ideas to the music, thus adding to the mix.

My central point, then, is that jazz did not arise from some generalized "black culture" or "black experience." As I believe, the Creoles were key to the process, and they possessed a culture that was substantially different from that of the Southern black laboring man that produced the spirituals and field hollers. They spoke French rather than English; were Catholic, not Protestant; were artisans and small businesspeople rather than day laborers; and most important, despite the obvious African residuals in their religious practices, language, and folkways, saw themselves as the inheritors of a European tradition. They were not people of the sanctified church with its ring-shouts, but of a voodoo-tinctured Catholicism; not of the work song, but of the Creole love ditty and to some extent the "French" opera; not of the slow drag, but the schottische and the mazurka; and perhaps most critically, most of them had no recent history of slavery.

But even if the role of the Creoles in the making of jazz was less than I take it to be, the music nonetheless appeared first in the environs of New Orleans, a city that possessed a unique culture. I have found no contemporary evidence—none whatever—that some form of incipient jazz was beginning to appear in the black enclaves of, for instance, Memphis, St. Louis, or Savannah; or in the cotton fields and turpentine camps of the South where most American blacks were still getting their livings in 1900. Doc Cheatham, growing up in Nashville at a time when jazz already being played in New Orleans, said, "There was nothing in Nashville—jazz."[71] Sam Wooding, an important black bandleader of the 1920s, who was in Will Vodery's famous army band during World War I, which contained many of the best black musicians available, said that the group played ragtime, "but there was nothing of what we call jazz today."[72] Tony Sbabaro, (later Spargo) drummer with the Original Dixieland Jazz Band, said that when he arrived in Chicago in 1915, "You couldn't find a jazz band in Chicago when we landed there."[73] It is abundantly clear from show-business newspaper accounts that there was no jazz in New York until the New Orleans bands arrived, and the same is true of the West Coast.[74]

With or without the Creoles—and it would be hard to deny them a considerable role in the creation of jazz—the music was first played by people whose "experience" was in a good many respects different from the experience of the black share-cropper or day laborer, most of whom had been slaves or had slave parents, who constituted the majority of blacks at the moment.

It is of course true that virtually all blacks of the time, wherever they grew up, shared the experience of being disenfranchised in America—as, in fact, did Jews, Asians, and members of other ethnic groups. But the degree of disenfranchisement of the New Orleanians, especially the lower-middle-class Creoles, and the rural sharecroppers was dramatically different. And given all of this, it seems to me difficult to say that jazz grew out of an undifferentiated "black experience," "black ethos," or "black culture."

In any case, by 1908, jazz music was spreading out from New Orleans, and by 1915 it was being played in the vice districts, dance halls, and occasionally the vaudeville stages of the big Northern cities for audiences that included substantial numbers of whites—which were, indeed, in many cases exclusively white, as on the vaudeville circuit the Keppard group worked in 1915, and the Chicago clubs where the first white New Orleans bands were playing.[75]

It is important for us to keep it in mind that large numbers of blacks were hostile to ragtime, jazz, and the blues.[76] Religious blacks tended to see jazz as "the devil's music,"[77] a term blacks themselves used. Lawrence Brown, Duke Ellington's star trombonist for years, was told by his preacher father to either quit playing dance music or leave home—Brown left home.[78] His case was far from unique: as late as the 1950s, Hamp Hawes' minister father refused to attend his performances in nightclubs.[79]

The music was also disliked by the black middle class. In the first decades of the twentieth century, these people were still clinging resolutely to the ideal of Victorian gentility that had been the ethic of the American mainstream for decades, and still had some weight with the middle class. To the Victorians, anybody in show business was only a cut above a prostitute. As a consequence, according to W. C. Handy, "minstrels were a disreputable lot in the eyes of a large section of upper crust

Negroes."[80] The cultural historian John Lax quotes the pioneer bassist Pops Foster as believing that "among a large segment of the black population, 'show people were classified as nothin' and musicians were rotten.'"[81] This was as true in the sophisticated cities as in the rural South. Clarinetist Garvin Bushell said, "Most of the Negro population in New York had either been born there or had been in the city so long they were fully acclimated. They were trying to forget the traditions of the South; they were trying to emulate whites. . . . You usually weren't allowed to play blues and boogie-woogie in the average Negro middle-class home. . . . You could only hear the blues and real jazz in the gutbucket cabarets where the lower class went."[82]

204

Finally, in this period a huge number of blacks were still trapped in the poverty and despair of the Southern sharecroppers' cabins: in 1920, two-thirds of blacks still lived in rural areas. The fine swing trumpeter Bill Coleman did not own a record player until he was over twenty and had been working as a professional for some time.[83] Sam Wooding, who had a popular show band in the 1920s, said, "Well, we didn't listen too much to records, because most blacks, there wasn't a lot of them had phonographs. . . . Sometimes they'd have phonographs in the cabarets."[84] As late as 1939, according to one survey, only seventeen percent of rural Southern blacks had radios, and twenty-eight percent had phonographs. As there was undoubtedly considerable overlap, it is likely that two-thirds of these people had no way to hear jazz on a regular basis at all. It has been estimated that, during the 1920s, the three largest record companies specializing in the blues sold about five to six million blues records annually.[85] This may seem a large figure, but given that the black population of the United States at the time was above ten million, it suggests that only a minority of blacks could have been regular buyers of blues records. Furthermore, as Lax points out, "Few members of the working class [blacks] had the time, money, or inclination to frequent the cafes on the South Side. . . ."[86]

In sum, in the early days large numbers of blacks were excluded from the jazz audience for religious, social, and economic reasons. This helps us understand why jazz did not at first spread out from New Orleans through the black community, but washed more generally through the population of the big cities, at first, San Francisco, Los Angeles, and Chicago, and then elsewhere. Jazz musicians, like the people in the Keppard group, had been playing for whites frequently back home; they took it as natural for them to play in white dance halls and cabarets—or at the fancy Winter Garden in New York where the Keppard group had a booking.

This does not mean, however, that blacks were ignoring jazz. Purcell's, on the Barbary Coast, where a number of black bands worked, was a black and tan. The Lincoln Gardens where the Oliver Creole Jazz Band made a long residency, was a black dance hall. There were many more black locations in Chicago's South Side, Atlantic City's black belt, and elsewhere, although many of these places drew a considerable number of white patrons.

The point is that most of these big-city blacks were only a generation away from the South, and a substantial number of them were recent immigrants. The black folk music of the South—the spirituals, the work songs—was their own, and insofar as jazz bore a family resemblance to this music, it came to them more naturally than it did to whites. Lax has written, "In contrast to black writers and actors, black musicians found themselves within a tradition of their own creation."[87] He goes on to quote the bassist Milt Hinton who, like many blacks, heard his first jazz in a black theater: "We'd sit and listen to this overture which had a European environment. . . . Then somebody would say, 'Hey baby, play so and so,' and when Louis stood up and played one of his great solos, you could see everybody letting their hair down and say, 'Yeah, that's the way it should be. This is it.'"[88]

Jazz, at the beginning, was a language that spoke more directly to blacks than to whites. Indeed, to whites, especially young whites, part of its appeal was its unfamiliarity, its exoticism, the simple fact that it was perceived as the music of more "primitive" blacks. This is an important point for us to bear in mind. The plantation songs of minstrelsy, the spirituals of the Fisk Jubilee Singers and similar groups, early ragtime, the blues, and jazz, were attractive to whites not simply for their musical values, but because they were perceived as the music of blacks. We remember the 1917 ad in *Billboard* for the Clarence M. Jones tune "The Dirty Dozen," and the advertising pitch to *Billboard's* mainly white audience that it had "caused a sensation in the 'Black Belt.'"[89]

Nonetheless, even though tens of thousands of blacks, many of them young, were drawn to the new hot music, it did not become the common property of the black subculture as a whole. There were simply too many subgroups in the black culture who had set their face against it to make it a universal cultural artifact for blacks. Louis Armstrong, growing up in the New Orleans "back o' town," might take to it; but Duke Ellington came out of a respectable middle-class family with ambitions for him who did nothing to encourage him in undertaking a career in jazz. And Fletcher Henderson's parents, when they heard that he was going on the road with Ethel Waters, then considered a blues singer, came to New York to make sure he was not lowering himself.

It should not, of course, be thought that all whites were enamored of the music. As we have seen, a lot of them hated jazz, and a very large number—probably the majority—were simply indifferent to it. My own parents, who were young during the Roaring Twenties, grew up dancing indiscriminately to the jazz and pop-jazz dance bands of the period.

They never made any objection when my brother and I began listening to it and went on to try to play it. On the other hand, they never went out of their way to listen to it, either; and I think their attitude was a very common one among whites of the time.

With the arrival of swing, jazz, or jazz-based dance music, became the popular music of America. Full-fledged jazz musicians, like Count Basie, Benny Goodman, Artie Shaw, and Duke Ellington, were stars, playing for huge audiences drawn from the general public. Although it is impossible to put numbers to this, it seems likely that the black audience for this music increased during the swing era. The Savoy Ballroom in Harlem attracted large numbers of blacks night after night; and when famous bands, black or white, came up to the Savoy to battle the black house band, frequently that of Chick Webb, police might have to be called out to control the mobs in the streets.[90] The Club DeLisa, on Chicago's South Side, which by 1941 could seat a thousand patrons, booked name black talent, and lasted well into the post–World War II period.[91] There were a dozen jazz clubs in Kansas City catering to blacks during the period, and more in the Central Avenue area of Los Angeles.[92] It is probable that every city with a black population of any size during the swing era had its jazz clubs catering to blacks, offering whatever big swing bands they could afford, as well as local small groups, boogie-woogie pianists, and later the rhythm-and-blues groups that were attracting a substantial black audience in the 1940s.

What happened next was unexpected and today partially unfathomable: at some point during the decade of the 1950s the black audience for jazz began to melt away. The most obvious cause was the disappearance of the swing bands and the arrival of bop. This prickly new music was not nearly so easy to grasp as swing, and only the most determined young people were drawn to it. Few of the older listeners, who had grown up on Armstrong, Ellington, Goodman, and the rest, were willing to make the effort to comprehend it. By 1952, the black Central Avenue district in Los Angeles, which during the 1930s and 1940s had housed a dozen black and racially mixed jazz clubs, was "a jazz ghost town. Most of the clubs had closed or would soon do so."[93] In Harlem the famous Apollo Theater, where nearly all of the famous bands of the swing era had played, had converted to rock and allied forms, and James Brown, Gladys Knight and the Pips, and the Temptations were setting box office records.[94]

Yet there were those who were drawn to bop, and they were mainly white. Young blacks continued to come into the music to play it, but they did not come as listeners. Art Blakey, one of the leading black drummers, said flatly that blacks had "never heard" of Charlie Parker, and the black novelist Ralph Ellison, who had grown up hearing jazz in Oklahoma City, agreed that Parker was a "white hero."[95] Ted Gioia, in his careful study of West Coast jazz, says that in the 1950s, "mimicking Southern California's growing urban sprawl, the jazz nightspots also moved to the suburbs. The next generation of clubs, such as the Lighthouse in Hermosa Beach, would reflect these changing demographics."[96] The few clubs that remained in the city proper were no longer on Central Avenue, but in prestigious white neighborhoods: The Haig, the best-known Los Angeles jazz club of the day, was on Wilshire Boulevard opposite the Ambassador Hotel.

I do not mean, of course, that no blacks listened to the boppers; some did, and a good many more were drawn back to the music with the arrival of the so-called soul or funk movement in jazz in the mid-1950s. People like Horace Silver, who had a hit with a church-based tune called "The Preacher," and Cannonball Adderley, who also had a hit with "Watermelon Man," attracted black audiences precisely because they were using in their music elements that reflected, however dimly, the music of the black churches. This was a deliberate effort by "the more commercially minded hard bop musicians . . . to win back audiences alienated by bebop's intellectual pretensions with hard-swinging grooves and a folksy sensibility that wore its ethnicity on its sleeve," according to Scott DeVeaux.[97] Others working in the "soul" style who drew blacks were the Hammond organ players like Jimmy Smith and Jack McDuff—the Hammond organ was familiar to many blacks from its use in churches. To some extent, other boppers, like Coltrane, Sonny Rollins, and Art Blakey, who also at times employed similar devices, interested black music fans.

But the general black public was no longer interested in jazz in the way it had been during the jazz age of the 1920s and the swing period that followed. In 1957, *Ebony* ran an article under the title, "Are Negroes Ashamed of the Blues?" which said, "There'll be no more musicians of the status of Art Tatum, Duke Ellington, and Count Basie . . . the roots that produced great jazz have been cut off."[98] The magazine was wrong on one point: there was plenty of great jazz to come. But the implication that jazz was no longer rooted in the black culture was correct.

Ahmet Ertegun, co-founder of Atlantic Records, and one of the first to record rhythm and blues, said that in the late 1940s, when he was studying at Georgetown University in Washington, D.C., "I hung around a record store not far from the [black] Howard Theatre. What I learned at Max Silverman's Quality Music Shop was that black people didn't buy jazz. They bought country blues singers like Washboard Sam; they bought city bluesmen like Charles Brown; and they bought rhythm-and-bluesmen like The Ravens."[99]

What is surprising about this is that black musicians dominated bop in a way that they had not dominated other forms of jazz since the early days in New Orleans. Black musicians devised the music without any help from whites, and they were its stars for a considerable period thereafter: Parker, Gillespie, Thelonious Monk, Bud Powell, and somewhat later, Fats Navarro, Clifford Brown, and Sonny Stitt were the quintessential boppers and they were all black. Some whites, like Red Rodney, Dodo Marmaroso, and Al Haig, began playing the music fairly early; but they were secondary figures. The stars were all black.

In part the continued flow of blacks into jazz as players was due to the fact that it was virtually impossible for a black to get work in classical music, as it would be for many years to come, and very difficult for them to break into the radio or film studios, although by the 1940s the studio doors were opening fractionally. Moreover, blacks were still generally kept out of professions and executive offices in industry; show business remained an area open to blacks, and those who were interested in music had no place to go but jazz or popular music. The chance to work as a bopper was a real opportunity for blacks.

Furthermore, there was a militancy to bop and its players that ought to have suited the more aggressive mood of blacks in the postwar period. Bop musicians refused to conform to the stereotype of the grinning black entertainer of the Armstrong school, who was particularly resented by young black musicians.[100] Some of them would be active in the civil rights movement, and in time a few would use their music to make statements about black rights; e.g., Charles Mingus' "Fables of Faubus," and Max Roach's "Freedom Suite." The new bop music ought to have become a theme music for young blacks. Instead, they turned their attention to Louis Jordan, Fats Domino, and the doo-wop groups that followed.

Why? What happened? I think there is not one answer, but several. To begin with, blacks coming of age in the postwar period, at least the more militant of them, in firmly and unequivocally rejecting the old tradition of the black performer, chose to throw out the baby with the bathwater. The 1949 appearance of Louis Armstrong as "King of the Zulus" at the New Orleans Mardi Gras was significant. The Zulus were a black group that both emulated and parodied the white "krewes" that had annually mounted floats for the Mardi Gras parade from well back into the nineteenth century. These krewes elected kings, queens, and courts from among their members, and the Zulus had customarily parodied this practice by electing as their king somebody from well down the socioeconomic structure.

In 1949, however, in a departure, they chose Armstrong, who was nonetheless asked to wear the comic costume the King of the Zulus customarily wore. He appeared on national television and in major magazines and newspapers, in blackface, wearing a long black wig, a crown, and a grass skirt. Gerald Early has written: "To most blacks, especially the 'dicty' middle class, there was nothing funny about this. Armstrong simply looked ridiculous and he seemed to be holding the entire race up to scorn."[101]

The episode seemed to encapsulate for many blacks, especially the intellectuals who might have taken up bop, what was wrong with jazz: too many of its best-known black players, including Armstrong, Waller, many blues shouters with their crude double-entendres, and Jordan and Calloway, who were frequently lumped in with the jazz musicians, were performing in the old style of comic darky with rolling eyes and flamboyant manner. It did not matter that Armstrong's Hot Fives were being reissued in dignified packages and that white critics were writing about him as the genius of twentieth-century music. He and the others were unacceptable to many blacks, especially the better-educated among them.[102]

Conversely, none of this mattered to white listeners. A new generation of them was being drawn to these older black players. To them Armstrong was no disgrace, and those who liked jazz, but were put off by bop, turned to this older music, and began to play it in the dixieland bands that were a feature of high schools and colleges of the late 1940s and 1950s. [103] For young whites of the day, jazz posed fewer sociopolitical problems than it did for blacks—ironically, precisely because blacks saw jazz as "theirs." (One paradoxical result was that dixieland, the original jazz form that was unquestionably a black invention, came to be seen as the white man's music, denigrated or ignored by most jazz critics. Today it is virtually impossible to find blacks who can play dixieland, although at present in New Orleans there is a handful of blacks, some of them college professors, who are attempting to work in this older tradition.)

For a second matter, to quote Early again,

> Bebop musicians, despite their stance as militant, socially aware, artistically uncompromising professionals, were no more in tune with the black masses than the older Armstrong and, in some sense, were probably less so. The beboppers' insistence on seeing themselves as artists and not entertainers pushed them much closer to viewing their cultural function in more European terms. To Armstrong and to the black masses, the concept of the artist and of art as it is generally fixed by Euro-American standards is, quite frankly, incomprehensible. Armstrong saw himself as an entertainer who must, by any means, please his audience. And to the black masses generally there would scarcely be a reason for the public performer to exist if he did not feel that pleasing his audience was the prime directive. [104]

Indeed, the extent to which the boppers Europeanized themselves, not merely in music, but in their presentation, is astonishing. The new scales and harmonies were far more similar to those of Stravinsky and the modernists than to the old scales of black folk music; and while the new rhythms did relate back in the sense that there was a good deal of metric byplay in them, they were at so far a remove that they were incomprehensible not only to jazz fans of both races, but to the older musicians, as well.

But it was not just the music: Gillespie, Parker, Coltrane, and others eschewed the gaudy show-business costumes of Calloway and Ellington, and dressed like Westchester County stockbrokers. Their horn-rimmed glasses were the classic symbol of the overbred bookworm, and the berets they affected were standard with the Bohemian artists and intellectuals of the period, who in turn had adopted the style from the French painters and intellectuals of the generation before. Furthermore, both Parker and Gillespie would at times affect a sort of British accent, and on the stand refer to each other as "my colleague" in a formal manner.

A good deal of this of course, was parody—a put-on. But some of it was not; and the net affect was to give the boppers a Europeanized appearance which was markedly different from the vaudeville-derived tradition of the black entertainer most blacks were used to.

Finally, the movement of jazz into the academy in the 1950s also helped wall the music off from ordinary blacks. It was a time when there were still quotas for blacks at most colleges, although that was beginning to change. Not many blacks went to college, and if they did, they went to black colleges. A college campus was a foreign place to most blacks, and as jazz was drawn out of show business to academia, it was also being drawn away from its black audience. As Early has pointed out, the shift into the concert hall was something that many young black musicians were demanding, and it benefitted those, like John Lewis and the Modern Jazz Quartet, who broke into the college circuit. But in the process the black audience was lost.

This effect has persisted. A 1978 study of jazz education reported that only thirty-seven percent of seventy schools surveyed had a black instructor at the time of survey, and even when every school that had *ever* had a black jazz instructor, even on a part-time basis, was included, the number rose only to sixty-three percent. Fully a third of the schools surveyed had never had a black instructor. The authors conclude, "however, in 1978 prejudice did not seem to be a discernable factor. A more specific reasoning, by both black and white contributors to this study, suggests that the black jazz artist . . . finds the traditional European-oriented academic approach to music to be an alien and stifling environment which he/she tends to reject. . . . Consequently, many fine jazz performers and would-be potential instructors simply cannot or will not explain what they do in accepted academic terminology."[105] Readers who have come this far will suspect that I have a sneaking sympathy for the resistance to the academic approach many black jazz musicians feel; but that does not alter the fact that the movement of jazz into the academy caused many blacks to shy away from it, for whatever reasons.

Beyond all of this there is the simple fact that the new jazz of the postwar period—bop, and the related West Coast, or cool school, no longer bore much relation to the black folk music jazz had originally been drawn out of. As we have seen, during the 1920s and 1930s, jazz had an immediate appeal for blacks, because it had a family resemblance to the blues, the work song, and the music of the storefront church that blacks of the time were at home with. This was no longer the case. The blues and the fluid approach to pitch had been replaced by a more European scale; the old "barbershop" harmonies of jazz were going in favor of advanced harmonies using a high degree of dissonance; the earlier relaxed swing was becoming tenser. Jazz had moved farther away from its roots in black folk music, and for the majority of blacks, it was no longer a member of the immediate family. But the music of Jordan and Domino was, and they turned to it.

In sum, by the 1950s, jazz appeared to many blacks no

longer to be theirs. It now had, as the cultural historian Irving Louis Horowitz has put it, a "largely white middle class constituency."[106]

And this remains the case today. A study made in the early 1980s by Harold Horowitz, and supported by the National Endowment for the Arts, reported that, while some thirty-two million Americans listened to jazz at least once in the course of a year, only about ten percent of the population actually attended a jazz performance, and only about twenty percent listened to a jazz record.[107] The racial breakdown indicated that fifteen percent of blacks, as against nine percent of whites, attended a jazz performance in the surveyed year, and thirty-six percent of blacks against eighteen percent of whites listened to a jazz record. The black audience for jazz is *relatively* larger than the white audience; but it is also clear, given that a lot of the respondents had only listened to jazz a few times in the course of a year, that jazz is of serious interest only to a small percentage of blacks—probably not more than ten percent. It can hardly be said, therefore, that jazz today somehow reflects anything that can be called a "black ethos." And it is also clear that the bulk of the audience for jazz is white.

What is startling about this is that young blacks continue to come into jazz as *players* in disproportionate numbers. Once again, I have seen no figures on, say, the percentages of blacks in jazz courses, but many of the best-known of the younger jazz musicians, like Terance Blanchard, the Harper Brothers, and of course the Marsalis family, are black.

Yet despite the presence of Marsalis and other blacks, it is also clear that a lot of young white musicians are playing important roles in shaping jazz today: Chris Hollyday, Geoff Keezer, Joe Lovano, Benny Green. Black musicians no longer dominate the music as they have done in the past. Up until perhaps 1960, or even later, any reasonable list of the most significant working jazz musicians of the day would have been predominantly black. Perhaps more important, the colossi of the music were almost all black, and whenever the white musicians threatened to take over the music, a black messiah appeared to hold them at bay. In about 1925 the white groups following after the Original Dixieland Jazz Band and similar New Orleans groups were coming to dominate jazz, and white improvisers like Beiderbecke, the underrated Adrian Rollini, Miff Mole, Red Nichols, and Jimmy Dorsey were catching the ear, not merely of the public, but of the musicians, both black and white, as well. Then came Louis Armstrong, who changed the rules of the game. In the mid-1940s some of the most advanced music in jazz was being written for the Goodman, Herman, and Barnet orchestras, and white improvisers like Goodman, Teagarden, Hackett, Pee Wee Russell, Bunny Berigan, and more, were the peers of the best black jazz players. But then came Charlie Parker, who once again changed the rules. In the mid-1950s, the whites of the cool school, like Getz, Brubeck, Desmond, and Bill Evans, were developing a somewhat intellectual approach that could compete with the boppers. But then came John Coltrane.

We have not had a black messiah in jazz since. Wynton Marsalis comes the closest to being one, but I doubt that even his most impassioned fans would put him in a class with Armstrong and Parker.

One reason why we have not had a dominating black presence in jazz is, I think, because blacks, by and large, are learning about jazz the same way that whites are: in high school and college lab bands and jazz composition courses, as the survey mentioned earlier makes clear.[108] This is a point of critical importance: blacks are not reaching back into their own cultural backgrounds for something new to bring to jazz. The great innovators, like Ellington, Armstrong, Parker, and Coltrane, brought something to jazz that came out of personalities shaped in a black subculture. It is possible to trace critical elements in Armstrong's "West End Blues," Ellington's "Black and Tan Fantasy," and Parker's "Now's the Time" directly to the folk music of the black slave culture.

But young jazz musicians today, black or white, are finding little of interest to them in the music of the black culture, in part, as the critic Krin Gabbard has pointed out, because a unified black culture does not really exist. And this has been the case for half a century: the innovations of the beboppers and then the avant-garde, were not drawn from the American black culture. In fact, not since the 1930s, when the riff-based blues bands came out of Kansas City to add an element to swing, has a significant musical idea for jazz been drawn from the black culture. Perforce, young blacks learn about jazz in school.

There are, of course, first-rate black instructors in high schools and colleges. But as we have seen, the great majority of jazz teachers today are white, and they are setting the tone for jazz education today. And that tone is distinctly more European, less "black" than has been the case heretofore in jazz. The emphasis in schools and colleges is on clean playing, standard technique, a knowledge of theory heavily indebted to the European harmonic system, good sight-reading skills, the ability to compose and arrange.

I have written elsewhere that jazz has always swung between its European and its African side, now emphasizing one, now the other. Whenever it began to lean too far in one direction it would be tugged back toward the middle. In the mid-1920s the symphonic jazz school was drawing the music away from its New Orleans roots; but by the end of the decade the demands of audiences had forced the dance bands to heat up their music, and Armstrong was capturing mainstream fans. In the mid-1940s the music was coming to be dominated by elephantine bands playing arrangements that owed much to Stravinsky and even Schoenberg; then came bop, which despite its advanced harmonies, had frequent recourse to the blues. But I do not see today any counter-movement back towards the use in jazz of a more black vocabulary. To some extent the new conservatism in jazz, which has drawn a good many younger players to look back to the boppers and swing musicians of the 1930s and 1940s, has had the effect of reintroducing the black elements in the work of Young, Parker, and others. But this has been only incidental to the backward-looking impulse.

To be sure, this slide towards the European side of jazz is not absolute. There are plenty of stone beboppers out there making records and playing in clubs. Furthermore, some of the avant-garde are making somewhat self-conscious efforts to employ black elements in their work. Nonetheless, the concert orchestras, lab bands, and repertory groups that have become so important to jazz are mainly playing composed music based on the European harmonic system, and generally using formal structures also taken from European practice.

And now, finally, we can return to the question I posed at the outset: to what extent is it reasonable to describe jazz as black music, and what does it mean to do so?

Jazz was originally devised by blacks, albeit a very anomalous group of blacks, many of whom refused to admit they were in fact black; and the music bore a clear relationship to nineteenth century black folk music, which traced its roots back to both Africa and Europe. At that early stage it was certainly possible to say that jazz was, if not black music, at least the music of blacks. After the diaspora, from about 1925 to 1935, most of the leaders in the development of the music were black. True enough, by the late 1920s whites dominated in clarinet playing, and there existed very influential whites like Beiderbecke, Miff Mole, and Teagarden on other instruments. But Hines, Waller, and other stride players were the leaders on piano; Hawkins, Hodges, and others set the pace on saxophone; blacks like Jimmy Harrison, Benny Morton, and Dickie Wells—not Teagarden or Mole—were establishing the basic trombone style; the Duke Ellington Orchestra was charting new paths, and Louis Armstrong was supreme overall. Once again it could at minimum be said that blacks dominated the jazz world.

Furthermore, from time to time jazz continued to dip back into the black culture for refreshment: for example, when the Kansas City bands brought into swing the riff style, developed out of the black boogie-woogie system; and when the *white* players of the dixieland revival looked back to New Orleans jazz for a hot antidote to the well-groomed swing of the big bands. Thus, up until 1940, I should judge that jazz could be considered a black province more than a white one.

But today jazz has had a primarily white audience for perhaps seventy-five years. Jazz criticism was devised by whites and has been mainly in white hands ever since. Jazz education, since it began to have a real existence in the early 1950s, had been dominated by whites. And ever since jazz began to revive in the 1970s after the onslaught of rock, white players like Dave Liebman, John Scofield, Scott Hamilton, and others have done as much to give the music direction as blacks have.

Perhaps more critically, it is my hunch that today a white child from a middle-class suburb is as likely to encounter jazz growing up as is a black child from the ghetto. The audience for jazz today lies mainly in the white middle class: The N.E.A. study mentioned earlier shows that the better educated any group is, the more likely it is to be interested in jazz.[109] As I hope to show in a later chapter, there is a surprising amount of jazz being played in mainly white suburbs. It may be true—although I can find no figures—that the black middle class is as interested in jazz as its white counterpart; but as their numbers are substantially smaller, they cannot constitute a major portion of the jazz audience.

For another, the commercial big-city radio stations play little or no jazz, and neither do the black oriented stations. The jazz programs are almost always found on small radio stations—college stations, publicly funded ones, and smaller suburban ones—which are by and large aimed at the better-educated middle-class market.

Finally, the market for jazz records is lodged primarily in the mainly white middle class. Most middle-class people who listen to recorded music at all will have at least a few jazz records of one kind or another on the shelf. It is a terrible irony that jazz has for most of its life got its main support from the very people the jazz world has seen as the enemy, quintessential squares—accountants, car salesmen, high school teachers, insurance brokers, advertising copywriters.

The consequence of all of this is that most white middle-class kids will encounter jazz in some form occasionally as they grow up; and some of them will hear a good deal of it in their homes or the homes of their friends, where somebody regularly listens to the music.

I do not think that that is the case any more in the majority of black homes—at least in such homes where the parents are under fifty. Recently a woman I know who teaches in a black high school—my wife, as it happens—out of curiosity asked her students if they knew who Louis Armstrong was. Only one student even dared to volunteer, and she suggested that he might have been an astronaut. These kids had been born in the mid-1970s when Armstrong was only recently dead. Their parents, who were themselves growing up when Armstrong was becoming the most celebrated American black in the world, could hardly have been unaware of him. And yet so little did Armstrong mean to them that they left no idea of him in the heads of their children. Jazz was simply not part of these children's heritage.

All of this is, of course, anecdotal and only suggestive. It may be that if careful studies were made, they would unearth greater interest in jazz among blacks than this indicates. But I doubt it: it is a simple fact that jazz clubs exist mainly in white, not black areas, that jazz is broadcast on radio aimed at affluent, not ghetto audiences, that jazz educators come mainly from white college-educated groups.

What this means is that if we are to understand how jazz was shaped, we have to stop focussing solely on black culture, however defined, and look as well at the middle-class whites who have provided the bulk of the jazz audience for decades. It is crucial to realize that in Harlem the incipient Ellington band was playing "cocktail" music: when it moved to Broadway, Ellington reached out for the hot musicians Bechet and Miley; and when it went to the white Cotton Club, Ellington had to expand it and play the arranged hot music white audiences wanted. Fletcher Henderson, with the black-owned Black Swan label, was producing mainly psuedo-blues and pop records; when it moved into the white venues it rapidly evolved into a hot big band playing complex arrangements. In the late 1920s Armstrong had to abandon the blues-oriented small band style blacks preferred and front a big band. In sum, as it became clear that there was a large white audience for jazz, it was redesigned to suit white, not black, tastes. Later, it was whites, mainly middle class, who populated Birdland to hear Parker, bought those hundreds of thousands of copies of "A Love Supreme" and "My Favorite Things," made Davis wealthy, and Marsalis a star. Jazz does not simply blossom from the black culture: it is shaped by an audience who will buy this and not buy that. Yet to my knowledge no jazz critic has ever looked at this group to see why they have chosen what they did. Almost universally they continue instead to look at jazz as if it were purely a product of "the black experience." As a consequence, we have a *Down Beat* writer denominating as "African-American music" a record by white trumpeter Warren Vaché, accompanied by the Beaux-Arts String Quartet playing Tin Pan Alley tunes like "With the Wind and the Rain in Your Hair."[110] This is simply ludicrous.

Second, it does not do jazz any good—or jazz studies at any rate—when we by reflex turn to blacks as authorities on the music simply because they are black, as has been the case for example of Lincoln Center in New York. Nobody has racial knowledge of jazz history or the ability to analyze a jazz solo. Black scholars who are interested in black music usually choose some other form of it to study: gospel, the spirituals, black classical composers. Black jazz historians are extremely rare.

As a consequence, a jazz lecture program, repertory series, and the like must perforce depend on many whites. Any program that attempts to rule whites off the turf (as has happened) will be impoverished.[111] I am by no means saying that there are no blacks out there capable of running such jazz programs, or that they all ought to be turned over to whites. There are certainly qualified blacks available, and it is equally true, as we shall shortly see, that there are a lot of white jazz journalists running jazz programs of one kind or another who are not qualified to do so.

My point simply is that we ought to be choosing people to review jazz books, run jazz studies programs, sit on grants committees and so forth on the basis of their qualifications, rather than on skin color. And yet as obvious as this would seem, there remain a large number of people in the jazz world who continue to use race as a critical guidepost, as the cases of Schuller, Williams, Perotti, and others suggest.

The jazz world was the first area in American life to become reasonably well racially integrated, and it remains in the forefront today: in sports it is still difficult for blacks to get into the "front office," but they have been in the front offices in jazz for a long time. Do we really wish to polarize jazz into white and black camps? In the short term the insistence that jazz is black music and that blacks ought to run it may do a few blacks, who get jobs out of it, some good. I cannot see how it is going to be for the good of anybody, white or black, in the long run.

Bruce Boyd Raeburn has said:

> I have always found it ironic that many jazz adherents will make claims (usually with political implications) on behalf of "jazz" that the originators of the music themselves would never have endorsed. The willingness to let talent or innovation serve as the standard (as opposed to "race" or "class") was a major breakthrough and helped to cement relations within the broader jazz community. Isn't the point of *contact* exactly where we should be focusing our efforts? Emphasis on a *black* or *white* ethos for heuristic purposes is fine, as long as we finally come to grips with the *American* ethos—what ties it all together—more than a composite of African and European. [112]

Gerald Early makes the same point: "Where else, other than in the popular culture arenas of sports and music, have the races really come together, really syncretized their being? And has it not been, in many compelling ways, that society has experienced its greatest changes for the better through just these avenues of marginalized culture suddenly taking center stage in the culture for one crucial moment?" [113]

It is only human for people to feel proprietary about a cultural artifact they love. The English educated classes have always resented hearing Shakespeare played with American accents, and they think of English literature as *theirs*, something that Americans might do well to study, but surely should not offer any comment on. The French laugh viciously at foreigners who attempt to speak their language without doing so perfectly, and Americans have equally resented claims by the French that they appreciate jazz more than Americans do.

Yet can we really claim that a cultural artifact, like the plays of Shakespeare, the sculpture of classical antiquity, the music of Bach, "belongs" to anybody? Can Italian opera be performed only by Italians, English literature written only by the English, Chinese painting criticized only by the Chinese? It seems to me that a cultural artifact belongs to anyone who brings to it passion and effort—that English literature, Italian opera, French painting, or African drumming belong to any of us who will cherish them.

How then can we conclude that jazz belongs to anyone? It is worth pointing out that today Europeans are beginning to insist that jazz, far from being black music, is not even American music, but an international form whose practitioners need not look to the United States for leadership. Jazz has been modified by too many forces to assign it an ethnicity. Surely it belongs to us all, and just as surely, the masterpieces of Armstrong, Coltrane, Beiderbecke, and the rest are as much the heritage of the kid from the suburban middle class as they are of the child from the ghetto.

9

Criticism has a long history. Its practitioners include some of the most imposing names in arts and letters, from Plato to George Bernard Shaw, from DaVinci to Ezra Pound. Yet, despite the fame of some workers in this field, the craft has always been somewhat suspect. What, really, does the critic contribute? Who elected him to his office? What business does he have to tell artists, who are presumed to be able to do something the critic cannot, how to achieve their efforts, and indeed what effects they ought to achieve?

It has seemed to a good many working artists—if we must use that dreadful term—that the primary function of criticism is to assert the superiority of the critic over the artist. That, certainly, was the case with the deconstructionists, who managed blandly to assert that the writer had no idea what his work meant, and it was up to the critic to explain it to him.[1] Given how dubious the calling of criticism has seemed to many, I have always been cagey enough to deem myself a historian, a craft it is at least possible to write a job description for.

But whatever one may think of the critics, the appearance of a new form—the novel, free verse, the film, jazz—seems, as spring rain coaxes flowers from the ground, to give rise to a body of clamoring, quarrelsome critics, eager to air their opinions on the attractive new subject. If art comes, the critic cannot be far behind.

And that, certainly, was the case with jazz. The music had hardly surfaced before the critics began to appear, and they have been with us ever since.

The first piece of printed jazz criticism I have been able to discover is the *Literary Digest* piece for August 25, 1917, that included the notable discussion of rhythm by William Morrison Patterson.[2] The same year saw Walter J. Kingsley's similar comments on jazz rhythm in the *New York Sun*.[3]

Over the next few years, American newspapers and magazines gave jazz a good deal of attention. Most of these stories were straightforward reportage, but mixed in was a modest amount of more serious analysis that could qualify as criticism. Typical was a piece in the *Musical Courier* in 1922, which said in part, "'Jazz' is just fun and foolishness . . . musically much of it is of a high order; that is to say, contrapuntal and colorful . . . [it] expresses our American nature—and as long as our nature is expressed by anything so simple and straightforward we will have no cause to worry. When our nature becomes so complex that we need the high art of Europe, or something similar, to express it, it will then be time to realize that we are getting old and effete."[4]

In the same year the highbrow *Atlantic* carried a piece by Carl Engel, a trained musician and composer who would eventually become head of the music division of the Library of Congress. Engel said:

Jazz finds its last and supreme glory in the skill for improvisation exhibited by the performers. The deliberately scored jazz tunes are generally clumsy, pedestrian. . . . Jazz is abandon, is whimsicality in music. . . . Each player must be a clever musician, an originator as well as an interpreter. . . . The playing and writing down of jazz are two different things. When a jazz tune is written on paper, for a piano solo, it loses nine tenths of its flavor. [5]

These early critics were talking about the jazz of the five-piece dixieland ensemble that dominated the music at first. By 1925, however, the new solo style was beginning to be manifest, and jazz criticism was becoming more sophisticated. Carl Van Vechten, writing in *Vanity Fair*, noted that, "like the Spirituals, the Blues are folk songs and are conceived in the same pentatonic scale, omitting the fourth and seventh tones—although those that achieve publication or performance under sophisticated auspices are generally passed through a process of transmutation."[6] A year before, the composer Virgil Thomson, writing in the *American Mercury*, observed that in jazz, notes were frequently played "an instant before the beat."[7]

Then, in 1926, Abbe Niles produced for the *New Republic* an excellent description of the blues, which said in part:

The melody would be a four-bar phrase favoring a syncopated jugglery of a very few notes; the second phrase would vary somewhat the first, suggesting to the musical ear an excursion into the sub-dominant; the third would give a final version. Play between the keynote and its third was particularly frequent, and the tonic third characteristically coincided with the antepenultimate syllable of the line. And in these, as in other Negro songs, the singer was apt, in dealing with this particular note, to slur from flat to natural or vice-versa.

And in speaking of W. C. Handy, already celebrated for his blues compositions, Niles said, "In writing down this music, he chose to represent the primitive treatment of the tonic third, in some case by the minor, simple, sometimes by introducing the minor third as a grace note to the major, or vice-versa."[8] This was very good analysis for its time—better, I regret to say, than many present-day critics would be able to produce. Within a couple of years, Niles was reviewing with considerable acumen jazz records for the *Bookman*. His taste grew surer and surer over time, and by his last columns he was singling out for special praise Ellington, Armstrong's Hot Fives, Bessie Smith, and other important musicians of the time.[9]

The most important jazz critic from the period, however, was Robert Donaldson Darrell, who signed himself "R. D. Darrell." I have written about Darrell at length elsewhere and I will limit my comments here.[10] A Bostonian, Darrell had attended the prestigious New England Conservatory. He was also interested in writing, and was part of an intellectual circle that included R. P. Blackmur, to become one of the country's leading literary critics.

The idea of the critic, then, was something that Darrell was familiar with. In time he concluded that he would never be another Beethoven. He gave up composing, and set about making himself into a music critic. He was interested in the new music of the time, which was upsetting a lot of the old ideas—the by-now-well-known work of Stravinsky, Ravel, Debussy, and others—and like many intellectuals of the day was particularly concerned with promoting new American music, which seemed to reflect the country's growing position as the point man in the artistic vanguard. He wrote an early appreciation of Charles Ives, and one scholar who has studied his writing on classical music has said that Darrell was "one of our first major record critics," and "someone who, in the 1920s and 1930s championed a number of American composers before it was fashionable to do so."[11]

In 1926, Darrell was asked to go to work on a new magazine

called *Phonograph Monthly Review*. This was a shoestring operation located in Boston, where it was removed from the recording industry centered in New York. It was primarily concerned with classical music, and carried long discussions of the most recent recordings of Beethoven, Wagner, and the rest, many of which Darrell wrote himself under pseudonyms. He was not particularly interested in jazz, but he felt he had to give popular music some attention. Working at a distance from the music industry, he was simply opening the boxes the record companies sent him, and putting the discs on the turntable. He said:

> The first two or three months there I didn't pay any particular attention. Then all of a sudden a couple of Red Nichols' records, and particularly Ellington's "Black and Tan Fantasy" really snapped me to attention. The reason why I was so taken with Ellington—one of the reasons—was [that he] struck me as an orchestrator in the class of Ravel, Respighi, and Strauss. It was the serious element in it that got me at first, although with the Red Nichols thing it was the dry, ironic jazz wit. That was something brand new to me. [12]

With little access to the musicians who were rapidly bringing the music to its first maturity, and the close fans who were developing an informal aesthetic to judge the musicians by, Darrell was running somewhat behind those who had discovered Oliver in the 1923 recordings, Armstrong and Bechet in 1924 and 1925, or had been trailing around after Bix in the Midwest. At first Darrell distinguished between white and black orchestras, and classified Armstrong's Hot Sevens as the "noisy" side of jazz.

But his taste grew surer and surer, and by 1929 he was again and again singling out for praise records today acknowledged to be among the classics of the time—Ellington's "Creole Love Call" and "Ring Dem Bells," Armstrong's "Dear Old Southland," Earl Hines' "A Monday Date," and others by King Oliver, Red Allen, Goodman, Beiderbecke, Nichols, and Venuti.

Finally, in a last flowering, in 1932, Darrell wrote long appreciations of Armstrong and Ellington for a small magazine published in Philadelphia called *Disques*. His *Disques* piece on Ellington is, to my mind, the best piece of jazz criticism written by anyone to that date, and for that matter, a good many years after. It remains one of the finest brief discussions of Ellington's work ever published. A short selection will give some idea of Darrell's manner:

> Harmonically Ellington is apt and subtle rather than obvious or striking. Except for sheerly declamatory lines, his melodies are clothed on the harmonies they suggest. He thinks not in chordal blocks, but in moving parts. . . . In exploitation of new tonal coloring . . . Ellington has proceeded further than any composer—popular or serious—of today. His command of color contrast and blend approaches at times an art of polytimbres.[13]

With the Depression, *Phonograph Monthly Review* sickened and died, and in any case Darrell had begun to lose interest in jazz, preferring to concentrate on classical music. It is hard to know how influential Darrell's work was on the jazz public. *Phonograph Monthly Review* had a small circulation, and as it was heavily weighted toward classical music, with the jazz reviews constituting only a few pages in each issue, it was probably not read by many jazz fans. Surprisingly, musicians of the time seem to have been unaware that their work was frequently being praised in it; in none of the many reminiscences, oral histories, and autobiographies of jazz musicians have I seen any reference to Darrell's reviews.

This is all the more puzzling because John Hammond had begun to read *Phonograph Monthly Review* as a schoolboy; he corresponded with Darrell, and eventually the two became friends, to the point where Darrell visited Hammond in the

Fifth Avenue mansion he grew up in. Hammond was in constant touch with musicians and other jazz fans, and it is curious that he never showed this or that one what Darrell had written about them.

For another thing, Darrell was eager to write a bio-discography of Ellington. He corresponded with Ellington and eventually went to see him; Ellington, however, was made uneasy about the whole idea and it never came off. So far as I have been able to discover, he never mentioned the incident, even though Darrell had sent him the *Disques* piece in manuscript.[14]

But if Darrell's influence at home cannot be easily traced, we can be more certain of it abroad. It is known that Darrell's *Phonograph Monthly Review* pieces and the *Disques* articles were being read by the small band of jazz fans in England.[15] The English, particularly the writers for *Melody Maker*, were working at a considerable distance from the source. They were not receiving representative samplings of the records, and they were further handicapped by the practice in the record industry of the time of sometimes issuing the same record in several guises. *Melody Maker* usually had an American correspondent who provided gossip and reports on the American scene; and from time to time American musicians turned up in London who could straighten out the editors on this or that point. But Darrell was otherwise the only regular source of information the English had on American jazz records. They read him carefully, and eventually his *Disques* piece on Ellington was reprinted in England.[16] Darrell's enthusiasm for Ellington and Armstrong in particular alerted the English to these musicians at a time when they were primarily following the white players, whose records were more easily available in England.

In the 1928 to 1932 period when Darrell was publishing his most significant jazz criticism, *Melody Maker* editors, and the English fans in general, were well ahead of nearly everybody elsewhere in their understanding of jazz. Jazz fans on the Continent were looking to the English for guidance to one extent or another, and thus through them did Darrell's influence spread out into France, Belgium, Germany, Sweden, and elsewhere.

These early American jazz critics—Darrell, Van Vechten, Niles, and others—had enough in common to constitute a school. For one thing, jazz had sprung upon them when they were adults, or nearly so. It was not for them an adolescent crush, but one of several interesting phenomena representative of the new spirit sweeping America. They wrote about it with enthusiasm, but they were also able to view it with a certain dispassion—to fit it into a larger musical whole.

They could do this because they were intellectually broad-based; indeed, they were typical intellectuals of the 1920s, filled with a zest for the new ideas and new art forms they saw coming out of America, which would shove into the ash bin the decadent soul of a corrupt Old World. They took it for granted that they should know Ravel as well as Armstrong, the "Work in Progress" James Joyce was publishing bit by bit in *transition* as well as the designs of Frank Lloyd Wright and the paintings of Matisse.

Furthermore, they all had training in music. Darrell had studied at the New England Conservatory, Niles had made a specialty of folksong, Thomson and Engel were trained composers. They were able to write about the new jazz music and the blues with intelligence because they understood how it worked musically and could place it against the vast canvas of world music. They could compare Hines to Stravinsky, Ellington to Delius, because they knew the music of Stravinsky and Delius.

The weakness evident in the work of these early jazz critics was that they were not as thoroughly at home in the music as later critics would be. Few of them—Van Vechten was the exception[17]—spent a lot of time in cabarets listening to the music, or knew many of the musicians, club owners, and close fans who understood the practicalities of the jazz life. This distance had a certain virtue, because it saved these early critics from the hero-worship and massive conflict of interest that would entangle so many jazz critics thereafter. But it nonetheless left them outsiders, viewing the phenomenon with discernment, but without truly having the feeling for it that an insider might acquire. Still, Darrell, Van Vechten, Niles, and the others laid a base for what promised to be a solid discipline of jazz studies, built around a technical understanding of music and an uncompromising intellectuality that, as it should, coupled enthusiasm with skepticism.

During the years immediately following the 1929 stock market crash, the whole entertainment business suffered serious damage. The record industry collapsed, the dance halls disappeared, and suddenly a lot of jazz musicians found themselves out of work.[18] It appeared to many that jazz had been a fad, a phenomenon of the boom times of the Roaring Twenties, and that its day was done. Magazines and newspapers were no longer much interested in running pieces on what now appeared to be a *passé* form; and some of the people who might have written about jazz found other matters, like breadlines and strikes, more important: John Hammond, for example, in the early 1930s wrote pieces on political matters like the trial of the Scottsboro Boys.[19]

But although there were now fewer places to hear live jazz, and less published about it, interest in the music did not die. There were still the records—a surprising number of jazz classics were issued in the early 1930s in the face of the utter collapse of the recording industry—and the numbers of intense fans seem to have, if anything, increased.

Among these fans was a group who would constitute what can be considered a second generation of jazz critics. John

Hammond, Marshall Stearns, Rudi Blesh, William Russell, Frederic Ramsey, Steve Smith, Charles Edward Smith, George Simon, Dave Dexter, George Fraser, Walter Schaap, Gene Williams, and Helen Oakley, were perhaps the best known, but there were others, including a few blacks working for the black press, like Franklin Marshall Davis; and two transplanted Englishmen, Leonard Feather and Stanley Dance.[20] Some of these people were not much younger than Darrell and Van Vechten, but most of them began writing about jazz ten years later than the first group, and would go on doing so for decades thereafter in some cases, by which time Darrell's role in jazz had been entirely forgotten, and Van Vechten was seen only as a bohemian who had written a bad novel about Harlem.

This group was different in certain respects from the generation who had preceded them. They had been excited by jazz as adolescents, or even younger. They did not have merely the intellectual enthusiasm for it that was typical of the 1920s critics, but were passionate about it. Where Darrell lost interest in jazz relatively soon, and Niles, Van Vechten, Thomson, and others eventually relegated it to a minor role in their lives, many of the people in this second generation were bent on devoting their lives to it, and some of them did.

It is therefore not surprising that they did not always view the music with dispassion, but brought to it a sense of mission; that they did not try to fit it into a larger framework, which many of them did not possess in any case, but organized their view of the music around a belief system that included gods and devils, high priests, commandments, and scripture that could not be questioned.[21]

One of these critics, Russell Sanjek, later a historian of popular music, said, "There was a standard of prejudice. It was a party line and you had to adhere to it. 'Jelly Roll Morton is no good. Red Allen is a clown. There is no God but Louis. . . .'

There were all kinds of dogmatic statements made in print by these people."[22]

There were, of course, exceptions. Some of them did have other intellectual interests, and Stearns and Ulanov eventually had academic careers, although not in jazz. Others, like Otis Ferguson, Charles Edward Smith, and Wilder Hobson, were working journalists who wrote on a variety of subjects and understood the ordinary rules of journalistic objectivity.

But most of this generation of critics wrote little outside of jazz; not all of them were thoroughly enough versed in arts and letters to enable them to see parallels and discordances between jazz and other arts. Most surprisingly, few of them felt it necessary to study music theory or learn to play a musical instrument. John Hammond was a fairly well-trained amateur cellist, William Russell played violin at a professional level, Leonard Feather played a little piano, George Simon had actually worked professionally as a drummer, and others, like Marshall Stearns, had struggled with one instrument or another as adolescents in an attempt to play the music they loved. But unlike their predecessors, many of them lacked the ability to analyze in technical terms the music that was so important to them.[23]

The most important of this second wave of jazz writers, and probably the most influential critic jazz has ever had, was John Hammond. Born in 1910 to a wealthy family with connections to the Vanderbilts, he was destined to follow his father into law and oversee the family money.[24] But Hammond's mother was not quite cut to the mold of the people in her social class. She was deeply religious and, as Hammond himself said, had "a compulsion to save the world." She devoted much of her energy and a good deal of the family's money to causes she thought important, and she endowed her son with the sense that he had a duty to aid the helpless and the downtrodden. Hammond became committed to the cause of blacks and working people in general, and remained so all his life. Inevitably, as a young man he was also involved with left-wing groups, writing in support of strikers and the union movement of his time.

Hammond became interested in jazz when he was quite young, through recordings that came into the house, and especially through the experience of hearing, quite by chance on a trip to London, the American jazz pianist Arthur Schutt, a highly regarded jazz musician in the early days. As a teenager he began visiting the black theaters of Harlem from time to time, where he heard a lot of the then-popular blues singers. He dutifully went off to Yale, but dropped out after a year or so to devote his time to music. In 1931, when he reached twenty-one, he came into an inheritance. He moved out of the family mansion into a small apartment in Greenwich Village, and plunged into the world of jazz, with time out for the other causes that interested him. Blessed with immense energy, enthusiasm, and the presumption that is often part of the emotional equipment of the rich, he very quickly insinuated himself into the record industry, and by 1933 was producing records featuring his favorite musicians, among them Bessie Smith, Billie Holiday, and Benny Goodman. He went on to discover the Basie band, promote the careers of Basie, Holiday, and others, and supervise scores of important jazz recordings, almost invariably using mixed black and white groups, all the while churning out a steady stream of reports and articles on his favorites for whatever periodicals would publish them, including the *Brooklyn Eagle*, *New Masses*, *Down Beat*, and the *Melody Maker*.

In time Hammond became so celebrated that he was the subject of profiles in *Newsweek*, *Harper's*, and *Society Rag*,[25] the last written by one of his peers, Otis Ferguson, who said that Hammond's "idea of giving a musician a hint is to hit him in the face with a shovel."[26] Hammond was a force in jazz, and his influence was felt everywhere. Musicians were afraid to cross him, and his readers tended to see him as the source of all knowledge.

Second only to Hammond in his influence was Marshall Stearns. Born in 1908, Stearns was thus hearing the new jazz music in his early teens. He played various instruments in local bands, but eventually dropped music for an academic career. While at Yale, with Hammond and others he founded the United Hot Clubs of America, whose treasurer and president he was at times. He went on to earn a doctorate in 1942 in medieval literature, with a specialty in Chaucer; he taught at Cornell and then Hunter College in New York City.[27]

His interest in jazz, however, never slackened. He later reported that during the 1930s, he was "trying to read all the writings on jazz, listen to all the recordings of jazz, and talk to all the musicians who play jazz," he could discover.[28] This research resulted in a long series of articles on the history of jazz that ran in *Down Beat* from 1936 to 1938. Stearns was also contributing articles to *Variety* and other magazines, and was involved with various jazz organizations and periodicals. He taught an early course in jazz at New York University, and in 1952 founded the Institute for Jazz Studies, now at Rutgers University in Newark, New Jersey, using his own extensive collection of recordings, books, and clip files as a base.[29] Finally, in 1956, Stearns published *The Story of Jazz*, one of the first books on the subject pretending to scholarship.

But if Hammond and Stearns were the most influential of this generation of jazz critics, there were others who contributed as well. George Simon was for some twenty years the band reviewer for *Metronome*, and his opinions were accepted by many readers.[30] Leonard Feather provided early support for the modernist movement of the 1940s and later.[31] George Hoefer wrote regularly for *Down Beat* on jazz history and discography and helped alert readers to neglected figures and recordings. To this must be added the work of the little magazines, like *Jazz Information*, *Society Rag*, *The Record Changer*, and several others that came and went over the years. Taken together, this group of jazz writers produced a substantial body of periodical literature—argumentative, unscholarly, even unjournalistic, and passionate, which fed the appetite for jazz even as it created it.

This second generation of jazz writers was also responsible for writing the first books about jazz that were anywhere near satisfactory. There had been jazz books before, among them Henry O. Osgood's *So This Is Jazz*, published in 1926, Paul Whiteman's autobiography from the same year, the Belgian Robert Goffin's *Aux Frontières du Jazz*, in 1932, and Hugues Panassié's famous *Hot Jazz*, which appeared in the United States in 1936.[32] The first two books were quick, superficial discussions of symphonic jazz that barely mentioned blacks, and the Goffin and Panassié books were simply awash in misinterpretation and factual error; neither was taken seriously in the United States by knowledgeable jazz people.[33]

It was in part in reaction to the Panassié volume, which annoyed a lot of the American critics, that Americans began to write their own books. The first of these was *Jazz: Hot and Hybrid*, written by Winthrop Sargeant, a trained musicologist with an interest in folk music. Sargeant was something of an outsider, who did not have as deep a knowledge of jazz as people like Stearns and Hammond. Furthermore, he believed that the music "has not proved itself an art of sufficient poetic or intellectual scope to take the place in civilized society occupied by the great art of concert and operatic music."[34] But his solid music training gave him a weapon that none of the writers around him possessed, and he was able to produce the kind of analysis of elements like the blue notes and metric shifts that has so often been lacking in jazz criticism.

In 1939, two more books appeared: Wilder Hobson's *Ameri-

can Jazz Music and Frederic Ramsey, Jr., and Charles Edward Smith's *Jazzmen*. Hobson had some technical understanding of music, and was, moreover, a professional writer who over his career worked for both *Time* and *Fortune* magazines. He was also a devoted jazz fan, and it is not surprising that "American Jazz Music" proved to be the best general introduction to jazz before the Stearns book some twenty years later.

But it was the third of these books that caught the imagination of jazz fans, and proved to be most influential. *Jazzmen* was a collection of essays, a substantial proportion of them written by Smith, William Russell, and Stephan Smith. It was particularly important for its exploration of the early days of the music in New Orleans, which had come and gone before there was any jazz criticism to speak of, and it sparked a lot of somewhat romantic interest in the jazz pioneers and helped to prepare the ground for the New Orleans revival, which began at the same moment.

More recent research into jazz history has shown the weaknesses of these three books, but much of what they contain remains valid, and in any case they were important for sorting out for the public a lot of the myth and legend that had already encrusted jazz.

These three books were followed by more, among them Rudi Blesh's 1946 *Shining Trumpets*, Sidney Finkelstein's *Jazz: A People's Music*, and Ralph de Toledano's *Frontiers of Jazz*; the last two published in 1948.[35] The Blesh and Finkelstein books were written from a left-wing perspective—Blesh coined the term "collective improvisation" for the New Orleans ensemble and referred to swing, which he hated, as "reactionary music."[36] The de Toledano book was marred by excessive romanticism. But all three writers knew jazz well and had interesting things to say about it.

In sum, by the late 1940s there existed a literature of jazz that included a number of books, several "little" magazines, and a good deal of ephemera. Little of this writing was scholarly in the academic sense, or anything like it; much of it was partisan and frequently belligerent; but it made it possible for jazz to be studied in a more or less serious way by interested people.

The fad for collecting hot records, which, as we have seen, began in the late 1920s, was important in establishing the science of discography.

It should be pointed out that formal discography has been largely the creation of Europeans. The first such work was put together by a Frenchman, Charles Delaunay, and his colleagues.[37] Subsequently massive discographies were produced by Brian Rust, an Englishman; W. Brunincks and Jorgen Grunnet Jepson, a Dane, among others.[38] But these discographers have been heavily dependent upon the data gathered by these early collectors, at least insofar as the early records are concerned.[39]

These hot collectors were not precisely the same group who became the second generation of jazz critics, but there was considerable overlap. What is surprising is that the very high level of scholarship that the hot collectors brought to their avocation did not create a scholarly mentality among the critics, who for the most part went on operating from passion rather than cool appraisal. Their primary accomplishment was to force on American society the idea that jazz was an important element in the culture, something that not only could, but should, be taken seriously. It is true that the first generation of critics had tried to turn the attention of the artists and intellectuals of their time to jazz as representative of the new American age. But they tended to see it as a symptom, one of the "lively arts" that, however seriously they might be treated, could not be put on a level with the great literature, painting, and music rolling majestically down from classical antiquity.[40] To the contrary, the Hammonds, Stearns, Bleshes, and the rest were insisting, to one degree or another, that jazz was as important an art form as Italian opera or the Elizabethan theater.[41] And in so doing they created a climate of opinion that allowed the movement of jazz out of show business into the academy.

But there was a less salutary effect to their proselytizing for jazz. Unlike the first-generation critics, few of these people, despite their college degrees, evidenced in their writing anything like the breadth of taste exhibited by the early writers. Many of them do not appear to have known much about classical music, nor do they manifest much interest in the musical ideas of Schoenberg, Stravinsky, and others, which by then were second-nature to music students. They do not appear to have had any interest in the philosophy or sociology of art in general, or in the relationship of jazz to American culture, except to regularly announce that it was the only art form produced by that country, and that it was despised at home and only recognized for its merits in Europe, neither of which was true.[42] They were, first, last, and always, jazz fans, and they brought to their writing passion, but not objectivity; intensity, but not scholarship. They were, concluded Ron Welburn in his thorough examination of jazz criticism, "arrogant and opinionated, impatient with musicians and critic peers alike. Their image . . . gave the impression of amateurism and immaturity as they argued in record stores or at performances over their favored musician's merits. . . . The esoteric nature of jazz coupled with their pomposity shrouded their enthusiasm in pretense."[43]

Regrettably, this attitude of being all-out-for-jazz frequently justified rounding off corners when the canons of good journalism ran head on into some previously staked-out position. In particular, concern for conflict of interest was simply heaved out the window. Almost all of this group of critics were deeply enmeshed in the very industry they were supposed to be reporting on.[44] The problem was that many of them were hoping to make their living from some involvement with the music they loved. They formed friendships with musicians; alliances with record producers, band bookers, song publishers, in the hope of picking up free-lance jobs. Hammond, Feather, Dave Dexter, Helen Oakley, and others produced records for both major and minor labels. Hammond, Harry Lim, Helen Oakley, Dance, and others arranged concerts and public jam sessions, which put them in the position of hiring and firing musicians. Some, like Feather, wrote songs, which they hoped the musicians they knew would record. Virtually all of them, after the advent of the long-playing album, wrote liner notes for the companies whose records they routinely reviewed.

The whole system was, to put no fine point on it, hopelessly compromised. It should be remembered that many of the people responsible for producing and promoting jazz were also engaged in more lucrative aspects of the music industry. Irving Mills, who managed Ellington, owned a vast publishing business and record companies, and controlled a lot of bookings. Joe Glaser, who was critical in making Armstrong a commercial success, eventually built a small empire in music. Willard Alexander, who as a novice band manager went out on a limb with his employer for the Benny Goodman orchestra, quickly became a maker and shaker in the swing band industry. And of course there was always Hammond, who himself became a major figure in the music industry.[45]

People like these wanted the support and good will of the jazz writers; they also controlled a lot of work in the music industry that many of the writers were eager for, not only because of the money, but because it helped make them insiders in the jazz world. This was conflict of interest with a vengeance. Trade presses have never been noteworthy for attacking the industries they report on, but in general, reporters will get fired if it turns out they have a financial interest in the industry they are covering. In jazz, by contrast, nobody seemed to care that many writers were working in the music business—in part because the trade press publishers were paying so badly they could not complain.

How often these critics found it necessary to tailor their reports to protect an ally or avoid annoying a client, only those involved can know. But the risk was there, and it would be naïve to suppose that it did not routinely occur. It is, of course, too much to expect human beings to be always perfectly just regardless of circumstances; even the most virtuous of scholars are not above citing in their work people who might matter to them in the future, and to praising with faint damns. But in jazz the conflict of interest was palpable.

In sum, this second generation of jazz writers had lost some of the intellectual high-mindedness of the people who had gone before them, like Darrell, Van Vechten, *et al.* They were essentially fans, and they took the fan's approach to their criticism. They were non-professionals—neither trained musicians, trained scholars, nor, in most cases, even trained journalists. And they established the tradition in which jazz criticism has been done ever since.

The third generation of critics, the one that dominates jazz criticism today, is made up of people who came into jazz in the swing and bop eras. They grew up reading *Metronome, Down Beat, Jazz Information, Society Rag, The Record Changer,* and the Hobson, Sargeant, Blesh, Finkelstein, and Ramsey-Smith books. They formed their first attitudes and beliefs about jazz from their reading of Stearns, Hammond, Hoefer, Frazier, Simon, Ulanov, and the others. Needless to say, most of them revised their early opinions as they matured; but they did not abandon the fan approach to jazz writing, which today remains the way most jazz critics work.

The most influential of them, probably, are the late Martin Williams, Whitney Balliett, Gary Giddins, Nat Hentoff, Stanley Crouch, Dan Morgenstern, and Gunther Schuller; the last of whom is, however, a special case. To these should be added Leonard Feather and Stanley Dance, who, although they began writing in the 1930s, had their major influence later. Where the first generation of jazz critics were frequently trained people who did a lot of musical analysis, and the second generation were jazz fans interested in historical and discographic research, this generation has concentrated on what can be called the journalistic essay, written mainly for weekly or monthly periodicals, although occasionally also for daily newspapers, as liner notes, and the like. Such essays are usually short, to fit the requirements of the media they appear in; and the essayists are more interested in stylish prose and the insightful comment than they are in fresh research, historical detail, or close analysis. As a consequence of appearing often in respectable and even prestigious periodicals, this group of critics has gained more public prominence than did most of the early jazz critics, John Hammond being the exception: where R. D. Darrell, William Russell, Marshall Stearns, and the others were hardly known to the general public, writers like Williams, Giddins, and Crouch have developed modest names for themselves. Although they all write on a variety of subjects, they are the best known for their jazz essays.

Such critics appear regularly in the national press, write important series of liner notes, turn out documentaries for television, and produce radio shows. Many of them from time to time collect their newspaper and magazine pieces into hard covers. They are likely to be present for seminars, and conferences, celebrating this or that jazz hero, or one anniversary or another. Taking it all together, their opinions are widely exposed, at least in the rather confined world of jazz.

Yet they cling resolutely to the tradition of the journalist-critic—the enthusiast guided by gut feelings rather than careful study. Schuller and Feather aside, none of these people has had much training in music, and many of them have had none at all. Most of them cannot read music or play a musical instrument with any degree of skill. It is a simple truth that there are thousands of high school music students around the country who know more music theory than our leading jazz critics.[46]

The question immediately arises whether it is necessary for an art critic to have a technical grasp of his subject. It has been pointed out that few literary critics are successful novelists or poets: neither Edmund Wilson nor Malcolm Cowley, two of the best-known American literary critics of the twentieth century, was given high marks for fiction or poetry. Recently jazz writer Will Friedwald has said flatly that "being a layman" gave him a "distinct advantage" in getting his ideas across, as he would not—indeed could not—confuse his readers with technical language.[47] Another jazz writer, Francis Davis, has accepted his position, saying, "I am sympathetic to that viewpoint, since I don't have much technical knowledge of music myself."[48]

Neither of theses arguments is without flaw. The idea that it is better for the critic to be without technical knowledge that might confuse readers is refuted every day in tens of thousands of classrooms, where people with a good deal of technical knowledge are expected to make the subject clear to people without it. It is the primary function of the teacher—and the good writer, for that matter—to make difficult subjects understandable to the untrained. Our whole philosophy of education is based on the idea that the better one understands a subject, the better one is able to impart it to others.

Concerning the other argument—the idea that the literary critic need not be a novelist to contribute insights into novels— it seems to me that the parallel to the music critic is inexact. The point is that literary critics do in fact possess a great deal of technical knowledge of their subject: to wit, an understanding of English grammar and syntax, a knowledge of dramatic structure, forms of poetry, a lot of the social history the works under study rose out of, and much else. We do not expect literary critics to be novelists, but we do expect them to be well-versed in the forms and language of the literature they study. We would not, for example, accept as a critic of French literature somebody who had to read the works in translation. Similarly, we do not expect music critics to be great composers, or composers at all; but we do expect them to be versed in the "language" of the art—that is to say, the forms and syntax of music. That is the case, at least, with classical critics; and it is hard to see why it should not be the case with jazz.

Among other things, it is simply true that many of our major jazz critics are unable to read with complete comprehension many of the signal works of jazz literature, because they are written in part in a language they do not understand; that is to say, musical notation. Examples are Winthrop Sargeant's *Jazz: Hot and Hybrid*, André Hodeir's *Jazz: Its Evolution and Essence*, Gunther Schuller's *Early Jazz*; some less-well-known but valuable works like Billy Taylor's *Jazz Piano*, Edward A. Berlin's *Ragtime*; a considerable number of doctoral dissertations and master's theses; and a good deal more.[49]

Finally, musicians do not talk about their work in the abstractions, metaphors, and impressionisms that the musically untutored critic is forced to fall back on. They talk in technical terms about physical realities, like intonation, chord changes, note selection, fingering, embouchure, and that whole immensely complex matter subsumed under the heading of "time." The journalist-critic, lacking musical training, is unable to converse with musicians about their art in the musicians' own terms. They instead have to talk about the musicians' life stories, "influences," and feelings about things.

The results show up in the hundreds of oral histories housed in the jazz archives at Yale, Rutgers, Tulane, and elsewhere, as well as in the thousands of published interviews with musicians. Because so many of these interviews were conducted by people with little or no musical training, a lot of crucial questions about the *music* never got asked. In these interviews we read endlessly about the kind of liquor that was drunk, the gangsters who owned the clubs, that Mom played the organ in church, that Dad was a clarinetist with the town band. That is all useful information, but not nearly so useful as it would be to know why Gillespie decided to start employing the hitherto forbidden diminished ninth; how much of the introduction to "West End Blues" Armstromg had worked out in advance; what, exactly, Ornette Coleman's "harmolodic" theory really amounts to. These questions do not get asked, because the musically untutored interviewer does not really understand that they *are* questions.

As a consequence, in my experience at any rate, it frequently takes some understanding of music to puzzle out what is being said in these interviews. Many of the older musicians who supplied the bulk of the earlier oral histories did not have a lot of technical training themselves, and they frequently used home-brewed terminology, which has to be translated.

In sum, the music critic without much technical background is handicapped in a number of ways. Certainly, such critics can and do write illuminatingly about jazz; but there is always that limitation.

And inevitably, when they do attempt to use technical terms, they are likely to come a cropper. For example, Martin Williams refers to the "four evenly accented beats-to-the-measure of the New Orleans style," when in fact the New Orleans rhythm sections invariably play the first and third beats distinctly differently from the second and the fourth. He says that "the source of the syncopated $\frac{2}{4}$ of jazz may well be the tango,"[50] when surely ragtime, which is what these early jazz musicians thought they were playing, is the likelier source. The English writer Christopher Hillman, who has the sense to admit that he had little technical training, says that Bunk Johnson "may well have been the first to introduce minor and diminished chords in 'hot' music, using them to provide variation in the otherwise monotonous cornet lead,"[51] when it would hardly have been possible to play the standard New Orleans band repertory without constantly coming across minor and diminished chords. Another writer says "swinging is taking the rhythmic value of any given note to its extreme breaking point before release,"[52] a statement I do not even pretend to understand. It is hardly the case that the work of the journalist-critics is rife with this kind of error, for they usually keep their distance from technical terms; but anybody who wants to look for them will find plenty.

What I find more troubling than this lack of technical knowledge in so many critics is the almost total absence of anything even remotely approaching a scholarly attitude in their work. I am aware that the idea of "scholarship" puts off many jazz fans. One writer has said, "I do not believe that the weighty, respectable, scholarly approach does jazz any favors. Jazz—never the most popular manifestation of musical endeavour, can easily be turned into a worthy subject deserving of study and therefore dull and a turn off."[53] I have a certain sympathy with this view, for I lack scholarly credentials in the form of a doctorate and the journal publications scholarly reputations are based on, and I, too, resent the notion, unfortunately common in the academy, that unless you have a Ph.D., your ideas do not count.

On the other hand, there is something to be said for the scholarly method, which requires original research expected to add something to a body of knowledge, scrupulous checking of facts, peer review, and in general an unwillingness to put an idea into print until good evidence for it has been marshalled. Key to the process is "documentation"—that is to say, giving the evidence. Who said it? Where do the figures come from?

What do other sources say? To nonscholars this at times seems like nitpicking, but it is necessary: a body of knowledge is built up painstakingly, brick by brick, and if even a few of the bricks are unsound, the structure will fall. It is a bit like what goes on in a court of law: guilt or innocence may hang on some tiny bit of evidence—was the stain on the glove blood or ketchup, the hair on the axe human or canine?

The well-known jazz critics—Hentoff, Giddins, Crouch, Morgenstern, Williams, Balliett, Dance—do none of this. (Schuller and Feather are special cases and I will discuss their work separately.) Not one of them has ever produced any significant work that would even remotely qualify as scholarly, if for no other reason than that they never provide the documentation that is essential to scholarship. Their work is simply awash in hunch, guess, dubious assertions that by their nature cannot be documented, and a good deal of outright error. It is clear that very frequently they do not bother to do anything so simple as to pull down a discography from the shelf to check dates and personnel. They seem, often, to take it for granted that what they believe is correct, simply because they believe it.

I have taken the trouble, during the course of writing this, to examine several hundred pages of the work of these critics. I estimate that in this work there is one doubtful statement, or outright error, for every one and a quarter pages. Some of these are small—a date that is off by a year or two, an incorrect citing of personnel. Some, however, are fairly sweeping. To cite just two examples: Whitney Balliett says, "The big bands grew indirectly out of the New Orleans ensemble of trumpet, clarinet, trombone, piano, guitar, bass and drums,"[54] apparently unaware of the influence of the immensely popular Whiteman and Hickman bands. Martin Williams says, "Most of our slang comes from the gallion (as the black ghetto was called) . . . ,"[55] oblivious to a vast literature on American slang showing it has roots in many sources and ethnic groups. Clearly, these writers did not look into these matters, but simply wrote down what they thought.

What is even worse is that these critics often repeat old myths and legends that more careful students have called into question. Both Nat Hentoff and Martin Williams have written about Billie Holiday as if John Chilton's scrupulously researched book on Holiday did not exist.[56] Hentoff and Williams are not required to agree with Chilton: but at least they should acknowledge his work, and if they disagree, tell us why.

I am here making a serious accusation, which is that however interesting the work of these critics is to read, it is for practical purposes not a wholly reliable guide to anybody who really wants to know what jazz is about. I cannot, of course, in even a fairly long chapter, make a line by line analysis of their work to show what is wrong with it. I will therefore concentrate my attention on the recently published proceedings of a conference on jazz held in Racine, Wisconsin, in 1986.[57] I choose this event precisely because it was presented as a scholarly proceeding, the purpose of which was "to reexamine the field for those involved in it, explain it for those not familiar with it, and direct it for those responsible for its future."[58] The conference was sponsored by several universities and the National Endowment for the Arts, and was funded by several established granting organizations, and the proceedings were published by the Smithsonian Institution Press under the editorship of the distinguished jazz educator David N. Baker. Papers were read, and there were formal responses to each paper, as is customary at scholarly conferences of this sort. Among the participants were such "leaders in American jazz"[59] as Gunther Schuller, Gary Giddins, Dan Morgenstern, Amiri Baraka, and Stanley Crouch. (Martin Williams, who did not attend, contributed a paper, which was published with the proceedings.)

On the surface, then, the event had all the earmarks of a scholarly convention. In fact, it was nothing of the kind. There was one paper based on careful research, a report by Harold Horowitz on his study of the American jazz audience. Others, like Billy Taylor's discussion of the economic condition of jazz, were, if not based on new research, commonsensical. But too many of the papers consisted of the same dreary mish-mosh of half-truths, guesswork, and ancient myths, many of them long since refuted. None of the presenters or responders provided any documentation whatever, or indeed any sort of scholarly apparatus. It was all speculation.

To cite just a few examples: Schuller says that Whiteman's father encouraged him to enter jazz; but Whiteman's most recent biographer says he was appalled by the idea.[60] Schuller says, "The fact that jazz everywhere is loved and understood, studied and taken seriously everywhere in the world except in the land of its origin is, of course, a tragic reality"; but there is more serious jazz interest in some American cities, like New York and Chicago, than in whole countries, indeed whole continents, elsewhere, such as Spain, Portugal, Turkey, Bulgaria, Greece, Brazil, the Balkans generally, and large areas of what was the U.S.S.R.[61] Giddins says, "When Louis Armstrong opted to record "Body and Soul," he asserted his independence and increased his options"; but far from asserting his independence, in recording popular tunes like "Body and Soul," he was doing what his manager of the moment, Tommy Rockwell, told him to do.[62] Amiri Baraka says that jazz was created for the "black mass audience,"[63] an idea I have been at some pains to refute earlier in this book. These papers are simply filled with such incorrect assertions.

In order to see why those critics so frequently go wrong, we might examine in a little more detail two examples from these papers. Gunther Schuller's paper is called "The Influence of Jazz on Concert Music." He is especially interested in Darius

Milhaud's "La Création du monde," which Milhaud himself said was the only one of his works in which he was consciously influenced by jazz.[64] Schuller says that Milhaud heard "authentic black in jazz in 1922 in Harlem. . . . He also brought back to France a stack of records he bought in Harlem, mostly of the Black Swan and Gennett labels . . . of artists such as Fletcher Henderson, Ethel Waters, King Oliver, and the New Orleans Rhythm Kings."[65] Now, in fact, Waters has never been considered by most critics an authentic jazz singer; Fletcher Henderson did not have his own orchestra until 1923, and early records issued under his name—some of which he had nothing to do with—were hardly authentic jazz, but commercial dance tunes like "Bamboo Isle" and "The Last Waltz"; the New Orleans Rhythm Kings was a white group; and Oliver did not begin to record until 1923.[66]

What went wrong here is not merely that Schuller did not bother to check any of this—he has the correct dates for the Oliver recordings in his own *Early Jazz*—but that he did not do any significant research at all. It would indeed be interesting to know what jazz Milhaud heard in Harlem, especially for students of twentieth-century music. Was it authentic jazz? Or was it, as I think more probable, some sort of pseudo-jazz-cum-ragtime played by show bands? Were there any authentic black jazz musicians in Harlem at the time? Bechet returned to New York from Europe late in 1922, but he was working with Ford Dabney, a society bandleader, and at times touring with a show.[67] Did he play in Harlem? Who else was around? Milhaud may have heard authentic black jazz in 1922, but Schuller has not convinced me at any rate. Yet regrettably, because students of twentieth-century music not familiar with jazz studies are likely to be impressed by Schuller's mammoth reputation, the idea will become embedded in music history.

This same lack of precision and unwillingness to do any

legwork is exhibited in a debate between Giddins and Morgenstern, who was asked to respond to Giddin's paper, on whether the jazz audience has "savagely narrowed." Giddins says it has; Morgenstern does not think so.[68] It is not always easy to determine the size and nature of the jazz audience at a given moment, but it is something that can be studied through figures for record sales, numbers of jazz clubs in operation, concert grosses, numbers of radio and television broadcasts, and so on. And this is precisely what a scholar does, or is supposed to do at any rate—find ways of attacking questions that seem worth answering. But neither Giddins nor Morgenstern has done this. Instead, they have given us their opinions in the matter, making no attempt whatever to provide supporting evidence, and we are left knowing no more than we did before we read their papers.

What is most astonishing about this debate is that present at the conference was Harold Horowitz, who reported on his study of the American jazz audience and distributed copies of the study. As Giddins and Morgenstern stood there arguing about the size of the American jazz audience, sitting in front of them was the world's greatest authority on the subject. Neither of them alluded to the Horowitz study or, as far as I can discover, bothered to ask him what he thought.

Why did these highly regarded jazz critics fail to do the research that would allow them to tell us whether the jazz audience had grown or shrunk, or the kind of jazz Milhaud heard when he was in New York? In part it is because doing this sort of research requires a lot of tedious labor: it is not a whole lot of fun to spend days turning ancient issues of *Variety* through a microfilm viewer. But I think the real problem lies elsewhere. These jazz critics are not really interested in discovering the facts about this or that aspect of jazz. They are primarily concerned with supporting viewpoints that they have become emotionally tied to. I am hardly the first to suggest that, for many, jazz has become a species of religion, with a gospel, commandments, a pantheon of gods, a set of devils.[69] For such people to be forced by good research—theirs or anybody else's—to give up portions of this belief system is to confront them with a crisis of faith. And this, really, is why they not only refuse to do proper research themselves, but ignore—or actively attack—the work of others that undercuts the accepted gospel, as, for example, Chilton's study of Billie Holiday: they are fearful that the temple will collapse.

A particularly disturbing aspect of this preference for myth over scholarship is the rule against criticizing blacks as whites are.[70] Implicit in this is the assumption that the work of blacks cannot stand up to dissection. This idea is unacceptable, not only because it is racist—which it is—but because it is obviously untrue. How is the jazz student to evolve critical standards if his mentors appear to have none? How is the aspirant musician to discover what is at the heart of the music if he is told that Armstrong's relentlessly commercial All Stars records are the equal of the Hot Fives?

I have said that exceptions have to be made of Leonard Feather and Schuller. Feather, like Stanley Dance, overlaps an earlier generation of jazz writers, but his influence has been felt mainly in more recent decades. While, in my view, he has swallowed a lot of the standard jazz scripture, it is also true that his various encyclopedias constitute a respectable body of research. They are not without flaws: jazz scholars consider them less accurate than John Chilton's similar work, and also less complete than the more recent New Grove Dictionary of Jazz;[71] but for a period they were the only source for a good deal of information about jazz, and Feather deserves much credit for creating them. Furthermore, Feather plays the piano and has a good deal of technical knowledge of the music, and as a consequence his opinions on musical matters are likely to have more substance than those of his peers.

The case of Gunther Schuller, regarded by many as our most imposing jazz authority, is both curious, and I think, saddening. Schuller has taken the trouble to listen carefully to thousands of jazz recordings, and to transcribe a great deal of music from them, a considerable task, as anyone who has tried his hand at it knows. His musical analyses are always interesting, and frequently brilliant. Although he tends, as do many jazz musicologists, to look at the music too much through the glass of European music theory, he may well be the finest analyst of jazz *as music* we have ever had.

The assiduousness he brings to his music analysis makes all the more puzzling the fact that he fails so dismally when it comes to other aspects of jazz. His historiography is not merely poor; it is virtually nonexistent. For his recent *The Swing Era* he appears not to have done something so rudimentary as to thumb through the pages of *Down Beat* for the period. (As he provides no scholarly apparatus it is difficult to know what sources he consulted.) The late Edward Pesson, a distinquished American historian, discussed the book in *Reviews in American History*. He entitled his review "A Less Than Definitive Nonhistorical Account of the Swing Era," and said, "The nonmusical context is for the most part ignored and, when it is invoked, the results are best described as facile pop sociology of the thinnest sort." Citing "lapses in taste and judgement," and "not insignificant" errors, Pesson concludes: "Schuller regards himself as a 'cultural historian' who is writing history. The book does not sustain this self-appraisal."[72] And Lewis Porter, in a lengthy review of the book for the *Annual Review of Jazz Studies*, says, "*The Swing Era* is the most thorough and erudite guide ever compiled to the jazz recordings of the period, and as such it is absolutely indispensable. But this tome is purported to be a history of the era, and that is where it falls short. Schuller's primary research consisted of thousands of hours listening to recordings, and properly so. But there is little idea of history here outside of the recordings, little sense of the world at large for these musicians."[73]

If the journalist-critics had been content to deem themselves what they in fact are, jazz journalists reviewing performances, spotting trends, interviewing the new hotshot come to town, there could be no quarrel with them. Jazz needs its journalists to promote the music and to keep fans informed of what is going on. Moreover, most jazz fans lack technical knowledge of music, and have little patience for the careful weighing of evidence that constitutes a lot of scholarly writing. They need those impressionistic descriptions, that enthusiasm, that un-critical praise, and there is no reason why they should not have this kind of writing available to them. Many of the essayists write well, and in keeping the music before the public they perform a crucial service to jazz. Nor can they be taken to task for an occasional error of fact or the too-sweeping judgement. I have done a great deal of journalism in my time, and I am well aware that a writer on a short deadline cannot be expected to check everything he has been told in an interview, or do a lot of background reading before writing a piece on the newest trend. Journalism is often necessarily done in haste, which is why we have scholars to come along later and take a more studied look at matters.

There is, then, nothing wrong with the kind of journalistic criticism I have been talking about, as such. The problem comes in when the journalists allow themselves to be taken for scholars—authoritative in ways that they are not. As a conse-quence we have journalists serving in official capacities at jazz institutions that, in other fields, would be reserved for people with more appropriate training: Williams for years at the Smithsonian Institution, Crouch at Lincoln Center in New

York, Morgenstern at the Institute for Jazz Studies at Rutgers, Giddins with the American Jazz Orchestra (now, unhappily, dead), and others elsewhere. As a result of both their official positions and their more general reputations, these and other critics like them are frequently asked to review books filled with technical material they cannot understand, judge grant proposals in areas in which they have done no research, and evaluate scholarly manuscripts in the absence of a complete grasp of the scholarly method.

For example, Stanley Crouch was asked to review Schuller's *The Swing Era* for the *Sunday Times Book Review*.[74] Crouch is not able to make serious musical analysis, and therefore failed to grasp that Schuller's technical dissection of the records was what made the book important. On the other hand, he has not studied the swing period in depth himself, and he also failed to see how badly flawed Schuller's historiography was. As a consequence, his review was largely irrelevant.

Again, Gary Giddins took it upon himself to review Lewis Porter's book on Lester Young,[75] which is based on a computer analysis of Young's solos, and contains a great deal of musical notation. Giddins said, "Those who cannot read music or have no access to Young's recordings will find it rough going if not impenetrable."[76] In fact, Giddins did not have sufficient musical training to follow the technical discussions in the book, and of course it seemed impenetrable. Surely he ought not to have accepted the assignment to review the book. Once again, these are not isolated examples: a search of the literature will turn up dozens of examples of books and other material being reviewed by critics who do not have the necessary training.

In their defense, it must be said of the journalist-critics that they know a great deal about jazz, love the music, and frequently have good insights into this or that playing style. Furthermore, many of them have performed noble service for jazz, as for example Gary Giddins' efforts at keeping the American Jazz Orchestra going, Martin Williams' work on a number of projects that came out of his association with the Smithsonian, Balliett and Hentoff's production of the television classic, *The Sound of Jazz*. Furthermore, Lewis Porter has pointed out that Williams in particular was very supportive of a number of younger jazz scholars, getting them assignments of various kinds when he could, and publishing their work when the opportunity arose.[77] These people have brought a great deal to the music, and must be commended for what they have done.

But their eminence in the jazz world has brought into effect a Gresham's Law of jazz studies, by which poor scholarship drives out good. Resources for the study of jazz, although more abundant than they were twenty years ago, are limited. According to Bruce Boyd Raeburn, "Most graduate students who contact me share one overwhelming problem—lack of funding for the conduct of research in remote locations. It's still a struggle for the budding jazz historian, even if conditions have improved somewhat."[78] A considerable part of the problem is that a lot of funding is falling into the hands of the jazz essayists. Whenever somebody who has not done serious scholarship in an area is asked to speak at a conference, join a seminar, contribute to a documentary film, design a representative record collection, review a book, somebody who might have offered a more carefully researched contribution goes unheard. Two cases in point are the aforementioned Giddins and Crouch reviews of important books in major review media. A third was the Racine conference. There are many first-rate jazz scholars around the country who would have been overjoyed to be asked to participate in an important conference like that one, and would have willingly spent months preparing carefully crafted studies of one kind or another for it. Indeed, they might well have arranged for the funding of their own expenses. We would have had, as a result, at least some contribution to our understanding of jazz. Instead, we got speculation and the rehashing of old myth.

There was a time, twenty or thirty years ago, when the employment of the journalists for evaluating manuscripts and running conferences on jazz made sense, simply because there were so few jazz scholars available. That time has long since passed. Today there are at least three dozen holders of the Ph.D. in jazz, as well as dozens of other students with degrees in related areas—African music, twentieth-century social history, American popular music—who are better qualified to do these tasks than the journalists are. The discipline of jazz studies is still struggling to be born; the journalists control a great deal of the institutional machinery of jazz studies, and they will not easily relinquish their grip in favor of trained scholars who are likely to "deconstruct" much of the work they have built their reputations on. Nonetheless, the scholars are out there, waiting to be put to use.

One serious consequence of the Gresham's Law of criticism is that much of what is taught in jazz history courses is simply untrue. The fault does not lie with the jazz educators; it lies instead with those of us who are supposed to be doing jazz studies. The truth is that there is not a single satisfactory history of jazz—anywhere in the world, as far as I can discover—and that includes my own earlier work, *The Making of Jazz*. (It is to be hoped that a new jazz text by Lewis Porter and his collaborators will remedy this situation.[79]) Why? Simply because major areas of the music's history have not been systematically studied. As we have seen in an earlier chapter, we really are not sure who invented jazz, and how it came into being. We do not know how much of a role the black Creoles played, although it is to be hoped that Curt Jerde's long-awaited study of New Orleans jazz will close the gap. There is no careful study of the exodus of jazz from New Orleans, and the San

Francisco–Chicago axis where it first established itself. The whole development of bop in the early 1940s has not yet been given anything but the most impressionistic accounting—who really was producing all those new musical ideas? There are no good musical biographies of such major figures as Bunny Berigan, Jimmy Noone, Sonny Stitt. And yet every month there arrives in the bookstalls one more collection of casual essays, bereft of research, musical knowledge, or even thought: one self-appointed jazz expert has recently proposed that the blue notes came into being because early black jazz players could not afford instruments that could be played in tune,[80] in the face of a literature on the blue notes that dates back to H. E. Krehbiel's 1914 study of black folk music.[81] Jazz educators have simply not been given the tools to work with. The fault lies squarely with the people who control jazz archives, institutions of jazz studies, jazz seminars, and conferences, for it is these people who ought to be guiding young jazz enthusiasts into the kind of research that would contribute to our knowledge of the music. But they are not doing it, and they are not because too many of them are certain that they already possess the truth.

Curt Jerde has said, "Far too many myth makers and tendentious minds dominate the world of jazz history writers. I cannot even recount all of the 'scholars' whose research I've directed, thinking that I've helped them see the forest and not merely the trees, only to have them revert to mythical constructs and tendential assertions just to 'play it safe.'"[82]

The jazz journalists, I am sure, are not aware of how much they are resented by many trained jazz scholars, because the academics usually find it advisable to keep their mouths shut: not long ago one young jazz scholar said to me, in the course of discussing a controversial subject, "I agree with you, but can I afford to get into the wrong with Martin Williams and Dan Morgenstern?" Academics, of course, should be above this sort of resentment; nonetheless, it is easy to understand the feelings of a scholar who, after months or years of researching a topic, finds himself in the audience at a seminar where a jazz journalist reads a badly researched paper on the subject in ignorance of the scholar's work.

It has been suggested by some people that the discipline of jazz studies is today about where film studies was in the 1960s and 1970s—knocking at the door, but "not universally accepted into the universities," as Krin Gabbard puts it.[83] He suggests that the problem is that even the best jazz scholars keep reverting to the fan mentality, suddenly bursting out of the confines of rigorous analysis into sentimental encomiums in which Hot Lips Smithers is presented as some combination of Santa Claus and the Virgin Mary, and his music a summation of the goodness inherent in all humankind. Gabbard concludes that when film studies finally forced its way into the academy, it was faced with "a stiff, cold wind" that threatened to blow away a lot of the legend, half-baked theorizing, and impressionistic criticism film writing was then encumbered by. Similarly, Gabbard says, "Having boarded the windows against the winds for some time now, jazz scholars now face two significant choices: they may continue developing and protecting a jazz canon, or they may take the consequences of letting in some fresh, if chilling, air."[84]

A lot of readers, I am sure, will object, believing that jazz is better off in the hands of the people who love it, in however unscholarly a way, than left to the technocrats of the academy who might analyze it to death. They may well be right. As must be clear, I have a somewhat dishonorable preference for jazz in the nightclub, where people are drinking, talking, and dancing, to jazz in a classroom where students sit in silent rows listening to a professor analyze Smithers' use of the Lydian Scale. It may be that jazz is better fostered outside of the academy; that it does not need the kind of rigorous scholarship I have been talking about; that it can get along perfectly well with critics who are essentially fans, and criticism that is essentially legend and impressionism. I would not have any complaint if that decision were made.

But we cannot have it both ways. We cannot go on pretending we are doing scholarship when all we are doing is rummaging through the refrigerator for leftovers to run through the processor one more time. We cannot go on applying for grants normally reserved for scholars in order to produce yet another collection of undocumented opinion. We cannot go on asking for institutional support unless we are willing to adhere to the same rules of scholarship expected of students of Renaissance art or liturgical music. In sum, if we are to have a discipline of jazz studies worthy of the taxpayers' support, it must bring itself up to the standards of the academy.

10

Local

Jazz

I have been saving for last the discussion of a phenomenon in jazz that is little remarked, but that may be more important to the vitality of the music than other aspects I have talked about. It is, in any case, one of the happiest ones. That is what might be called the "local" jazz scene.[1]

Jazz criticism and jazz history have always concentrated on the big names, the stars, and the famous clubs and dance halls where they worked. In fact, jazz history is usually written around a chain of major figures—Oliver, to Armstrong, to Beiderbecke, to Ellington, to Goodman, to Parker, to Davis, to Coltrane, to Coleman—to the point where it might appear to the outsider that these great players *were* jazz history.[2]

But, in fact, perhaps ninety percent of the music has always been made by unknown players working in local bars and clubs for audiences drawn from the surrounding neighborhood, town, and county. Right from the beginning, all over the United States, there have been thousands of jazz bands manned by people who, in the main, play the music only part-time.[3] Some of these are outright amateurs offering a very rough version of the music for the amusement of their friends at tailgate parties, anniversaries, or fraternity beer busts. Others are semi-professionals who play for money on some more or less regular basis in restaurants, bars, lake cruises, clubhouses, campus lounges, community centers—almost anywhere that it is possible to make music. Many are high school music teachers. Still others are professional musicians who make the bulk of their living playing club dates in their area, but keep together trios and quartets that find jazz work two or three times a month. Finally, a fairly considerable number of full-time professional jazz musicians dip into the local jazz scene from time to time when they have nothing else booked, in order to "keep their chops up," as a favor, or because they would rather be out playing than sitting home watching television. I have seen notables like Al Haig, Max Kaminsky, Wild Bill Davison, and Eddie Gomez playing with semi-pros, and even Armstrong, Goodman, and Parker have been known to sit in with such groups on occasion.[4]

It should be borne in mind that this "local" jazz scene exists in big cities as well as small towns and suburban communities. New York, Chicago, Boston, Philadelphia, San Francisco, and other cities have their contingents of part-time players who find bars and restaurants where they can work regularly for modest sums.

It is difficult to calculate how extensive this local jazz scene is. The Horowitz survey gives us some clues, however. It reports that about .8 percent of Americans play jazz in public from time to time—about 1,300,000 adults. There are about 144,500, members of the American Federation of Musicians, which most full-time professional jazz musicians belong to;

and as many of these people are not jazz players, it is clear that, as Horowitz says, the 1,300,000 jazz players aforementioned are "largely amateur performers."[5]

My own experience suggests that there is some sort of regular local jazz activity in most cities with populations of 50,000 and above. There are about 500 such cities in the United States, and as the larger cities will have several—even dozens of regularly constituted jazz bands working part-time—the total number of such bands must run into the thousands, and the players in them to the tens of thousands.

But it is not just in the cities, large or small, that these local jazz bands are found. Startling numbers of them are to be found in suburban restaurants, and even roadhouses in rural areas. I have repeatedly been astonished to find in a local barroom in a rural backwash a jazz musician of the first quality playing for an audience of working people out for a little fun. (It often turns out that such players were once "on the road with Woody.")

To this must be added the 20,000 college, high school, and even junior high school stage bands and jazz units that rehearse regularly and give occasional concerts. Admittedly, the audience for most of these student groups is artificial, consisting of parents and fellow students dragged out two or three times a year to dutifully applaud the carefully rehearsed version of "Little Darlin'." Nonetheless, it is a jazz experience for everyone involved.

Thus, even though we can only put rough numbers to this local jazz scene, we can be sure that in bulk it vastly outweighs the big-time professional arena in any terms we wish to use— numbers of musicians involved, numbers of gigs played, the size of the live audience. At this moment the *New Yorker* lists nine well-known jazz clubs in New York City that usually feature name jazz musicians. I can think offhand of at least twice that many clubs in Manhattan alone that use semiprofessional jazz bands several nights a week. And this is in the heart of the supposed jazz capital of the world, where every night the unsung must compete with the likes of Phil Woods, Barney Kessel, and Gerry Mulligan, all of whom are playing in Manhattan as I write. In most small cities and suburban towns, there are *no* locations that regularly hire big-name jazz musicians: the Mulligans and Kessels appear at such places only for occasional concerts. Here the locals dominate by a factor of at least ten to one, and perhaps many times that: there are thousands of towns in which the appearance of a star jazz musician is a rare event, but that offer local jazz bands on a weekly basis.

This is especially true of dixieland. With the recent deaths of the last of the dixieland veterans, like Wild Bill Davison, there are virtually no professionals left playing in this style. There are a few exceptions, like the Jim Cullum Happy Jazz Band, but almost all of the some one hundred bands that show up at the Sacramento Dixieland Festival each year are manned, in the main, by part-timers. It is one of the paradoxes of jazz that this basic form has virtually disappeared from the repertory of the professionals: it is kept alive by the local players.

These local jazz players come from everywhere in the society and include every class and ethnic group. Nonetheless, a disproportionate number of them are middle-class, both black and white, many of them from the higher end of the socioeconomic spectrum.[6] We would not be surprised to find among them a fair number of writers, painters, or college professors, for whom jazz is part and parcel of the intellectual or semi-bohemian lifestyle many of them adopt. It is more surprising to find in this group a large number of doctors, lawyers, dentists, and captains of industry, many of them political conservatives, a strain not generally thought to be widespread in jazz. This phenomenon is important to note, for it contradicts the stereotype of the jazz player as outsider or political radical. It is simply true that there are plenty of skilled, sensitive jazz players around who vote for conservative candidates, oppose gun control, and believe that welfare cheats are responsible for the present federal budget deficit.

Part of the explanation for the disproportionate number of upper-middle-class professionals in the ranks of the part-time players is that there were paths open to them other than music. Most of them, black and white, came from middle-class homes where it was taken for granted that they would go on to college and have professional careers. Despite that, many of them considered careers in music, some even trained at it, and a fair number actually tried it for a few months or even years. But most quickly began asking themselves why they should settle for the risky, even marginal lives most musicians lead, when they could be doctors, lawyers, government officials, and upper-level corporate executives, with the prestige and money that go along with such careers. For these people, the critical decision to give up music usually followed the realization that they would be spending the bulk of their lives in music playing club dates, or if they were lucky, working in the studios or in pit orchestras. For a kid from a working-class home who may have dropped out of high school to go out on the road, a lifetime of club dates sounds a good deal better than thirty years in the canning plant or the post office. To the young adult with a college degree, there are other alternatives: if you are not going to be playing jazz in any case, why not aim for a professional career and play jazz on the side?

But it is hardly the case that the part-timers among the local players are all surgeons with half-million-dollar annual incomes. The local scene is very democratic. Any local jazz band is likely to include a high school music teacher, a mail carrier or cab driver, one or two full-time club date musicians, as well as a doctor, lawyer, or college professor. They frequently include a retiree who finally has the time to work at his music. Most revealingly, the pecking order on the bandstand forms up along musical, rather than occupational, lines. The clarinet-playing bank president will take his cues from the club-date pianist who earns a fraction of the banker's income but knows Bird's changes to the bridge to "Cherokee."

One factor that keeps the local jazz scene in good health is the fact that the players come cheap. To a few the money is important; some bands of part-timers develop local reputations and can work a hundred or more gigs a year, often for seventy-five, a hundred, or more dollars a man, and for some players the extra five thousand dollars a year is significant. But most of the gigs local bands of this kind work pay twenty-five to fifty dollars a man, and many are what the musicians call "free-bies." For many local players, the earnings do not cover their expenses—travel costs, reeds and strings, and instrument repair, to say nothing of the between-set beers, which may not always be on the house.

What matters to these people is the chance to play jazz, and especially to play it in public, and that is as true of the working club-date musician as it is of the rank amateur. There are many busy professional musicians who will give up a Sunday afternoon and travel an hour or more each way, to play a jazz gig with agreeable companions for nominal money. Exactly why it is important for them to play in front of a real audience is difficult to know; obviously, the experience of playing, of itself, is no different in a basement den or a rehearsal hall from what it is in a club. But it does matter to the local players to work before an audience. For the part-time musician this is to some extent a matter of credentials: a player who is working in public for a fee, however small, can savor the idea that he is a jazz musician, in the same way that a school teacher who occasionally places a short story with a little magazine can think of himself as a writer.

But I think there is more to it than that. Ordinary local jazz players, whether they work in music full-time or not, lead the same sort of daily life that most Americans do: a routine job, marriage and family life with the normal ups and downs; births, deaths, commuting trains, vacation trips, the flu, office parties. The experience of playing jazz in the local gin-mill, however seedy, is the plus, the added factor that lifts them out of their daily lives and enables them to accept more easily the graying hairs, the children's failures, the grind of the job. It heals the battered ego, provides a sense of being on the inside of something, a feeling of doing something wholly worthwhile for a change.

Beyond this, the experience of playing regularly with the same people is like belonging to a bowling league. There is a genuine camaraderie among people who play jazz together frequently. This sense of good fellowship is an important aspect of the gig, especially where the musicians have been working together for a period of time, as is likely to be the case with local groups, who do not have the vast pool of first-rate jazz musicians to call on that exists in big cities. A sense of good feeling on the bandstand is an attraction for audiences, too, who notice the players kidding each other about mistakes, cheering each other on, and indulging in a certain amount of good-natured banter. Good spirits like these are infectious. It is common to hear audiences say, "You all seem to have such a good time playing."

Having a good spirit on the bandstand is more important to local players, who are not doing it for money or prestige, than it is for professionals who more frequently have something to prove—a reputation to uphold, a leader to impress. As a consequence, big egos and domineering personalities are not well tolerated among the locals, and such people are likely to find themselves excluded, no matter how good they are, in favor of less adequate musicians who are more personable, more willing to play the supporting roles that a jazz band, like a football team, requires. Most jazz musicians—and that includes professionals as well—feel a *responsibility* for the music. You don't cheat, you don't look for the showy effect, you don't push yourself forward at the expense of others. You remain humble in the face of the difficulty of playing jazz well, and the example of the great players who manage to do so consistently. Local players generally have little use for musicians who lack this humility.

It is probably here that the line between the full-time jazz player and the part-timer is most clearly drawn. Professionals are working in a very tight market and are perforce more competitive than those who are not dependent on jazz for their living, or just as important, a place in the world. They are more likely to endure the abrasive but gifted player who draws audiences, and to tailor their playing to the demands of the market in order to keep the gig. Local jazz players—and once again we remember that they include a lot of professional club-date musicians—are not immune to commercial pressures, because they, too, want to keep their gigs. But their attitude is more likely to be, "I'm not doing this for the money; why am I driving all the way over here just to play this stuff?" The non-professional has the luxury of principle, which the professionals do not always have.

Jazz critics have usually looked down on the nonprofessionals with, at best, amused condescension, and, at worst, outright scorn. They have written virtually nothing about the local jazz scene, one exception being John S. Wilson of the *New York Times*, who occasionally reports on clubs where the unsung groups play. To the average critic, this local jazz scene, with its tens of thousands of players and its huge audience, does not exist.

Professional jazz musicians take a far more tolerant view. As I have pointed out, most professionals, even very big names, find themselves from time to time working with local groups, and they are almost always very accommodating in such circumstances. Rarely do they pull rank or try to dominate the proceedings. As a rule they try to fit themselves into the circumstances as best they can in order to make the gig go smoothly.

It is important for us to keep in mind that "part-time" or "local" is not synonymous with poor musicianship. Among the local players are many who could have had careers in music if they were so impelled, and who from time to time are asked to work with name jazz players. As a rule, the professionals tend to hire other professionals, in part because they need the gigs more than the part-timers do, in part because other pros are more likely to be hiring people for their own gigs. But the professionals usually keep in their books the phone numbers of a certain number of part-timers whose work they respect, and call them on occasion. In fact, the line between the part-timer and the full-time jazz player, the professional and the semi-pro, is fluid. Not only are semi-professionals often hired to work with established musicians, but more frequently than is realized, professionals accept jobs with local players. Professionals get married, have families, find day jobs, and become local players working once or twice a week to bring in a little extra money and to remind themselves that they are, really, musicians. Part-timers take early retirement and attempt to establish themselves as professional. The line is regularly crossed.

But it must be admitted that the majority of the part-time jazz musicians who make up the local bands do not play at a professional level. Many of them are strictly avocational players who like to get out one evening a week and bang around on "Lady Be Good" or "Bernie's Tune" in the best way they can. Others with some training will make a better showing—can indeed sound very professional when they are working in the genre they are most at home in. And this, really, is the point. It is characteristic of the part-time player to be musically limited one way or another. Many of them cannot read very well, and some cannot read at all. Many have only an intuitive grasp of theory, enough to work for them in their genre, but not beyond it. Most have one or another technical weakness—good tone but a poor upper register, a lot of speed but questionable intonation at moments, a fine inventive mind but inconsistent, a big ear and no chops. And it is therefore not surprising that many of them have little experience playing other kinds of music: they cannot sit down in the local concert band and produce the legitimate sound called for; cannot walk into an ordinary club date and play the Latin tunes, recent pop hits, or ethnic specialties such jobs require. They are specialists in jazz who know the jazz standards and the conventions of the music, and can frequently produce an acceptable, even exciting, level of jazz. But they are not—most of them—broad-based musicians.

It could hardly be otherwise. It is very difficult to play a musical instrument well, especially at the level expected of musicians today, when the woods are full of young music school graduates who fly around their horns and read anything in seven clefs. It takes thousands upon thousands of hours of practice, over many years, to reach a competitive level, and it takes constant playing to keep the skills sharp. Many professionals, even after they are well established, continue to practice several hours a day: Benny Goodman practiced obsessively long after he was able to frighten most of the people around him with his technical skills.

The most dedicated of the part-timers make a point of picking up their instruments regularly if they can, if only for fifteen minutes a day. But blessed with regular jobs, commuting time, family responsibilities, and community obligations, they often find themselves going for days at a stretch without touching their instruments. Some make it a point to keep their instruments unpacked so they can practice for a few minutes while waiting for a spouse to finish dressing, or for the children to get out of the bathroom. That is no way to improve.

Some of these local jazz players, especially the younger ones who are making their livings on the club date circuit in Evanston, Marin, or Westchester, have ambitions to move onto a larger stage. Someday they will "get to New York," start playing with the big names, make records under their own name, work in the well-known clubs. But most no longer dream those dreams. They know enough about the music business to be shy of it; they recognize their limitations; they realize that they could play music full-time only by sacrificing their families. Maybe some day—when the kids are older, when they retire— they will woodshed, take some lessons, get their theory together, and see what happens. But for now, it is enough that they can get out once or twice a week, once or twice a month, and play the music.

Nonetheless, these local, part-time jazz players are a far more important part of jazz than has been generally recognized. For one thing, anyone sufficiently devoted to music to endure the often painful struggle to play it as well as they can in constrained circumstances, is bound to care for jazz with something of the fervor of an acolyte. These tens of thousands of local players constitute an important audience for jazz. They listen regularly to the jazz radio programs; they buy tapes and CD's; they tape scores and even hundreds of hours of music for their personal jazz libraries; they go to clubs and concerts when their favorites are appearing.

Moreover, they are an extremely knowledgeable audience. They can hear, to one degree or another, what is going on in the jazz they listen to. They know how So-and-so's version of a tune differs from the standard way of playing it, because they have played it a hundred times themselves. They know which technical stunts are easier to bring off than they sound, and which lazy passages are actually very difficult to play. They are more appreciative of the *musicianship* required of a particular performance, even where the jazz content is not very important. Their experience over the years of playing from time to time with solid professionals, even big-name players, gives them a very clear idea of what goes into a first-rate jazz performance. They are likely to be better critics of the music than many of the well-known jazz writers whose pieces they frequently read. In sum, they make up the best kind of audience jazz musicians can have, because they know what is going on in a performance, they approach their art with humility, and they respect those who can do it well.

For another thing, they make available to the public a tremendous amount of live music that otherwise would not exist. Big-city jazz clubs today often charge customers as much as twenty-five dollars admission, and may require a minimum as well. A couple can easily spend fifty dollars to hear a set or two by a big-name musician, and few people can afford this very often.

The local players, on the other hand, mainly work in places that charge at most a five-dollar music fee, and the majority of them do not charge anything beyond the price of a couple of beers. Furthermore, where a lot of the stars working the big-name clubs are not scheduled to start until ten at night, and may not actually get going until well beyond that, the local bands will start at eight or nine and quit by midnight, simply because many of the musicians have day jobs to get to the next morning. This schedule makes it possible for ordinary people who happen to like jazz to go out to the neighborhood Italian restaurant for a couple of hours to hear the local band, have a couple of drinks and the pizza, and be home in bed at a reasonable hour.

In fact, these local players provide a lot of free music, for they are frequently asked to play concerts for retired people on small incomes, the weddings and anniversaries of friends and relatives, school concerts meant to educate children about jazz, political rallies, and, inevitably, memorial services for other musicians. In some cases, a well-known local jazz band will be seen as a community resource, and will find itself being asked to provide free music at community functions—the opening of the new library, the Christmas party for the indigent, the block association's annual fund-raiser. As such, these local groups are integrating jazz into the community in a more real and personal way than the professionals do, who by and large resent being asked to perform for nothing on the reasonable grounds that they ought not be required to compete with themselves.

Early in this book I made the point that jazz stopped being a folk music long before it escaped New Orleans. But in the hands of the local players, jazz remains, in a certain sense, folk music. They are providing for nominal sums, or indeed for nothing, functional music to people who share this aspect of a common culture. And this is why these players are so important to the music: they are not playing jazz for fame and money, but sheerly because they love the music. They are the pure in heart, and they should be condescended to by critics no more than we condescend to the club tennis player who gets onto the court every Sunday for the love of the game.

These local players are essential to jazz. They are the foot soldiers in the army, and in the end it is the foot soldiers, not the generals, who win wars. If the record companies suddenly stopped recording jazz, the radio stations stopped playing it, the jazz clubs switched to hip-hop, and the name players disappeared into the studios, jazz would endure, because these foot soldiers, the local musicians, would go on playing it in neighborhood taverns, high school auditoriums, tailgate parties, or if need be, in their own basement game rooms. As long as these, the true acolytes, go marching on, the music will live.

Notes

The following abbreviations are used in the notes. Tulane refers to the William Ransom Hogan Archive of Jazz, Tulane University, New Orleans. Rutgers refers to the Institute for Jazz Studies at Rutgers University, Newark. JOHP refers to the Jazz Oral History Project, lodged at Rutgers. Jazz Grove refers to *The New Grove Dictionary of Jazz*, ed. Barry Kernfeld (London and New York: Macmillan, 1988).

Notes for Chapter 1

1. Henry Kmen, *The Music of New Orleans* (New York: Da Capo, 1979), is the standard work on musical New Orleans.

2. James Lincoln Collier, *Louis Armstrong: An American Genius* (New York: Oxford, 1983), 46–55; James Lincoln Collier, *The Making of Jazz: A Comprehensive History* (New York: Delta, 1979; orig. pub. 1978 by Houghton Mifflin), 57–71.

3. *New Orleans Times-Picayune*, June 20, 1918. Clipping in Nick LaRocca scrapbooks, Tulane.

4. Letter dated July 2, 1918, in the *New Orleans Times-Picayune*. Ibid., clipping.

5. The literature on the rise of modernism is substantial. Among the standard works are Stowe Persons, *The Decline of American Gentility* (New York: Columbia Univ. Press, 1973); and Henry F. May, *The End of American Innocence* (New York: Knopf, 1959). Also useful

in the context of jazz is Lewis A. Erenberg, *Steppin' Out* (Westport, Conn.: Greenwood Press, 1981). I have discussed the question in some detail in *The Rise of Selfishness in America* (New York: Oxford, 1991).

6. Once again, the literature on the Victorian age is voluminous. I found useful Daniel Walker Howe, ed., *Victorian America* (Philadelphia: Univ. of Pennsylvania Press, 1976); and Jack Larkin, *The Reshaping of Everyday Life* (New York: Harper and Row, 1988).

7. See, in particular, Ray Ginger, *Age of Excess* (New York: Macmillan, 1965); and Robert Weibe, *The Search for Order* (New York: Hill and Wang, 1967).

8. Of value on immigration are John Higham, *Strangers in the Land* (New Brunswick, N.J.: Rutgers Univ. Press, 1988); Maldwyn Allen Jones, *American Immigration* (Chicago: Univ. of Chicago Press, 1960); John Bodnar, *The Transplanted: A History of Immigrants in Urban America* (Bloomington: Indiana Univ. Press, 1985); and Alan Kraut, *The Huddled Masses: The Immigrant in American Society 1880–1921* (Arlington Heights, Ill.: Harlan Davidson, 1982).

9. Emmett Dedmon, *Fabulous Chicago* (New York: Random House, 1953), 10.

10. For figures on the shift of the population from rural areas to the cities, see *Historical Statistics of the United States* (Washington D.C.: U.S. Dept. of Commerce, Bureau of the Census, 1975).

11. Particularly important for feminism is Nancy F. Cott, *The Grounding of Modern Feminism* (New Haven: Yale Univ. Press, 1987).

12. Here again the literature is immense. For philosophy, a brief review is A. J. Ayer, *Philosophy in the Twentieth Century* (New York: Vintage, 1984). The psychologists are discussed briefly in Henry F. May, *The End of American Innocence*.

13. Bennard B. Perlman, *Painters of the Ashcan School: The Immortal Eight* (New York: Dover, 1979), 87–88, 90.

14. The rise of modernism in literature is treated most recently in Julian Symons, *Makers of the New: The Revolution in Literature, 1912–1939* (New York: Random House, 1987).

15. See May, *End of American Innocence*, 106 and passim, for a discussion of the coalescing of the new spirit in the young.

16. *The Bulletin*, San Francisco, 1913, quoted in Tom Stoddard,

Jazz on the Barbary Coast (Chigwell, Essex, England: Storyville Publications, 1982), 132.

17. Robert L. Herbert, *Impressionism: Art, Leisure, and Parisian Society* (New Haven: Yale Univ. Press, 1988), 219.

18. The literature on the rise of the entertainment industry is considerable. I have given a summary in *Rise of Sefishness*, Chapters 7 and 8.

19. For a good discussion of the institution of the *cafés-concerts* and its relationship to the new class system, see T. J. Clark, *The Painting of Modern Life: Paris in the Art of Manet and His Followers* (Princeton: Princeton Univ. Press, 1984), 205–55.

20. Kathy Peiss, *Cheap Amusements: Working Women and Leisure in Turn-of-the-Century New York* (Philadelphia: Temple Univ. Press, 1986), 142.

21. The best sources for vaudeville are Douglas Gilbert, *American Vaudeville* (New York: Whittlesey House, 1940); and Don B. Wilmeth, *Variety Entertainment and Outdoor Amusement* (Westport, Conn.: Greenwood Press, 1982). Also useful is Joe Laurie, Jr., *Vaudeville: From the Honky-Tonks to the Palace* (New York: Holt, 1953).

22. For the recording industry, the standard work is Roland Gelatt, *The Fabulous Phonograph, 1877–1977* (New York: Collier Books, 1977); for the movies, John L. Fell, *A History of Films* (New York: Holt, Rinehart and Winston, 1979); for music publishing, Charles Hamm, *Yesterdays: Popular Song in America* (New York: Norton, 1983).

23. The role of the immigrants in show business is covered in the works cited in note 22.

24. Fell, *History of Film*, 17.

25. The primary source for information on the vice districts is a substantial number of "reports" by ad hoc city and state "vice commissions" published in the early years of the twentieth century. Many are lodged in the New York Public Library. For a good overview, see Ruth Rosen, *The Lost Sisterhood: Prostitution in America, 1900–1918* (Baltimore: Johns Hopkins Univ. Press). Collier, *Rise of Selfishness*, Chapter 5, has a briefer discussion.

26. See, for example, David Lawrence, *Washington—Cleanest Capital in the World* (New York: American Social Hygiene Associa-

tion, 1917), 315; *Report of the Commission for the Investigation of the White Slave Traffic, Called February, 1914* (no other data given). This was the Massachusetts Vice Commission's report.

27. There is no study of the black-and-tan cabarets; they are rarely mentioned in jazz literature. This information has been abstracted from show business newspapers, oral histories, musicians' memoirs, etc. See James Lincoln Collier, *The Reception of Jazz In America: A New View* (Brooklyn: Institute for Studies in American Music, 1988), 3.

28. Charles Dickens, *American Notes and Pictures from Italy* (Oxford: Oxford Univ. Press, 1957), 90–91.

29. See Eileen Southern, *The Music of Black Americans*, 2nd ed. (New York: W. W. Norton, 1977), passim.

30. Stoddard, *Jazz on the Barbary Coast*, 10.

31. James Lincoln Collier, *Duke Ellington* (New York: Oxford Univ. Press, 1987), 38–39.

32. Pops Foster, *Pops Foster* (Berkeley: Univ. of California Press, 1971), 64.

33. *Variety*, Vol. 83 (May 26, 1926), p. 50.

34. Stoddard, *Jazz on the Barbary Coast*, 96.

35. Quoted in Whitney Balliet, *American Musicians: Fifty-six Portraits in Jazz* (New York: Oxford Univ. Press, 1986), 84.

36. Author's interview with Tom Thibeau, a musician active in Chicago in the 1920s, Jan. 31, 1982.

37. Doc Cheatham, JOHP, 9.

38. *Billboard* (Feb. 14, 1925), 52; (Nov. 3, 1923), 56.

39. Bruce Kellner, *Carl Van Vechten and the Irreverent Decades* (Norman: Univ. of Oklahoma Press, 1968), passim.

40. John Hammond with Irving Townsend, *John Hammond on Record* (New York: Summit Books, 1977), passim.

41. Kathy J. Ogren, *The Jazz Revolution: Twenties America and the Meaning of Jazz* (New York: Oxford, 1989), 146, discusses the idea of primitivism in relation to jazz.

42. *Arts and Decoration* (April 1924).

43. *Vanity Fair* (September 1925), 62.

44. *New York Times*, February 13, 1924.

45. *Billboard* (Nov. 21, 1917), back page.

46. Al Rose, *Storyville, New Orleans* (Tuscaloosa: Univ. of Alabama Press, 1974), 106.

47. Ibid., 177.

48. Stoddard, *Jazz on the Barbary Coast*, 11.

49. Kathy Peiss, *Cheap Amusements*, 102.

50. Irene Castle, *Castles in the Air* (Garden City: Doubleday, 1958), 85–86.

51. Edward A. Berlin, *Ragtime: A Musical and Cultural History* (Berkeley: Univ. of California Press, 1980), 147.

52. Samuel B. Charters and Leonard Kunstadt, *Jazz: A History of the New York Scene* (New York: Da Capo, 1981; orig. published Doubleday, 1962), 32.

53. For Prohibition, useful books are Herbert Asbury, *The Great Illusion* (Garden City: Doubleday, 1950); Norman H. Clark, *Deliver Us from Evil* (New York: Norton, 1976).

54. The extent to which jazz was welcomed into American society at large has been debated both within and without the scholarly world for many years. Morroe Berger, "Jazz: Resistance to the Diffusion of a Cultural Pattern," in Charles Nanry, *American Music: From Storyville to Woodstock* (New Brunswick, N.J.: Transaction, 1972; orig. in *Journal of Negro History*, Oct. 1947), concluded that "leaders and representatives of the white community, especially those who concern themselves with 'public morality' and education, opposed the acceptance of jazz music. . . ." Berger's sample was small and unrepresentative, however. Neil Leonard, in *Jazz and the White Americans* (Chicago: Univ. of Chicago Press, 1962), took the position that the society was generally opposed to jazz; and more recently Kathy Ogren, in *The Jazz Revolution: Twenties America and the Meaning of Jazz* (New York: Oxford, 1989), has asserted that "the more lively and improvisational jazz performances remained segregated in black communities—known primarily to black audiences. This was as true for phonograph recordings and radio as it was for live performances" (87–88). Another position was taken by Ronald G. Welburn, in "American Jazz Criticism, 1914–1940" (Ph.D. diss., New York Univ., 1983), who said that the American position on jazz was not an attack, but "a debate." Finally, in my *The Reception of Jazz in America*, I took the position that, while there were elements in the

society that disapproved of jazz, the reception of the music was generally favorable, or at least neutral. Lawrence W. Levine, "Jazz and American Culture," 6–22, in *Journal of American Folklore* Vol. 102, no. 403 (Jan.–Mar. 1989), says that "American Society" has "denigrated [jazz], and distorted its meaning and its character." (6). Levine seems unaware of the abovementioned Welburn, Leonard, and Collier contributions, however. Serious students of jazz will want to examine the evidence for themselves. It should be clear from the present text that many whites were hearing the best jazz musicians in black and tans and elsewhere, were buying the best jazz records, and were certainly hearing it on radio, which was intended almost wholly for a white audience.

55. William Howland Kenney, *Chicago Jazz: A Cultural History, 1904–1930* (New York: Oxford, 1993), 102.

Notes for Chapter 2

1. Lewis Porter, *Lester Young* (Boston: Twayne, 1985), 66–67.
2. Lee Young, JOHP, reel 5, 29.
3. For example, sworn depositions in the lawsuit over ownership to "Livery Stable Blues" by members of the Original Dixieland Jazz Band make it clear that the music was carefully rehearsed. LaRocca collection, Tulane.
4. Chink Martin oral history, Tulane, 7.
5. Hitchcock, *Music in the United States*, 118.
6. See J. H. Kwabena Nketia, *The Music of Africa* (New York: Norton, 1974), Chapter 2 and passim; and John Miller Chernoff, *African Rhythm and African Sensibility* (Chicago: Univ. of Chicago Press, 1979) passim, for discussion of group function in African music.
7. Chernoff, *African Rhythm*, 50.
8. Eileen Southern, *The Music of Black Americans* (New York: Norton, 1971), passim.
9. See *Folk Music of the United States, Negro Work Songs and Calls*, B. A. Botkin, ed., Library of Congress Music Division AAFS L8, for examples.

10. This nineteenth-century black music was not, of course, recorded. Little of it was transcribed, and that was forced into Western notation. The standard works are Dena J. Epstein, *Sinful Tunes and Spirituals* (Urbana, Ill.: Univ. of Illinois Press, 1977); and Southern, *Music of Black Americans*. Henry Edward Krehbiel, *Afro-American Folksongs: A Study in Racial and National Music* (New York: G. Schirmer, 1914), remains useful. Much of my discussion has been abstracted from contemporary descriptions of this music; e.g., Jeanette Robinson Murphy, "The Survival of African Music in America," *Popular Science Monthly* (Sept. 1899), 660–72; William E. Barton, "Old Plantation Hymns," *New England Magazine*, Vol. XIX, no. 4 (December 1898), 443–56, and Vol. XIX, no. 5 (Jan. 1899), 609–24; Thomas Wentworth Higginson, *Army Life in a Black Regiment* (New York: Norton, 1984; orig. published Collier, 1869).

11. Once again, there is no thorough study of this early New Orleans music. My discussion is abstracted from a considerable number of oral histories of pioneer jazz musicians, lodged at Tulane.

12. Shown in James Lincoln Collier, *The Making of Jazz* (Boston: Houghton Mifflin, 1978), 70.

13. Based on an analysis of photographs in Al Rose and Edmond Souchon, *New Orleans Jazz: A Family Album*, 3rd edition (Baton Rouge: Louisiana State Univ. Press, 1984).

14. I observed this practice when playing with the Harold Dejan band in 1981, which was working in what was assumed to be the old tradition.

15. Collier, *Louis Armstrong*, 93.

16. Dan Havens, "Oh Play That Thing," 67–79, *Jazz Research Papers*, published by National Association of Jazz Educators, Charles T. Brown, ed., 72.

17. For example, Whitney Balliet, *New Yorker* (Oct. 14, 1991), 97. Balliet has confused Oliver's Creole Jazz Band with a later group that was by that time playing in the new solo style.

18. Thibeau interview, Jan. 31, 1982.

19. Reported to me by James T. Maher, personal communication.

20. Quoted in Nat Shapiro and Nat Hentoff, *Hear Me Talkin' to Ya* (New York: Dover, 1966), 120.

21. I have discussed the development of the "symphonic" jazz

band in some detail in *Benny Goodman and the Swing Era* (New York: Oxford Univ. Press, 1989), 28–38.

22. For example, Mark C. Gridley, *Jazz Styles: History and Analysis*, 3rd edition (Englewood Cliffs, N.J.: Prentice Hall, 1988), 68–69; Collier, *Making of Jazz*, 160; Gunther Schuller, *Early Jazz* (New York: Oxford, 1968), Chapter 3.

23. The standard work on Bechet is John Chilton, *Sidney Bechet: The Wizard of Jazz* (London: Macmillan, 1987). Bechet's autobiography, *Treat It Gentle* (New York: DaCapo, 1975: orig. Cassell, 1960), is extremely unreliable.

24. Danny Barker, *A Life in Jazz* (London: Macmillan, 1986), 29.

25. Chilton, *Sidney Bechet*, 23.

26. Quoted in ibid., 40.

27. *Down Beat*, June 7, 1962.

28. Collier, *Louis Armstrong*, 143, 297; Chilton, *Sidney Bechet*, 64–65.

29. Bob Wilber, assisted by Derek Webster, *Music Was Not Enough* (London: Macmillan, 1987), 26.

30. Edward A. Berlin, "Ragtime and Improvised Piano: Another View," 4–10, *Journal of Jazz Studies*, Vol. 4, no. 2 (Spring/Summer 1977), passim.

31. I have discussed the question of European interest in jazz at length in *Reception of Jazz*. See especially Chapter 4.

32. Ibid., 42.

33. Chilton, *Sidney Bechet*, 96–97.

34. Ibid., 58.

35. Collier, *Duke Ellington*, 82–83.

36. Chilton, *Sidney Bechet*, 58.

37. What follows is based on Collier, *Rise of Selfishness*, Chapter 9.

38. Walter Harding, *The Days of Henry Thoreau* (New York: Knopf, 1965), 340.

39. Shapiro and Hentoff, *Hear Me Talkin' to Ya*, 157–58.

40. Bud Freeman, *You Don't Look Like a Musician* (Detroit: Balamp Pubs., 1974), 8.

41. Quoted in Martin Williams, *Jazz Changes* (New York: Oxford Univ. Press, 1992), 98.

42. Donald Jay Grout, A *History of Western Music* (New York: Norton, 1960), 382–83.

43. Herbert, *Impressionism*, 192.

44. H. O. Brun, *The Story of the Original Dixieland Jazz Band* (Baton Rouge: Louisiana State Univ. Press, 1960), 92.

45. Collier, *Louis Armstrong*, Chapter 14.

46. Kenney, *Chicago Jazz*, 118.

47. Ibid., 141.

48. Wilber, *Music Was Not Enough*, 27.

Notes for Chapter 3

1. Shapiro and Hentoff, *Hear Me Talkin' to Ya*, 147.

2. Much of what follows is based on several thousand hours of playing experience, coupled with hundreds of conversations with jazz musicians about their methods, as well, of course, as a great deal of reading in the jazz literature.

3. Collier, *Louis Armstrong*, 236.

Notes for Chapter 4

1. See, for example, Milton Metfessel, *Phonophotography in Folk Music* (Chapel Hill, N.C.: Univ. of North Carolina Press, 1928), who discusses some early mechanical analyses of melody.

2. William Morrison Patterson, *The Rhythms of Prose* (New York: Columbia Univ. Press, 1917). I have not seen the dissertation itself, but I assume it is not much different from the published book.

3. William Morrison Patterson, "The Appeal of the Primitive Jazz," *Literary Digest*, 55 (Aug. 27, 1917), 28–29.

4. Quoted in the *New York Sun*, Nov. 4, 1917, in an otherwise unidentified clipping in the LaRocca scrapbooks, Tulane.

5. Virgil Thomson, *Modern Music* (Jan.–Feb. 1927), 9.

6. Don Knowlton, *Harper's* (April 1926), 581.

7. Virgil Thomson, "The Future of American Music," *Vanity Fair* (Sept. 1925), 62.

8. Winthrop Sargeant, *Jazz: Hot and Hybrid* (New York: Da Capo, 1975; orig. New York: Dutton, 1938), 57.

9. Wilder Hobson, *American Jazz Music* (London: J. M. Dent, 1956; orig. New York: Norton, 1939), 48, 49.

10. Richard Alan Waterman, "African Influence on the Music of the Americas," in *Acculturation in the Americas: Proceedings and Selected Papers of the XXIXth International Congress of Americanists* (New York, 1949), Sol Tax, ed., 207–18.

11. Ibid., 211.

12. Marian McPartland, *All in Good Time* (New York: Oxford, 1987), 26–27.

13. Most of my information on the psychology of rhythm was developed through conversations with Geoffrey L. Collier, whose dissertation was on that subject: see Geoffrey Lincoln Collier, *A Single-timer Model for Rhythmic Performance* (Columbia University, 1990).

14. Carl Seashore, *Psychology of Music* (New York: McGraw-Hill, 1938; repr., Dover 1987).

15. R. F. Rose, "An Analysis of Time in Jazz Rhythm Section Performance" (Ph.D. diss. Univ. of Texas, 1989).

16. Mark C. Ellis, "An Analysis of 'Swing' Subdivision and Asynchronization in Three Jazz Saxophonists," *Perpetual and Motor Skills*, 73 (1991), 707–13. Geoffrey L. Collier and James Lincoln Collier, "An Exploration of the Use of Tempo in Jazz" (submitted).

17. G. L. Collier, *A Single-timer Model*, 52.

18. I have discussed issues of time, particularly in connection with my biography of Benny Goodman, with rhythm players like bassist Sid Weiss, pianists Jess Stacy, John Bunch, and Mel Powell, who all insisted that although a band might play "on top of the beat" or "behind the beat," there should be no acceleration or deceleration. See Collier, *Benny Goodman and The Swing Era* (New York: Oxford, 1989), 153–54.

19. *Down Beat* (July 1936), 8.

1. Carl Van Vechten, "The Negro Theatre," *Vanity Fair*, Vol. 25, no. 2 (Oct. 1925), p. 57.

2. Charles Edward Smith, "Jazz: Some Little Known Aspects," *The Symposium*, Vol. 1, no. 4 (Oct. 1930), p. 513.

3. See S. Frederick Starr, *Red and Hot: The Fate of Jazz in the Soviet Union* (New York: Oxford, 1983), 101–3, for a discussion of Communist policy toward jazz. I have also discussed this issue in *Reception of Jazz in America*, 72–74.

4. George T. Simon, *The Big Bands*, 4th edition (New York: Schirmer Books, 1981), 296.

5. Author's interview with Adderley, spring, 1963.

6. Marshall W. Stearns, *The Story of Jazz* (New York: Oxford, 1970), 174. The highly regarded Stearns says that Crosby's efforts to play jazz were only "tricks." Gunther Schuller, *Early Jazz*, mentions Crosby only once, in passing.

7. Sidney Finkelstein, *Jazz: A People's Music* (New York: Citadel Press, 1948; repr. New York: Da Capo Press, 1975), 4.

8. Otis Ferguson, *The Otis Ferguson Reader* (Highland Park, Ill.: December Press, 1982), 31.

9. Collier, *Reception of Jazz*, 5.

10. Alan Lomax, *Mister Jelly Roll*, 2nd edition (Berkeley: Univ. of California Press, 1970), 43.

11. Donald M. Marquis, *In Search of Buddy Bolden* (Baton Rouge: Louisiana State Univ. Press, 1978), 47.

12. Jelly Roll Morton, Library of Congress, *Classic Jazz Masters CJM9* Vol. 8, side one. Morton plays "Maple Leaf Rag," first in ragtime, and then in a jazz treatment.

13. Reb Spikes, JOHP, reel 5, 18.

14. Interview with New Orleanian musician George Baquet, *Down Beat* (Dec. 15, 1940), 10.

15. Stoddard, *Jazz on the Barbary Coast*, 55, 134. Other sources give later dates, but Sid LeProtti, a San Francisco musician of the day, says Johnson came in 1907, and Stoddard has seen an ad from a black newspaper for a dance on Dec. 21, 1907, with music by the "Creole Orchestra."

287

16. Lawrence Gushee, *Record Research*, 157/8 (Sept. 1978), 12–13. Also, the *Chicago Defender* carried an advertisement for the "Original Creole Band" at the Grand Theater in its issue for January 30, 1915, p. 6.

17. Interview with Tom Brown, leader of an early New Orleanian group, *Down Beat*, Vol. 3, no. 8 (Aug. 1936), 1.

18. Henry O. Osgood, *So This Is Jazz* (Boston: Little, Brown, 1926), 39.

19. See LaRocca scrapbooks, Tulane.

20. Chilton, *Sidney Bechet*, 23; Collier, *Louis Armstrong*, 71.

21. See Allan H. Spear, *Black Chicago: The Making of a Negro Ghetto* (Chicago: Univ. of Chicago Press, 1967), passim.

22. For Palmer, Smith, Duhé, Morton, and Oliver, see Rose and Souchon, *New Orleans Jazz*, 283–85, 319. For Original Memphis Five, see *Variety*, Vol. LVI, no. 4 (Sept. 19, 1920), p. 17. For the Original Dixieland Jazz Band, see the *New York Clipper*, April 18, 1917, p. 4.

23. *Billboard* (Sept. 1, 1916), in LaRocca scrapbooks, Tulane.

24. Rose and Souchon, *New Orleans Jazz*, 279.

25. Stoddard, *Jazz on the Barbary Coast*, passim.

26. *Variety*, Vol. XLVI, no. 9 (April 27, 1917), 14; also no. 10 (May 11, 1917), 14.

27. Ibid., Vol. XLVIII, no. 17 (July 13, 1917), 13.

28. Ibid., Vol. XLVI, no. 12 (May 26, 1917), 16; *Jazz Grove*, Vol. 2, p. 198.

29. Ibid., Vol. XLVIII, no. 11 (Aug. 10, 1917), 14.

30. Erik Barnouw, *A Tower in Babel: A History of Broadcasting in the United States*, Vol. 1 (New York: Oxford, 1933), 210.

31. A good survey of black jazz musicians on early radio is William Randle, Jr., "Black Entertainers on Radio, 1920–1930." *The Black Perspective in Music* (Spring 1977), 68.

32. Anon., *Record Research*, Vol. I, no. 2 (April 1955), 7, reports that the group made some experimental records for Aeolian in 1916.

33. Chris Albertson, *Bessie* (New York: Stein and Day, 1972), 60.

34. *Variety*, Vol. XLVI, no. 12 (May 26, 1917).

35. The best coverage of this early jazz activity is in *Variety*, which was generally more sympathetic to the music than *Billboard* and the

Clipper. There was some mention of jazz in virtually every issue of *Variety* through the spring and summer of 1917.

36. See note 35. By the fall of 1917, *Billboard* was increasing its coverage of jazz, probably because a lot of its readers were attempting to play the music.

37. *New York Clipper*, Vol. LXV, no. 6, March 14, 1917, 16.

38. *New York Clipper*, June 20, 1917, p. 4.

39. *The Chicago Defender*, May 19, 1926.

40. *Billboard* (Aug. 4, 1917), 42; also June 22, 1917, p. 34.

41. Ronald G. Welburn, *American Jazz Criticism, 1914–1940* (Ph.D. diss., New York University, 1983), contains the best discussion of the published attacks on jazz during the early years.

42. Wilder Hobson, *American Jazz Music* (New York: Norton, 1939; repr. New York: Da Capo Press, 1975), 51.

43. *Literary Digest*, Vol. 59, no. 3 (Oct. 19, 1918), 27.

44. Collier, *Duke Ellington*, 44.

45. W. C. Allen, *Hendersonia* (Highland Park, N.J.: Jazz Monographs #4, 1973), 86. Allen is the authority on Henderson, and believes that the band went into the Club Alabam on Jan. 24, 1924.

46. *Jazz Grove*, Vol. 2, p. 193.

47. Ibid., 205.

48. Collier, *Benny Goodman*, 24.

49. The literature on French art of the nineteenth century is immense. A brief, if somewhat dense, discussion of the audience for this work is in Arnold Hauser, *The Social History of Art: Vol. Four* (New York: Knopf, 1958; repr. New York: Vintage, 1985).

50. Sam Wooding, JOHP, 133–35.

51. Saxophones: see *Jazz Grove*, Vol. II, 418–24.

52. Much of what follows is drawn from Collier, *Duke Ellington*. See also Duke Ellington, *Music Is My Mistress*; and Mercer Ellington with Stanley Dance, *Duke Ellington in Person* (Boston: Houghton Mifflin, 1978).

53. Ibid., 80.

54. Sam Wooding, JOHP, 213–14.

55. Collier, *Duke Ellington*, 150.

56. Laurence Bergreen, *As Thousands Cheer* (New York: Viking, 1990), 365–66.

57. *Disques*, "Black Beauty", Vol. 6, no. 9 (June 1932), 153–57.

58. See, for example, *New York Times*, May 29, 1911, C11.

59. Almost all of the people who have supported my view of these pieces asked to be off the record. R. D. Darrell told me, however, "To me it was a letdown when these things came along" (quoted in Collier, *Duke Ellington*, 290).

60. Much of what follows is drawn from Collier, *Louis Armstrong*. See also Max Jones and John Chilton, *Louis* (Boston: Little, Brown, 1971); Louis Armstrong, *Satchmo* (Englewood Cliffs, N.J.: Prentice-Hall, 1954); Richard Meryman, *Louis Armstrong: A Self-Portrait* (New York: The Eakins Press, 1971).

61. Undated letter from Charles Black, Spring, 1988.

62. There is substantial literature on blacks in show business. The standard work is Tom Fletcher, *100 Years of the Negro in Show Business* (New York, 1954). For the period in question, see also Arnold Shaw, *The Jazz Age* (New York: Oxford, 1987); Charters and Kunstadt, *Jazz: A History of the New York Scene*.

63. Chilton, *Sidney Bechet*, Chapter 13.

64. Max Kaminsky with V. E. Hughes, *My Life in Jazz* (New York: Harper and Row, 1963) 114–29; Eddie Condon, *We Called it Music* (New York: Holt, 1947), passim.

Notes for Chapter 6

1. Grout, *History of Western Music*, 8.

2. Frank P. Chambers, *The History of Taste* (New York: Columbia Univ. Press, 1932), 7.

3. Ibid., 243.

4. Andrew Martindale, *The Rise of the Artist in the Middle Ages and the Early Renaissance* (New York: McGraw-Hill, 1972), 9, 98.

5. Chambers, *History of Taste*, 245.

6. Hauser, *Social History of Art*, 51.

7. Chambers, *History of Taste*, 139–49.

8. Ibid., 148–49.

9. Ibid., 149–50, 175.

10. Christopher Collier and James Lincoln Collier, *Decision in Philadelphia* (New York: Random House, 1986), 23.

11. Paul E. Johnson, *A Shopkeeper's Millennium* (New York: Hill and Wang, 1978), 54.

12. Lawrence Levine, *Highbrow Lowbrow* (Cambridge: Harvard Univ. Press, 1988), 13–14.

13. Charles Hamm, *Yesterdays* (New York: Norton, 1983; orig. pub. 1979), 87.

14. John R. Reed, *Victorian Conventions* (Athens: Ohio Univ. Press, 1975), 7.

15. Levine, *Highbrow Lowbrow*, 146–55.

16. Harding, *Days of Henry Thoreau*, 35.

17. Louis Franklin Snow, *The College Curriculum in the United States* (Teacher's College, Columbia Univ. Press, 1907), 181.

18. Laurence R. Veysey, *The Emergence of the American University* (Chicago: Univ. of Chicago Press, 1965), 182–83.

19. Ibid., 188.

20. Ibid., 235, 427.

21. Snow, *College Curriculum*, 176.

22. *Statistical Abstract of the United States*, 1989 (Washington, D.C.: U.S. Department of Commerce, 1989), 157.

23. My estimate, based on advertisements for openings in symphony orchestras published in *The International Musician*.

24. My estimate, based on sales figures of books published in *The Bowker Annual Library and Book Trade Almanac* (New Providence, N.J.: R. R. Bowker, 1992).

25. See *Reader's Guide to Periodical Literature, 1890–1900*.

26. *Literary Digest* (April 26, 1924), 29–30.

27. Perhaps the best examples of this state of mind are magazines like *Vanity Fair* and *The New Yorker*, both of which were read by intellectuals of the 1920s, and which covered dance bands, popular music, the movies, and the popular theater along with highbrow discussions of literature, drama, art, and classical music. It was assumed by people like R. D. Darrell, Virgil Thomson, and Winthrop Sargeant, all of whom were essentially in the classical music field, that they could treat popular music seriously.

28. *Musical Courier*, May 2, 1922, p. 18.

29. *The Nation* (Oct. 25, 1922), 438.

30. *New York Times*, Feb. 13, 1924.

31. *Harper's* (April 1926), 578.

32. Finkelstein, *Jazz: A People's Music*, 4.

33. Rudi Blesh, *Shining Trumpets: A History of Jazz* (New York: Knopf, 1946; repr. New York: Da Capo Press, 1975), 5.

34. Warrick L. Carter, "Jazz Pedagogy," *Jazz Educator's Journal* (Feb./Mar. 1986), 10, 11.

35. Collier, *Duke Ellington*, 101, 148.

36. C. E. Smith, "Collecting Hot," 96, 143, *Esquire* (Feb. 1934), 289. Reprinted in Ramsey and Smith, *Jazzmen*, 287–99.

37. Ibid., 96.

38. Charles Delaunay, *Hot Discography* (New York: Commodore Record Co., 1943), 9. Delaunay's list of acknowledgees runs heavily to American musicians and collectors.

39. Details of Stearns' life are from a memorial note in *Journal of Jazz Studies* Vol. 1, no. 1 (Oct. 1973), 83.

40. Stearns, *The Story of Jazz*, v.

41. The Stearns jazz history ran in *Down Beat* from Vol. 3, no. 6 (June 1936) to Vol. 5, no. 8 (April 1938).

42. Jazz writer Otis Ferguson, for example, called it "a source of . . . misinformation." See my *Reception* for a discussion of this point.

43. Leonard, *Jazz and the White Americans*, 133–38. Bruce Boyd Raeburn, in his dissertation, "New Orleans Style: The Awakening of American Jazz Scholarship and Its Cultural Implications," discusses these events at length.

44. Much of this is based on my own memories of the events in question.

45. There is an excellent collection of these periodicals at Rutgers.

46. Winthrop Sargeant, *Jazz, Hot and Hybrid* (New York: Dutton, 1938; rev. and enl. ed. 1946; repr. with additions, New York: Da Capo, 1975); Hobson, *American Jazz Music*; Ramsey and Smith, *Jazzmen*.

47. The attitude of these older music educators was expressed by *Étude*, which was largely edited for them, in a two-part symposium on jazz in the issues for August and September, 1924.

48. *Down Beat* (May 1, 1940), 12.

49. *Metronome* (Spring 1943).

50. *Down Beat* (April 8, 1946), 14.

51. Stearns' obituary, *Journal of Jazz Studies*, 1966.

52. Morroe Berger, *Jazz: Resistance to the Diffusion of a Cultural Pattern*.

53. Richard A. Waterman, "'Hot' Rhythm in Negro Music" *Journal of the American Musicological Society*, Vol. 1 (1948), 24–37.

54. Alan P. Merriam, A *Bibliography of Jazz* (New York: Da Capo, 1970; orig. Philadelphia: The American Folklore Society, 1954).

55. A. M. Jones, "Blues Notes and Rhythm," *African Music Society Newsletter*, Vol. 1, no. 4 (June 1951), 9–12.

56. Quoted in Larry Austin, "Jazz in Higher Education," *Jazz 3* (Summer 1959), 243–53.

57. Alan Merriam, "The Dilemma of the Jazz Student"; *Record Changer*, Vol. 8, no. 11 (Nov. 1949), 8, 11.

58. Alan Merriam, "Jazz University," *Record Changer*, Vol. 9, no. 3 (March, 1950), 11–12.

59. By 1949, *Down Beat* was carrying reports of jazz activity on campuses at least once a month, and in its April 22, 1949, issue (Vol. 16, no. 7) announced that it would carry "a new special feature" on jazz in each issue.

60. *Down Beat*, "Brandeis University Adds Jazz Course"; Vol. 20, no. 4 (Feb. 25, 1953), 9-S.

61. Rita H. Mead, *Doctoral Dissertations in American Music* (Brooklyn: Institute for Studies in American Music, 1974).

62. Neil Leonard, *Jazz and the White Americans* (Chicago: Univ. of Chicago Press, 1962).

63. *Down Beat*, "Lewisohn Adds a Jazz Night." Vol. 23, no. 13, June 27, 1956, 7.

64. Ibid., Vol. 23, no. 14, July 11, 1956, 8.

65. Collier, *Louis Armstrong*, 319.

66. *Down Beat*, "Music Educators Will Talk Jazz," Vol. 23, no. 6 (March 21, 1956), 7.

67. *Down Beat* (April 18, 1956), Vol. 23, no. 8, 30.

68. See discussion of student interest in jazz in Collier, *The Reception of Jazz*, 21–22.

69. Advertisement in *Down Beat*, Vol. 20, no. 8 (April 22, 1953), 12-S.

70. *Down Beat*, Vol. 23, no. 20 (Oct. 3, 1956), 7.

71. *Down Beat*, Vol. 57, no. 6 (June 1990), 56.

72. Personal communication, May 27, 1992.

73. Information provided by the National Endowment for the Arts.

74. Grout, *History of Western Music*, 370–71.

75. Hauser, *Social History of Art, Vol. III*, 81, 83.

76. Herbert, *Impressionism*, 115.

77. Dore Ashton, *Fragonard in the Universe of Painting* (Washington, D.C.: Smithsonian Institution Press, 1988), 227.

78. Hauser, *Social History of Art, Vol. III*, 83.

79. Grout, *History of Western Music*, 117.

80. Collier, *Benny Goodman*, 160, 177.

81. J. F. "Bud" Gould, "The Jazz History Course: An Update." *Jazz Educator's Journal*, Vol. 61, no. 7 (Dec./Jan. 1981), 13–15, 61–67.

82. Jeff Jarvis, "The Improvised Jazz Solo: An Endangered Species," *Jazz Educator's Journal*, Vol. XXII, no. 4 (Spring 1990), 70–74.

83. Mark Gridley, *Jazz Styles: History and Analysis, Third Edition* (Englewood Cliffs, N.J.: Prentice Hall, 1988).

84. Milton Babbitt, "Who Cares If You Listen?" *High Fidelity*, Vol. 8, no. 2, 38–40, 126–27.

Notes for Chapter 7

1. Rust's *American Dance Band Discography, 1917–1942* gives Borbee's Tango Orchestra for this recording, but the copy at Rutgers is as I have given it. Apparently the group was recorded as the Tango Orchestra, its proper name, but Columbia changed the name to cash in on the jazz fad.

2. *Variety*, Vol. XLVI, no. 3 (March 16, 1917), 15.

3. R. D. Darrell, "A Glance at Recorded American Music," *Phonograph Monthly Review* (July 1927), 410–413.

4. Hobson, *American Jazz Music*, 15, 86–87.

5. James T. Maher, an authority on dance bands: personal communication.

6. Bill Challis, JOHP, reel 1, p. 7 says, "The usual band at the time [before 1920] was a fiddle, a saxophone . . . piano, banjo, drums."

7. See Collier, *Reception of Jazz*, 15–17; and Collier, *Benny Goodman*, 31–34, for fuller treatments of the development of the modern dance band.

8. Details of this visit are in a letter from Peter Tamony, who has studied the Hickman band, to James T. Maher, dated July 7, 1960, which Maher was kind enough to share with me.

9. *Variety*, Vol. XLVI, no. 9 (April 27, 1917), 14.

10. Peter Tamony, *Jazz Quarterly* (Oct. 1958), 33–42.

11. Hobson, *American Jazz Music*, 77.

12. Abel Green, in a letter to James T. Maher.

13. Joe Laurie, Jr., *Vaudeville: From the Honky-Tonks to the Palace* (New York: Holt, 1953), 77.

14. *Down Beat*, Aug. 15, 1959.

15. James T. Maher interview with Bob Haring, Jr.

16. For details of Whiteman's career, see Thomas A. DeLong, *Pops: Paul Whiteman, King of Jazz* (Piscataway, N.J.: New Century, 1983).

17. *Variety*, Vol. LIX, no. 3 (June 11, 1920), 6.

18. *Billboard* (June 22, 1917), 34.

19. Paul L. Specht, *How They Become Name Bands* (New York: Fine Arts Press, 1941), passim. See also *Down Beat* (Sept. 1940), 7.

20. Specht, *How They Become*, 105.

21. Personal communication from James T. Maher, who interviewed Don Redman at length.

22. Bud Freeman, JOHP, no. 2, p. 20.

23. There are many biographies of swing band figures, but no reliable study of the era as a whole. The standard work is George T. Simon, *The Big Bands*, 4th edition (New York: Schirmer Books, 1981). I have given a brief discussion in Collier, *Benny Goodman*, Chapter 14 and passim.

24. Collier, *Benny Goodman*, 261–62.

25. Collier, *Duke Ellington*, 275.

26. See, for example, issues of *Jazz Information* and *HRS Society Rag*.

27. Details of the development of the Harlam Hamfats are from Paige Van Vorst, liner notes to *Harlem Hamfats*, Folklyric Records, 9029; a briefer discussion is in *Jazz Grove*.

28. *New Grove Dictionary of American Music*, Vol. II, 603.

29. Arnold Shaw, *Honkers and Shouters: The Golden Years of Rhythm and Blues* (New York: Collier, 1978), 414.

30. Jason Berry, Jonathan Foose, and Tad Jones, *Up from the Cradle of Jazz* (Athens: Univ. of Georgia Press, 1986), 30, 98.

31. Shaw, *Honkers and Shouters*, 64.

32. See issues of *Variety* for the period, esp. Vol. XLVIII, no. 7 (July 13, 1917), 13, which lists four "jazz" tunes as currently popular in Broadway restaurants.

33. Harold Horowitz, *The American Jazz Audience* (Washington, D.C.: National Jazz Service Organization, 1986), 22, 23.

Notes for Chapter 8

1. Fate Marable, *Jazz Record* (March 1946).

2. Burton W. Peretti, *The Creation of Jazz* (Urbana: Univ. of Illinois Press, 1992), 31.

3. Kenney, *Chicago Jazz*, 102–8.

4. Collier, *Benny Goodman and the Swing Era*, 172–3, 175.

5. Scott DeVeaux, "Constructing the Jazz Tradition: Jazz Historiography," 526–60, *Black American Literature Forum*, Vol. 25, no. 3 (Fall 1991), 529.

6. Peretti, *Creation of Jazz*, 5, 54, 76.

7. Quoted in Larry Fisher, "Place Traditional Objections to Jazz," 78–88; *Proceedings of the National Association of Jazz Educator's Research*, Vol. 2 (1982), 80.

8. There is considerable literature on nineteenth-century black music. Best-known are William Francis Allen, Charles Pickard Ware, and Lucy McKim Garrison, *Slave Songs of the United States* (New

York: A. Simpson, 1867); and Lydia Parrish, *Slave Songs of the Georgia Sea Islands* (New York: Creative Age Press, 1942).

9. See *Reader's Guide to Periodical Literature*, 1890–1900.

10. See note 10, Chapter 2.

11. Gilbert Seldes, "Toujours Jazz," *Dial* (Aug. 1923) 75, 151–66.

12. Irving Schwerké, *Kings Jazz and David* (Paris: Les Presses Modernes, 1927), 41.

13. Bert Ralton, "The Original Havana Band," *Melody Maker* (Feb. 1926).

14. Frank Damrosch, *The Étude*, Vol. XLII, no. 8 (Aug. 1924), 518.

15. *Phonograph Monthly Review*, "A Glance at Recorded American Music," (July 1927), 410–413.

16. Constant Lambert, *Life and Letters*, Vol. 1, no. 2 (July 1928), 125.

17. Seldes, "Toujours Jazz," 158.

18. For example, by 1929, both Darrell in *Phonograph Monthly Review* and Abbe Niles in *The Bookman* were not generally identifying musicians by race in their reviews, or showing a preference for either whites or blacks.

19. See Porter, *Lester Young*, 34, for Young's debt to Jimmy Dorsey and Frank Trumbauer. The influence of Beiderbecke is evident from records, as in, for example, Fletcher Henderson's 1931 "Singing the Blues" and Dave Nelson's 1931 "Rockin' Chair." See also John Chilton, *The Song of the Hawk* (Ann Arbor: Univ. of Michigan Press, 1990), 142, for Hawkins' opinion of whites.

20. White players like Beiderbecke, Goodman, and the Austin High group routinely visited black-and-tans to hear black jazz musicians as many biographies and oral histories attest. See especially Shapiro and Hentoff, *Hear Me Talkin' to Ya*, Chapter 2 and passim. But they also took as models other whites. See Sudhalter and Evans, *Bix: Man and Legend*, passim; Benny Goodman and Irving Kolodin, *The Kingdom of Swing* (New York: Stackpole Sons, 1939), 29; Max Kaminsky, *My Life in Jazz* (New York: Harper and Row, 1963), Chapter 2; Eddie Condon, *We Called It Music* (New York: Holt, 1947), passim.

21. Blesh, *Shining Trumpets*, 5.

22. LeRoi Jones [Amari Baraka], *Blues People* (New York: Morrow, 1963), 131.

23. Quoted in Collier, *Making of Jazz*, 471–72.

24. Frank Kofsky, *Black Nationalism and the Revolution in Music* (New York: Pathfinder, 1970), 9, 10.

25. Alan Lomax, *Mister Jelly Roll* (Berkeley: Univ. of California Press, 1950), 62–66; Morton letter, *Down Beat*, Vol. 5, no. 8 (Aug. 1938), 3.

26. For the Creoles of New Orleans I found particularly useful Virginia R. Dominguez, *White by Definition: Social Classification in Creole Louisiana* (New Brunswick, N.J.: Rutgers Univ. Press, 1986). Also helpful were Alfred N. Hunt, *Haiti's Influence on Antebellum America* (Baton Rouge: Louisiana State Univ. Press, 1988); and Arther Agnes Anthony, "The Negro Creole Community in New Orleans, 1880–1920: An Oral History (Ph.D. diss., Univ. of California at Irvine, 1978).

27. Hunt, *Haiti's Influence*, 9, 15.

28. Dominguez, *White by Definition*, 102.

29. Hunt, *Haiti's Influence*, 15.

30. Ibid., 22.

31. Ibid., 42.

32. Thomas Fiehrer, "From Quadrille to Stomp: The Creole Origins of Jazz," *Popular Music*, Vol. 10, no. 1 (Jan. 1991), 21–38.

33. Dominguez, *White by Definition*, 102.

34. Hunt, *Haiti's Influence*, 58–68.

35. Edward Laroque Tinker, *Creole City* (New York: Longmans, Green, 1953), passim.

36. Dominguez, *White by Definition*, 103–18.

37. Ibid., 125–34.

38. Ibid., 134.

39. Fiehrer, *Popular Music*, 22–23.

40. Dominguez, *White by Definition*, 141.

41. Ibid., 141–49.

42. Jack V. Buerkle and Danny Barker, *Bourbon Street Black* (New York: Oxford Univ. Press, 1973), 10 and passim.

43. Fiehrer, *Popular Music*, 33.

44. Hunt, *Haiti's Influence*, 45.

45. Ibid., 41.

46. Dominguez, *White by Definition*, 210.

47. Richard A. Waterman, *African Influence on the Music of the Americas*, 207–18; in *Acculturation in the Americas: Proceedings and Selected Papers of the XXIXth International Congress of Americanists* (New York: 1949), Sol Tax, ed. (Chicago: Univ. of Chicago Press, 1952), 217.

48. Hunt, *Haiti's Influence*, 9. In 1788 alone, 30,000 slaves were brought to Haiti.

49. Mme Emilie LeJune, *Creole Songs*, 23–28. Music Teachers' National Association, 39th Annual Meeting, New Orleans, Dec. 27–29, 1917. *Studies in Musical Education, History and Aesthetics, 12th Series, Papers and Proceedings* (Hartford: Music Teachers' National Association, 1918), 26.

50. Maude Cuney-Hare, "Folk Music of the Creoles." *The Musical Observer*, Vol. XIX, no. 11 (November, 1920), 12; Henry C. Castellanos, *New Orleans as It Was* (New Orleans: L. Graham, 1905), 158.

51. Maude Cuney-Hare, *The Musical Observer*, Vol. XIX, nos. 9–10 (Sept.–Oct. 1920), 17. Cuney-Hare is paraphrasing the opinion of Albert Friedenthal, from *Musik, Tanz und Dichtung bei den Krolen Amerikas* (Berlin-Wilmersdort: H. S. Schnippel, 1913), 100.

52. Steve Brown, oral history, Tulane, reel 2, 25.

53. Art Hodes, *Selections from the Gutter* (Berkeley: Univ. of California Press, 1977), 120; quoting George Lewis, Don Albert oral history, Tulane; Shapiro and Hentoff, *Hear Me Talking' to Ya*, 48, quoting Edmond Hall.

54. Samuel B. Charters, *Jazz: New Orleans* (New York: Oak Publs. 1963), 42.

55. Paul Barnes, oral history, Tulane, 7.

56. Steve Brown, oral history, Tulane, 87.

57. Peter Bocage, oral history, Tulane, reel 3, 45–46.

58. Ibid., p. 7.

59. Manuel Manetta oral history, Tulane, reel 4, 13. The definitive work on Bolden is Don Marquis, *In Search of Buddy Bolden* (Baton Rouge: Louisiana State Univ. Press, 1978).

60. Manetta, oral history, Tulane.

61. Quoted in *Storyville*, 64 (April–May 1976), 136.

62. Curt Jerde, Letter to the author, June 8, 1992.

63. Reb Spikes, JOHP, 18, specifically refers to the New Orleans jazz musicians as "Creoles."

64. Bruce Boyd Raeborn, "New Orleans Style: The Awakening of American Jazz Scholarship and Its Cultural Implications" (Ph.D. diss., Tulane University, 1992), 80.

65. Curt Jerde, as for note 62.

66. Brunn, *Story of the Original Dixieland Jazz Band*, 251–53.

67. Horst H. Lange, *The Fabulous Fives*, revised by Ron Jewson, Dereck Hamilton-Smith, and Ray Webb (Chigwell, England: Storyville, 1978), passim.

68. Arnold Loyacano, oral history, Tulane, 9; Jack Laine, oral history, Tulane, reel 2.

69. Steve Brown, oral history, Tulane, 86–87.

70. Shapiro and Hentoff, *Hear Me Talkin' to Ya*, 123.

71. Doc Cheatham, JOHP, 201.

72. Sam Wooding, JOHP.

73. Emile Christian, oral history, Tulane, reel 2, 30. Sbabaro was also present.

74. *Variety*, Vol. XLV, no. 8 (Jan. 19, 1917), 8, reported that Max Lowe of Reisenweber's had gone to Chicago "to bring a Jazz Band from Windy Town . . . the first of its kind in New York." For the West Coast, see Stoddard, *Jazz on the Barbary Coast*, passim.

75. The first jazz bands into Chicago were white, and perforce played at white clubs, like Lamb's Cafe, Schiller's Cafe, Kelly's Stables. See oral histories, Tulane, of Tom Brown, Arnold Loyacano in particular.

76. John Lax, "Chicago's Black Jazz Musicians in the 'Twenties: Portrait of an Era," *Journal of Jazz Studies*, 107–127, Vol. 1, no. 2 (June 1974), 110 and passim.

77. Collier, *Duke Ellington*, 128.

78. Lawrence Brown, Stanley Dance, *The World of Duke Ellington* (New York: Scribner's, 1970), 120.

79. Ted Gioia, *West Coast Jazz* (New York: Oxford, 1992), 118.

80. Quoted in Lax, "Chicago's Black Jazz Musicians," 110.

81. Ibid.

82. Ibid.

83. Bill Coleman manuscript, lodged with oral histories at Rutgers, 5.

84. Sam Wooding, JOHP, 98.

85. For figures on radios and phonographs, see Peretti, *Creation of Jazz*, 152; for blues record sales, see Howard W. Odum and Guy B. Johnson, *Negro Workaday Songs* (Chapel Hill, N.C.: Univ. of North Carolina, Press, 1926), 34.

86. Lax, "Chicago's Black Jazz Musicians," 115.

87. Ibid., 120.

88. Ibid., 118.

89. See note 45, Chapter 1.

90. *Down Beat* (June 1937), 1.

91. *Jazz Grove*, Vol. II, 197.

92. See *Jazz Grove* entry, "Night Clubs," for details on these clubs. For Central Avenue, see Gioia, *West Coast Jazz*, Chap. 1.

93. Gioia, *West Coast Jazz*, 128.

94. Jack Schiffman, *Harlem Heyday* (Buffalo, N.Y.: Prometheus, 1984), 239.

95. Ralph Ellison, *Shadow and Act* (New York: Random House, 1964), 228.

96. Gioia, *West Coast Jazz*, 128.

97. DeVeaux, *Constructing the Jazz Tradition*, 548.

98. Quoted in Richard Hadlock, *The Record Changer*, Vol. 15, no. 2 (1957).

99. Quoted in Arnold Shaw, *Honkers and Shouters*, 397.

100. Gerald Early, *Tuxedo Junction: Essays on American Culture* (New York: Ecco, 1989), 296–300.

101. Ibid., 296.

102. Ibid., 295.

103. I was part of this movement. By the mid-1950s there were dixieland groups on many, if not most, college campuses.

104. Early, *Tuxedo Junction*, 297.

105. J. F. "Bud" Gould, "The Jazz History Course: An Update," *Jazz Educator's Journal* (Dec./Jan. 1981), 15.

106. Irving Louis Horowitz, "Authenticity and Originality in Jazz:

Toward a Paradigm in the Sociology of Music," *Journal of Jazz Studies*, Vol. 1, no. 1 (Oct. 1973), 62.

107. Harold Horowitz, *The American Jazz Audience* (National Jazz Service Organization, Washington, D.C. 1986), 22–28, 56–66.

108. Gould, *Jazz History Course*, 61. Gould says flatly, "Most young blacks are receiving their basic training from white musicians."

109. Alvin E. Amos and William C. Smiley, "An Investigation of Factors That Influence the Ability to Discriminate Jazz Music," 1–13, *Proceedings of the National Association of Jazz Educators Research*, Vol. 2 (1982). According to his study, blacks were no better able to "discriminate" jazz than whites. The critical factors were education, class status, family income, etc. See also Horowitz, *The American Jazz Audience*, 22–28.

110. Kevin Whitehead, *Down Beat*, Vol. 57, no. 3 (March, 1990), 43.

111. The recently installed jazz program at Lincoln Center, for example, has been criticized for the disproportionate number of blacks appearing as musicians and lecturers in its programs. See Whitney Balliett, "Wynton Looks Back," *The New Yorker* (Oct. 14, 1991).

112. Raeburn, personal communication.

113. Early, *Tuxedo Junction*, 52.

Notes for Chapter 9

1. Krin Gabbard has pointed out that others, such as some Marxist and Freudian critics, had earlier said that they knew better than the writers what they meant.

2. "The Appeal of the Primitive Jazz," *Literary Digest*, Vol. 55 (Aug. 27, 1917), 28–29.

3. Quoted in the *New York Sun*, Nov. 4, 1917, in otherwise unidentified clipping in LaRocca scrapbooks, Tulane.

4. Frank Patterson, "'Jazz'—the National Anthem," *The Musical Courier* (May 2, 1922), 18; also May 11, p. 6.

5. Carl Engel, "Jazz: A Musical Discussion," *The Atlantic Monthly*, 130 (Aug. 1922), 182–89.

6. Carl Van Vechten, "The Black Blues," *Vanity Fair*, Vol. 24, no. 6 (Aug. 1925), 57.

7. Virgil Thomson, "The Future of American Music," *Vanity Fair*, Vol. 24, no. 7 (Sept. 1925), 62.

8. Abbe Niles, "Blue Notes," *New Republic*, Vol. XLV, no. 583 (Feb. 3, 1926), 292, 293.

9. See especially Niles' round-up in *Bookman* Vol. LXVIII, no. 5 (Jan. 1929), 570–71, which gives a good indication of his knowledge and taste.

10. Collier, *Reception of Jazz*, 35–40. Details of Darrell's career come from interviews with him by the author on May 21, 1982 and Oct. 4. 1984, as well as several phone conversations.

11. Carol J. Oja, "R. D. Darrell: A Pioneer in American Music," *I.S.A.M. Newsletter* 15/2 (May 1986), 14–15.

12. Author's interview.

13. *Disques*, Vol. III, no. 4 (June, 1932), 152–61, Ellington; *ibid.* (Sept. 1932), Armstrong. I have given longer excerpts in *Reception of Jazz*, 38–39.

14. Information on this meeting and Darrell's ideas for a book on Ellington are in carbon copies of letters from Darrell to Ellington in author's files.

15. Letter from Edgar Jackson, publisher of *Melody Maker*, to Darrell, in author's files.

16. Leonard Hibbs, ed., *A Short Survey of Modern Rhythm on Brunswick Records* (London: Brunswick Record Company, 1934), 16–18.

17. Van Vechten, *Vanity Fair* (Aug. 1925), 92: "I myself have heard as many as fifty [blues] in Lenox Avenue dives and elsewhere. . . ."

18. For the record debacle, Roland Gelatt, *Fabulous Phonograph*, 255; for the dance halls, *Variety* (Nov. 12, 1930), 1, had a headline "Dance Halls All Starving."

19. *The Nation* (April 26, Dec. 20, 1933).

20. Welburn, *American Jazz Criticism*, has a good survey of the work of these writers.

21. See ibid., passim, for the early enthusiasm for jazz of these writers.

22. Welburn interview with Sanjek in Welburn, *American Jazz Criticism*, appendix.

23. Walter W. Schaap, a jazz writer of the time, is quoted in Welburn, *American Jazz Criticism*, 10: "By and large the writers were not very learned musically."

24. Details of Hammond's youth from Hammond, *John Hammond on Record*.

25. *Newsweek*, 22:108+ (Sept. 20, 1943), 108; *Harper's* 179:43 (Sept. 1939), 431–40; *Society Rag* (Sept. 1938), collected in Ferguson, *Otis Ferguson Reader*, 97–103.

26. Ferguson, *Otis Ferguson Reader*, 103.

27. Memorial note on Stearns, *Journal of Jazz Studies*, Vol. 1, no. 1 (Oct. 1973), 83.

28. Stearns, *Story of Jazz*, v.

29. See note 27.

30. Simon, *Big Bands*, 4th edition, XV.

31. Leonard Feather, *Inside Bebop* (New York: J. J. Robbins, 1949), was the earliest book on the new music.

32. Henry O. Osgood, *So This Is Jazz* (Boston: Little, Brown, 1926); Paul Whiteman and Mary Margaret McBride, *Jazz* (New York: J. H. Sears, 1926); Robert Goffin, *Aux Frontières du Jazz* (Paris: Editions du Sagittaire, 1932); Hugues Panassié, *Le Jazz Hot* (Paris: Editions Corréa, 1934).

33. I have discussed these works in more detail in *Reception of Jazz*, Chapter 5.

34. Sargeant, *Jazz: Hot and Hybrid*, 280.

35. Ralph de Toledano, *Frontiers of Jazz* (New York: Ungar, 1962).

36. Blesh, *Shining Trumpets*, 163, 289.

37. Delaunay began publishing discographies in the French magazine *Jazz Hot*; his collection of them in book form appeared in 1936 in French. The first American edition was Charles Delaunay, *Hot Discography* (New York: Commodore Record Co., 1938).

38. Brian Rust, *Jazz Records, 1897–1942*, 4th edition (New Rochelle, N.Y.: Arlington House, 1978); Jorgen Grunnet Jepsen, *Jazz Records* (Holte, Denmark: Knudson, 1966); Walter Bruyninck, *Sixty Years of Recorded Jazz* (Belgium, pub. by author).

39. For example, of the about 250 contributors to Brian Rust, *Jazz*

Records, 102 are Americans, 99 from the U.K., the remainder scattered through other nationalities.

40. Darrell, Thomson, Van Vechten, and some others began to lose interest in jazz early, and by the 1930s had stopped writing about it.

41. See Blesh, *Shining Trumpets*, vii, viii; Stearns, *Story of Jazz*, xi; Finkelstein, *Jazz: A People's Music*, 1, 2.

42. I have discussed this matter extensively in *Reception of Jazz*.

43. Welburn, *American Jazz Criticism*, 387.

44. See the brief biographies of these critics in *Jazz Grove*.

45. I have discussed the career of Glaser in *Louis Armstrong*; of Mills in *Duke Ellington*; of Hammond and Alexander in *Benny Goodman*.

46. I have known most of these people; some fairly well, some only slightly. This judgment is based on conversations with them, as well as on discussions with other people who have worked with them, who wished to remain off the record. The best evidence lies in their work, however, where technical detail is generally avoided, and not always correct when it appears.

47. Will Friedwald, *Jazz Singing* (New York: Scribner's, 1990), xv.

48. Francis Davis, quoted in Gene Lees' *Jazzletter*, Vol. 10, no. 4 (April 1991), 5.

49. Andre Hodeir, *Jazz: Its Evolution and Essence* (New York: Grove, 1956); Billy Taylor, *Jazz Piano: A Jazz History* (Dubuque, Iowa: Wm. C. Brown, 1983). A sampling of these theses may be found at Rutgers.

50. Martin Williams, *The Jazz Tradition*, revised edition (New York: Oxford, 1983), 14, 24.

51. Christopher Hillman, *Bunk Johnson* (New York: Universe Books, 1988), 26.

52. Stephen M. Stroff, *Discovering Great Jazz* (New York: Newmarket, 1991), 14.

53. Maurice Jennings, *The Musician* (England), April, 1986. I am grateful to Lewis Porter for supplying me with this item.

54. Whitney Balliett, *Goodbyes and Other Messages* (New York: Oxford, 1991), 166.

55. Williams, *Jazz Tradition*, 3–4.

56. Nat Hentoff, *Jazz Is* (New York: Random House, 1976), 52–53, repeats a number of stories taken mainly from Holiday's autobiography, written with a professional author—Billie Holiday with William Dufty, *Lady Sings the Blues* (New York: Doubleday, 1956). Much of the same legend appears in Martin Williams, *Jazz Changes* (New York: Oxford, 1992), 19–21. John Chilton, *Billie's Blues* (New York: Stein and Day, 1975), 6–8, makes it clear, however, that the Holiday autobiography is a hash of error and invention, and that the truth about her childhood will probably never be known.

57. David N. Baker, ed., *New Perspectives on Jazz* (Washington, D.C.: Smithsonian Institution Press, 1990).

58. Ibid, vii–viii.

59. Ibid, vii.

60. Baker, *New Perspectives*, 15. Thomas A. DeLong, *Pops: Paul Whiteman, King of Jazz* (Piscataway, N.J.: New Century, 1983), 64, quotes Whiteman's father as saying after his son had become famous, "It's not real music, just some honkytonk outpourings that don't mean a thing in the long run."

61. Baker, *New Perspectives*, 12. My assessment of the interest in jazz in the countries listed is based on personal visits, which included lengthy conversations with musicians and leading jazz authorities in these countries. I have discussed this whole question in more detail in my *The Reception of Jazz in America*.

62. Baker, *New Perspectives*, 38. I interviewed Hammond about Armstrong; he said that Rockwell deliberately moved Armstrong into this sort of popular material in order to increase his white audience. See my *Louis Armstrong*, 204–213, for Rockwell's role with Armstrong.

63. Baker, *New Perspectives*, 56.

64. Interview with Darius Milhaud in Marion Bauer, "Darius Milhaud," *The Musical Quarterly*, vol. XXVII, no. 2 (April 1942), 139–159.

65. Baker, *New Perspectives*, 17.

66. For a discussion of Waters' career, see the entry in *Jazz Grove*; for Henderson, see Walter C. Allen, *Hendersonia* (Highland Park: Jazz Monographs #4, 1973); for the New Orleans Rhythm Kings and Oliver, see *Jazz Grove*.

67. Chilton, *Sidney Bechet*, 55–56.

68. Baker, *New Perspectives*, 39, 50.

69. Neil Leonard, *Jazz: Myth and Religion* (New York: Oxford, 1987), treats this subject at length.

70. Good examples of this attitude are Gary Giddins' *Celebrating Bird* (New York: Beech Tree, 1987) and *Satchmo* (New York: Anchor, 1988), in which the personal and musical weaknesses of the author's heroes are ignored or glossed over.

71. This judgement is based on conversations with a number of jazz scholars who have examined the works in question closely. Much of this opinion was offered in confidence. My own experience with these works bears it out.

72. Edward Pesson, "A Less than Definitive Nonhistorical Account of the Swing Era," *Reviews in American History*, Vol. 17, no. 4 (Dec. 1989), 599–607.

73. Lewis Porter, review of Schuller's *Swing Era* in *Annual Review of Jazz Studies* 5 (1991), 183–200.

74. Stanley Crouch, "The Duke, the King and the City of Jazz," *New York Times Book Review* (April 2, 1989), 7.

75. Lewis Porter, *Lester Young* (Boston: Twayne, 1985).

76. (London) *Times Literary Supplement* (April 11, 1986), 402.

77. Lewis Porter, personal communication.

78. Bruce Boyd Raeburn, letter to the author dated May 14, 1992.

79. Lewis Porter, Michael Ullman, with Edward Hazell, *Jazz: From Its Origin to the Present* (Englewood Cliffs, N.J.: Prentice Hall, 1993).

80. Stroff, *Discovering Great Jazz*, 4.

81. Krehbiel, *Afro-American Folksong*, 71–72.

82. Curt Jerde, letter to the author dated July 3, 1992.

83. John L. Fell, letter to the author, Spring 1992; Krin Gabbard, "Jazz Among the Discourses," in *Representing Jazz*, ed. Krin Gabbard (Chicago: Univ. of Chicago Press, forthcoming).

84. Gabbard, *Representing Jazz*.

Notes for Chapter 10

1. Much of what follows is based on personal experience, coupled with hundreds of hours of talk with musicians involved in what I have called the local jazz scene.

2. See, for example, Collier, *Making of Jazz*; Gridley, *Jazz Styles*; Tirro, *Jazz: A History*.

3. *Popular Mechanics*, c. 1922, unidentified clipping in LaRocca files, Tulane, said that there were "thousands" of jazz bands in the country, and that every town of over 5,000 population had one.

4. Eyewitness reports from musicians involved.

5. Horowitz, *American Jazz Audience*, 23/29.

6. Ibid., 28/33.

Index

as entertainment, 160–62; and local jazz, 273–74; and the musician as audience, 70; need for pleasing, 212; and rhythm, 75; whites as primary, 219–21
Austin High Gang, 34, 43, 49, 161, 177. *See also specific musician*
Aux Frontières du Jazz (Goffin), 238
"Avalon," 181
Avante-garde jazz, 150, 159–60, 188, 217, 218

Babbitt, Milton, 158–59
"Baby Won't You Please Come Home" (Lavere), 86–87
Bailey, Buster, 151
Baker, Chet, 144
Baker, David N., 250
Ballads, 81, 173–74
Ballet. *See* Dance/dancing
Balliett, Whitney, 243, 249, 258
'Bama State Collegians, 132
"Bamboo Isle" (Henderson), 252
Banjo Jazz Boys, 97–98
Banks, Billy, 177, 178, 184
Baquet, Achille, 183
Baquet, George, 94
Baraka, Amiri, 188, 250, 251
Barbarin, Isadore, 198
Barker, Danny, 36, 38
Barnet, Charlie, 120, 164, 216
Barron's. *See* Wilkins, Barron
Baseball games, 23, 168, 184
Basie, Count, 55–56, 82, 153, 164, 207, 236
Beat, 75, 81–82. *See also* Rhythm
Beaux-Arts String Quartet, 221–22
Bechet, Sidney: and the commercialization of jazz, 95, 96, 101–2, 106, 119; Creole origins of, 193, 197, 199; criticism about, 229, 252; early career of, 36; and Ellington, 37–38, 41, 172; European tour of, 36–37, 41; fame/popularity of, 36, 37–38, 39, 40–42, 197; and improvisation, 39–40, 47; and jazz as popular music, 165, 172; personality of, 38; recordings of, 38–39, 41–42, 165; and the revival of dixieland, 116; as a role model, 38, 41–42; as a soloist, 39–42
Beiderbecke, Bix: college tours of,

22–23; and the commercialization of jazz, 101–2, 104; criticism about, 229–30; and the emergence of jazz, 22–23; and hot record collecting, 133; and improvisation, 42, 43, 47, 55, 63; individuality of, 155; influence of, 216, 218; and jazz as ensemble music, 35; and jazz as popular music, 172, 177, 181; popularity of, 41; recordings of, 35, 55, 63, 83, 102, 104, 136; as a soloist, 47, 63; and tempo, 80–81, 83; training of, 152; and the Whiteman orchestra, 47, 172
"The Bells of Saint Mary's," 181
Bennington College, 150
Benny Goodman Orchestra. *See* Goodman, Benny
Berger, Morroe, 138
Berigan, Bunny, 174, 216, 260
Berlin, Edward A., 20, 40, 246
Berlin, Irving, 12, 90, 109, 181
Berry, Chuck, 178, 179
Berton, Vic, 176
Bertrand, Jimmy, 176
Bigard, Barney, 41–42, 83
Big dance bands: and the academization of jazz, 153, 154; and audience demands, 217–18; and the commercialization of jazz, 105; decline of the, 116, 174–75; and improvisation, 35–36; and jazz as popular music, 165–75, 182; and music theory, 218; popularity of the, 103, 104; and radio, 170; and solos, 35–36. *See also* Swing
Birdland (New York City), 221
"Birth of the Blues," 181
"Bitches Brew" (Davis), 165
"Black, Brown, and Beige" (Ellington), 110–11
Black, Charles, 114
Blackmur, R. P., 228
Blacks: and the academization of jazz, 213–14; and their entertainment, 212–14; as an audience, 185, 204–5, 207–24, 251; and "authentic" jazz, 90–91, 100–101, 187; as authorities on jazz, 222–23; and the blues, 90, 203–4, 206, 209, 211, 214, 217; and bop, 207–14, 217; and classical music, 210; and the

312

cians, 151; urbanization in, 6–7; vice districts in, 13, 14
Chicagoans, 157
Chicago Loopers, 86–87
Chicago style, 176–77
"Chicago" (Whiteman/Grofé), 167
Chicago White Sox, 23
Chilton, John, 41–42, 250, 254
"Chimes Blues" (Armstrong), 32
Choate, Robert A., 142
"Choo Choo Ch'boogie" (Tympany Five), 179
Chord relationships, 50–51, 155
"Clarinet à la King" (Goodman), 120
"Clarinet Marmalade": by Beiderbecke, 104; by the Original Dixieland Jazz Band, 104
Clarke, Herbert L., 28
Classical music: and the academization of jazz, 137–38, 143–44, 150, 151; academization of, 146–47, 149; and the arts, 129; and the black community, 210; as ensemble music, 27–28; and free expression of feeling, 61; and individualism, 43, 44; repetition in, 58; and tempo, 78, 84
Class issues: and the academization of jazz, 149–50; and art as sacred, 127–28; and aspiring jazz musicians, 221; and the audience for jazz, 219–221; and the cáfes-concerts, 10; and dance, 20, 147–48; and dislike of jazz, 203–4; and the emergence of the entertainment industry, 12; and the emergence of jazz, 10, 11, 12, 20, 22–23; and jazz culture, 215; and local jazz, 266–68; and the music industry, 11; and radio, 220; and recordings, 220; and vaudeville, 11; and vice districts, 10, 11, 12, 20, 22–23
Clovers, 180
Club Alabam (New York City), 22–23, 96, 101
Cohan, George M., 12
Coleman, Bill, 204
Coleman, Ornette, 44, 105, 155, 179, 188, 247
Colleges: and the academization of jazz, 132–62; and the commercialization of jazz, 97–98, 99; and

dixieland jazz, 211–12; and the emergence of jazz, 22–23; jazz concerts at, 142–44. *See also* Jazz studies; *specific college or university*
Collier, Geoffrey L., 78–88
Collins, Lee, 178
Coltrane, John: and the academization of jazz, 149, 156, 162; and the art *vs.* entertainment controversy, 213; and the black community, 209, 216–17; and the commercialization of jazz, 105; fame/popularity of, 216; individuality of, 66, 155; as an innovator, 216–17; and jazz as popular music, 165, 179; recordings of, 162, 165
Columbia Records, 97
Columbia University, 129, 132–33
Commercialization: of art, 160; and writers, 103
Commercialization of jazz: as antithetical to art, 89–91; and audiences, 91–93, 102–4, 105; and blacks, 90–91, 95, 98–99, 100–101, 102–3, 115; and criticisms of jazz, 98–99; and the entertainment industry, 92, 101–3; and intellectuals, 109–10, 112; and jazz as a fad/craze, 97–98, 112–13; and jazz as popular music, 165, 173–74; and local jazz, 270; and radio, 92, 96–97, 107, 108; and recordings, 97, 101, 102, 108, 118; and the saxophone, 105; and sheet music, 108; and the spread of jazz, 93–96, 99; and suspicion of successful commercialization, 91; and World War I, 101
Como, Perry, 175
Concentration, 65–66, 69
Concert-saloons, 10–11, 12
Condon, Eddie, 25, 87, 116, 184
Contrasts, 58, 59
Cook, Will Marion, 36–37, 38, 39
Cool school. *See* West Coast school
Copland, Aaron, 74
Cotton Club (New York City), 22–23, 97, 102, 106–8, 149, 181
Cotton Pickers, 39, 47
"Cotton Tail" (Ellington), 109, 111
Coycault, Ernest, 94
"Crazy Rhythm," 181

315